Blackwell Readings in Philosophy
Series Editor: Steven M. Cahn

Blackwell Readings in Philosophy are concise, chronologically arranged collections of primary readings from classical and contemporary sources. They represent core positions and important developments with respect to key philosophical concepts. Edited and introduced by leading philosophers, these volumes provide valuable resources for teachers and students of philosophy, and for all those interested in gaining a solid understanding of central topics in philosophy.

Deontology

Edited by

Stephen Darwall

Blackwell
Publishing

BLACKWELL PUBLISHING
350 Main Street, Malden, MA 02148-5020, USA
9600 Garsington Road, Oxford OX4 2DQ, UK
550 Swanston Street, Carlton, Victoria 3053, Australia

First published 2003 by Blackwell Publishing Ltd

5   2008

Library of Congress Cataloging-in-Publication Data

Deontology / edited by Stephen Darwall.
p. cm. — (Blackwell readings in philosophy ; 9)
Includes bibliographical references and index.
ISBN 978-0-6312-3111-0 (hbk. : alk. paper) — ISBN 978-0-6312-3112-7 (pbk. : alk. paper)
1. Free will and determinism.   2. Ethics.   3. Duty.   I. Darwall, Stephen L.,
1946–   II. Series.

BJ1461 .D44 2002
171′.2—dc21   2002066426

A catalogue record for this title is available from the British Library.

Set in 10/12½ Palatino
by SNP Best-set Typesetter Ltd, Hong Kong
Printed and bound in Malaysia
by KHL Printing Co Sdn Bhd

For further information on
Blackwell Publishing, visit our website:
www.blackwellpublishing.com

Contents

Acknowledgments

I am indebted to Steven Cahn for initially suggesting the idea of this anthology, to Jeff Dean for patiently shepherding me through the production process, to Blackwell's anonymous referees for very helpful comments, to Anthony Grahame for expert copy-editing, and to Sue London for yeoman work in copying.

The editor and publisher gratefully acknowledge the following for permission to reproduce copyright material:

Chapters 1, 2, and 3: Immanuel Kant, from *Groundwork of the Metaphysics of Morals* (1998), and from *Practical Philosophy* (1996), both ed. and trans. Mary Gregor. Reproduced by permission of Cambridge University Press;

Chapter 4: Richard Price, from *A Review of the Principal Questions in Morals*, edited by D. D. Raphael, 1974. Reproduced by permission of the editor;

Chapter 5: W. D. Ross, from *The Right and the Good*. Copyright © 1967 by Oxford University Press. Reproduced by permission of Oxford University Press;

Chapter 6: Robert Nozick, "Moral Constraints and Moral Goals," from *Anarchy, State, and Utopia*. Copyright © 1974 by Basic Books, Inc. Reproduced by permission of Perseus Books;

Chapter 7: Thomas Nagel, from *The View from Nowhere* by Thomas Nagel, copyright © 1986 by Thomas Nagel. Reproduced by permission of Oxford University Press, Inc.;

Chapter 8: Stephen Darwall, "Agent-Centred Restrictions From the Inside Out" from *Philosophical Studies* 50 (1986). Reproduced by kind permission of the author and Kluwer Academic Publishers;

Chapter 9: Judith Jarvis Thomson, "The Trolley Problem". Reprinted by permission of the Yale Law Journal Company and William S. Hein Company from *The Yale Law Journal* 94, pp. 1395–1415;

Chapter 10: Frances Myrna Kamm, "Harming Some to Save Others" from *Philosophical Studies* 57 (1989). Reproduced by kind permission of the author and Kluwer Academic Publishers;

Chapter 11: Warren S. Quinn, "Actions, Intentions, and Consequences: The Doctrine of Double Effect" from *Philosophy & Public Affairs* 18 (1989). Copyright © 1989 by Princeton University Press. Reprinted by permission of Princeton University Press;

Chapter 12: Christine M. Korsgaard, "The Right to Lie: Kant on Dealing with Evil" from *Philosophy & Public Affairs* 15 (1986). Copyright © 1986 by Princeton University Press. Reprinted by permission of Princeton University Press.

The publisher apologizes for any errors or omissions in the above list and would be grateful if notified of any corrections that should be incorporated in future reprints or editions of this book.

Introduction

Deontological theories can be defined by their opposition to consequentialism on a fundamental point. Consequentialists hold that what it is morally right or wrong to do depends upon what would bring about the best consequences, where the latter are evaluated simply as states of the world, as good or bad things *to happen*. Moral values, consequentialists believe, are ultimately instrumental, consisting in the promotion of values that, because they are prior to morality, are "nonmoral."

Consider, for example, the species of consequentialism called "utilitarianism." Utilitarians believe that it is a good thing in itself, irrespective of any relation to conduct and character, when sentient beings experience pleasure and that it is intrinsically bad when they experience pain. Nonmoral values of two different sorts are thought to be involved. Most obviously, since pleasure and pain are in their natures good and bad *for* those who experience them, these states involve "agent-relative" good and evil, respectively.[1] But what is most distinctive about utilitarianism as a fundamental approach to moral philosophy is the idea that the experience of pleasure and pain are good and bad things to happen *period*, from an "agent-neutral" perspective. The state of the world in which a being experiences pleasure is, it holds, good in a way that gives *any* agent a reason to cause it to exist. This pattern is repeated, moreover, with consequentialism more generally. Consequentialists believe that moral conduct and character are instrumental to states of the world whose agent-neutral value gives any agent a reason to bring them about.

As against this, deontology holds that moral values and standards cannot be determined at any level of analysis by what would promote the best outcomes or states, assessed agent-neutrally. Indeed, deontologists are frequently skeptical of the very idea of agent-neutral, nonmoral evaluations of outcomes. And they unite in the belief that at least some fundamental moral principles or ideas are agent-relative "all the way down."

Consider the following example. Suppose a consequentialist holds that among the intrinsically bad things that can happen is someone's being betrayed by a friend. The thought here is not that it is wrong to betray friends, or even (exactly) that this is a bad thing *to do*, but that betrayals are bad things *to happen*. And again, it is not just that it is bad for the person betrayed (agent-, or in this case, patient-relatively), but that it is a bad thing period (agent-neutrally) for someone to be betrayed. If betrayals are bad things to happen, then it would be good, other things being equal, to prevent them. Suppose that there are two people, A and B, who are contemplating betraying their friends. Suppose also that circumstances are such that if you betray *your* friend, A and B will be so horrified that they will not betray theirs, although they would have otherwise. If we consider what you should do in light of what would be best to happen, you would seem to have reason to betray your friend since that would produce fewer intrinsically disvaluable states of betrayal. And, other things being equal, this is precisely what an act-consequentialist would say. Against this, deontologists argue that many moral duties are agent-relative. How an agent may or must act frequently depends on the various relations he or she stands in to others and this, they argue, is so in this case. The moral duty not to betray *one's* friends, deontologists claim, is agent-relative, irreducible to any agent-neutral values, even if we assume that betrayals have intrinsic (agent-neutral) disvalue themselves.

One example of a deontological theory is *contractualism*, since it holds that moral principles are grounded in the fundamental, agent-relative idea of living with others on terms of mutual respect.[2] But deontological theories and principles are also often defended directly, without attempting to ground them in some more basic theory or idea. Historically, these versions of deontology have been called *intuitionist* or species of *intuitionism*. In general, intuitionism is the view that there is an irreducible plurality of different right- or wrong-making features whose moral relevance cannot be derived from some more fundamental principle or reasoning but can only be confirmed by moral reflection or "intuition." This might be done directly as when, for example, it can seem obvious on reflection that the fact that an action would amount to a betrayal or a broken promise must count against it morally. Or it can occur in thinking about or analyzing a specific case, as, for instance, when we reflect on Judith Thomson's "trolley problem," it can seem evident that causing harm and allowing it to happen are morally different.[3]

Another example, defended by some deontologists, is the "doctrine of double effect," according to which there is a moral difference between causing harm or evil as an unintended side effect of an intended action or policy and intending the harm or evil directly, either as an end or as a means to an end.[4] Thus, for example, although it is a terrible thing whenever innocent civilians die during wartime, it would seem to be morally worse to target and kill a given number of civilians directly than it would be to kill the same number as an unavoidable side affect of bombing a military target, even if both would produce the same valuable end of victory over a repressive, aggressive regime. One place the principle of double effect has played an important role is in debate about the controversial issue of abortion. Since abortion aims directly at the death of the fetus, it is sometimes argued that it is morally worse than another action would be which caused the fetus's death only as an unintended side effect. While it might be permissible to perform a medical procedure that is necessary to save a pregnant woman's life even at the risk of killing the fetus, it is argued that aborting a fetus to save the woman's life is morally wrong because it is an impermissible intentional killing.

Deontological intuitionists have defended a wide variety of independent principles or doctrines of right- or wrong-making features of conduct. In addition to the doctrine of double effect and the distinction between "doing and allowing," there have been claimed to be: duties of beneficence or mutual aid, duties of non-maleficence ("do no harm") – along with the idea that these are weightier than duties of beneficence, duties of gratitude for benevolence shown, duties of restitution for wrongs and injuries done, duties of fidelity relating to promise and contract, duties of personal relationship (including those of friends, parents, children, family members, and caretakers more generally), professional duties, duties owing to desert (what people deserve), duties of reciprocity and fair play, further duties of justice, duties to other animals (to the extent that these have not been included already), duties to ourselves, and various others.[5] Of course, intuitionists do not agree about every doctrine or principle, not even about those just mentioned. But they are nonetheless agreed that *some* such list of independent principles or doctrines is correct and that the principles on the list cannot be derived from some more fundamental principle or theory, such as contractualism or, even more so, consequentialism.

Both intuitionist and contractualist deontologists hold that the right is, in Rawls's phrase, "prior to the good."[6] They believe that any attempt to derive the right from agent-neutral outcome value is bound to fail, since the question of what it is right or wrong to do is one that agents face from their place *within* the world, defined by a complex set of relations to others who make widely varying claims on them owing to these different relations. Which states of affairs would be good to exist, considered as from some agent-neutral observer's standpoint, may, if there be such values, be among the considerations that are relevant to what a moral agent should do. But deontologists believe that many moral duties depend on the agent's place *within* the states an observer might contemplate, specifically, on the myriad relations she stands in (and that her actions bring her to stand in) to other agents and patients, to her own past acts, to the histories of those with whom she interacts, and so on.

Many of these relations were mentioned above in passing, but it would be helpful to list them more explicitly. We cannot begin to exhaust them, but we can nonetheless gain some idea of their range.

Duties of beneficence and non-maleficence

Like consequentialists, many deontologists believe that how our actions affect the good of others (other persons, at least, and perhaps any other being who can have a welfare or good) always has some relevance to what we should do morally. But the relevance, again, is not just that these are valuable or disvaluable outcomes we can promote or prevent. It also matters what antecedent relations we have to the affected parties (and what relations our actions bring us to have). Harming another (an injury done to the other) is worse, other things equal, than forbearing to benefit. It is not just the causing of a disvaluable state; it is doing harm *to* some being. Doing harm is worse, also, than failing to prevent it. And directly intending harm is worse than causing it as an unintended side effect.

Duties of special care

Various special relations of caretaking give rise to special obligations of beneficence. Parents have obligations to promote the welfare of their children that are greater than the duties of beneficence we have to others in general. And similarly for trustees and other relations of more specialized concern, such as doctors, teachers, and so on, who are responsible for their patients' or students' medical or educational welfare.

Duties of honesty and fidelity

Obligations not to lie or intentionally mislead, to keep promises, not to violate contracts, and, more generally, not to encourage expectations we intend not to meet, all fit under the general category of keeping faith and not violating trust. Various personal relationships, like those of friends, lovers and spouses, can be placed under this rubric as well.

Duties deriving from agents' and patients' past conduct

Agent-fault
When we wrong and injure others, we incur duties to them to acknowledge fault and offer restitution.

Patient-benevolence
When others benefit us, we acquire duties of gratitude towards them.

Patient-desert
A person's past conduct may call for some appropriate response, especially from those who have special responsibilities to respond appropriately to merit and desert, such as judges of various kinds.

Duties of reciprocity and fair play

There is a duty to do one's part in mutually advantageous cooperation, especially when one voluntarily accepts cooperative benefits. Contractualists regard this duty as fundamental and the source of all others. For intuitionists, it is simply one independently important duty among others.

Further duties of justice

Various further duties of justice derive from political relations, for example, from that of equal citizenship. Here we have duties to support a just political order that establishes and protects basic rights and achieves distributive justice. Where actual political relations are lacking, as in the international context, justice may require that we do our part to help establish justice more widely through more extensive political forms.

Duties to other species

Here again, our duties depend on complex relations. In addition to duties of beneficence and non-maleficence, we can acquire special obligations to animals owing to our history of interaction with them. Even if other animals cannot be full partners in cooperative schemes, we can acquire duties to them owing to the ways we have involved them in our lives and ourselves in theirs. Pets are an obvious example, but no less significant may be cases where species are themselves shaped and cultivated for human purposes in ways that give them special needs and vulnerabilities.

This list, again, is hardly exhaustive. It should be obvious even at this point, however, that the decisions we face in actual situations will inevitably involve, not just a single principle or right- or wrong-making consideration, but complex combinations of principles or considerations. Since intuitionistic deontology rejects the idea that some overarching principle, idea, or process of reasoning exists in terms of which these principles or considerations might be integrated or prioritized, how do intuitionists believe that the messy business of moral reflection is to proceed in thinking about concrete cases?

W. D. Ross distinguishes between the claim that a given duty or right- or wrong-making consideration holds *prima facie*, that is, other things being equal, and the proposition that, in some actual circumstance, something or other is our moral duty, all things considered, or, as he put it, *sans phrase*.[7] It is only claims of the former sort that Ross holds to be self-evident to intuition. To render a moral judgment in any actual case, however, it is necessary to reflect on all the morally relevant features and, moreover, on how they interact. To take a familiar example, one may have promised to do something of relatively mundane importance only to find oneself placed in a position to give another vitally necessary aid. Here both promise and need continue to have weight, but one is weightier and so overrides. It would be wrong not to render life-saving assistance, but the moral force of the promise continues, giving rise to a residual obligation to compensate the promisee in some way. But this is not the only way in which moral considerations can interact. Sometimes one consideration can wholly defeat another. When, for example, a benefit one is in a position to provide is tainted by injustice, this may cancel the positive reason to provide the benefit and not just outweigh it.

Ultimately, on an intuitionist picture, there is simply no substitute for carefully considering ethical cases in all of their complexity. Analyzing or "factoring" a case into various right- or wrong-making features or *prima facie* duties is an important part of the process. But even here, because these can interact in ways that intuitionists believe defy general formulation, one may be able to do no better than come to grips with these complex interactions in ways that give a reflective sense of what moral verdict they will ultimately support.

The readings that follow fall into two main categories, with the latter including two subcategories. First, there are classical statements of deontological ideas in the writings of Immanuel Kant, Richard Price, and W. D. Ross. Second, there are contemporary essays, a first group discussing deontology's underlying rationale (Robert Nozick, Thomas Nagel, and myself), and a second group discussing specific ethical issues within a deontological framework (Judith Jarvis Thomson, Frances Myrna Kamm, Warren S. Quinn, and Christine M. Korsgaard).

Notes

1 A more appropriate qualifier in this context would be "patient-" or "subject-relative," but I will follow the more standard philosophical usage "agent-relative." A more fine-grained analysis might distinguish between more properly *agent*-relative value – what is good from the agent's point of view – and what is good for someone in the sense of their good, interest, benefit, or welfare. On this point, see my "Self-Interest and Self-Concern," in Ellen F. Paul, ed., *Self-Interest*, Cambridge: Cambridge University Press, 1997; and *Social Philosophy & Policy* 14 (1997): 158–78.

2 For a discussion of contractarianism, see the introduction to *Contractarianism/Contractualism* (Oxford: Blackwell, 2002).

3 See Judith Jarvis Thomson, "The Trolley Problem."

4 See Warren Quinn, "Actions, Intentions, and Consequences: The Doctrine of Double Effect."

5 For some examples, see the selection in this volume from W. D. Ross, *The Right and the Good*.

6 *A Theory of Justice*, pp. 30–3.

7 Since *"prima facie"* suggests something epistemological, philosophers nowadays are as likely to use the term *"pro tanto"* ("as far as it goes"). The central idea is that a right- or wrong-consideration is one that makes an act right or wrong, *other things being equal*, such that were that the only morally relevant feature then the action would be right or wrong, all things considered or *"sans phrase."*

Part I
Classical Sources

1

From *Groundwork of the Metaphysics of Morals*

Immanuel Kant

From the *Preface*

Since my aim here is directed properly to moral philosophy, I limit the question proposed only to this: is it not thought to be of the utmost necessity to work out for once a pure moral philosophy, completely cleansed of everything that may be only empirical and that belongs to anthropology? For, that there must be such a philosophy is clear of itself from the common idea of duty and of moral laws. Everyone must grant that a law, if it is to hold morally, that is, as a ground of an obligation, must carry with it absolute necessity; that, for example, the command "thou shalt not lie" does not hold only for human beings, as if other rational beings did not have to heed it, and so with all other moral laws properly so called; that, therefore, the ground of obligation here must not be sought in the nature of the human being or in the circumstances of the world in which he is placed, but a priori simply in concepts of pure reason; and that any other precept, which is based on principles of mere experience – even if it is universal in a certain respect – insofar as it rests in the least part on empirical grounds, perhaps only in terms of a motive,[1] can indeed be called a practical rule but never a moral law.

   Thus, among practical cognitions, not only do moral laws, along with their principles, differ essentially from all the rest,[2] in which there is something empirical, but all moral philosophy is based entirely on its pure part; and when it is applied to the human being it does not borrow the least thing from acquaintance with him (from anthropology) but gives to him, as a rational being, laws a priori, which no doubt still require a

Immanuel Kant, *Groundwork of the Metaphysics of Morals*, ed. and trans. Mary Gregor (Cambridge: Cambridge University Press, 1998), pp. 2–3, 31–9.

judgment sharpened by experience, partly to distinguish in what cases they are applicable and partly to provide them with access[3] to the will of the human being and efficacy for his fulfillment of them;[4] for the human being is affected by so many inclinations that, though capable of the idea of a practical pure reason, he is not so easily able to make it effective *in concreto* in the conduct of his life. . . .

Notes

1   *Bewegungsgründe.* Kant subsequently (4:427) distinguishes this from an "incentive" (*Triebfeder*), and the force of some passages depends upon this distinction. However, he does not abide by the distinction, and no attempt has been made to bring his terminology into accord with it. He occasionally uses *Bewegursache*, in which case "motive," which seems to be the most general word available, has been used.

2   Here, as elsewhere, the difference between German and English punctuation creates difficulties. It is not altogether clear from the context whether the clause "in which there is something empirical" is restrictive or nonrestrictive.

3   Or "entry," "admission," *Eingang.*

4   *Nachdruck zur Ausübung.*

From Section I

There is, therefore, only a single categorical imperative and it is this: *act only in accordance with that maxim through which you can at the same time will that it become a universal law.*

Now, if all imperatives of duty can be derived from this single imperative as from their principle, then, even though we leave it undecided whether what is called duty is not as such an empty concept, we shall at least be able to show what we think by it and what the concept wants to say.

Since the universality of law in accordance with which effects take place constitutes what is properly called *nature* in the most general sense (as regards its form) – that is, the existence of things insofar as it is determined in accordance with universal laws – the universal imperative of duty can also go as follows: *act as if the maxim of your action were to become by your will a* **universal law of nature**.

We shall now enumerate a few duties in accordance with the usual division of them into duties to ourselves and to other human beings and into perfect and imperfect duties.*

(1) Someone feels sick of life because of a series of troubles that has grown to the point of despair, but is still so far in possession of his reason that he can ask himself whether it would not be contrary to his duty to himself to take his own life. Now he inquires whether the maxim of his action could indeed become a universal law of nature. His maxim, however, is: from self-love I make it my principle to shorten my life when its longer duration threatens more troubles than it promises agreeableness. The only further question is whether this principle of self-love could become a universal law of nature. It is then seen at once that a nature whose law it would be to destroy life itself by means of the same feeling whose destination[1] is to impel toward the furtherance of life would contradict itself and would therefore not subsist[2] as nature; thus that maxim could not possibly be a law of nature and, accordingly, altogether opposes the supreme principle of all duty.

(2) Another finds himself urged by need to borrow money. He well knows that he will not be able to repay it but sees also that nothing will be lent him unless he promises firmly to repay it within a determinate time. He would like to make such a promise, but he still has enough conscience to ask himself: is it not forbidden and contrary to duty to help oneself out of need in such a way? Supposing that he still decided to do so, his maxim of action would go as follows: when I believe myself to be in need of money I shall borrow money and promise to repay it, even though I know that this will never happen. Now this principle of self-love or personal advantage is perhaps quite consistent with my whole future welfare, but the question now is whether it is right. I therefore turn the demand of self-love into a universal law and put the question as follows: how would it be if my maxim became a universal law? I then see at once that it could never hold as a universal law of nature and be consistent with itself, but must necessarily contradict itself. For, the universality of a law that everyone, when he believes himself to be in need, could promise whatever he pleases with the intention of not keeping it would

---

* It must be noted here that I reserve the division of duties entirely for a future *Metaphysics of Morals*, so that the division here stands only as one adopted at my discretion (for the sake of arranging my examples). For the rest, I understand here by a perfect duty one that admits no exception in favor of inclination, and then I have not merely external but also internal *perfect duties*; although this is contrary to the use of the word adopted in the schools, I do not intend to justify it here, since for my purpose it makes no difference whether or not it is granted me.

make the promise and the end one might have in it itself impossible, since no one would believe what was promised him but would laugh at all such expressions as vain pretenses.

(3) A third finds in himself a talent that by means of some cultivation could make him a human being useful for all sorts of purposes. However, he finds himself in comfortable circumstances and prefers to give himself up to pleasure than to trouble himself with enlarging and improving his fortunate natural predispositions.[3] But he still asks himself whether his maxim of neglecting his natural gifts, besides being consistent with his propensity to amusement, is also consistent with what one calls duty. He now sees that a nature could indeed always subsist with such a universal law, although (as with the South Sea Islanders) the human being should let his talents rust and be concerned with devoting his life merely to idleness, amusement, procreation – in a word, to enjoyment; only he cannot possible **will** that this become a universal law or be put in us as such by means of natural instinct. For, as a rational being he necessarily wills that all the capacities in him be developed, since they serve him and are given to him for all sorts of possible purposes.

Yet a *fourth*, for whom things are going well while he sees that others (whom he could very well help) have to contend with great hardships, thinks: what is it to me? let each be as happy as heaven wills or as he can make himself; I shall take nothing from him nor even envy him; only I do not care to contribute anything to his welfare or to his assistance in need! Now, if such a way of thinking were to become a universal law the human race could admittedly very well subsist, no doubt even better than when everyone prates about sympathy and benevolence and even exerts himself to practice them occasionally, but on the other hand also cheats where he can, sells the right of human beings or otherwise infringes upon it. But although it is possible that a universal law of nature could very well subsist in accordance with such a maxim, it is still impossible to **will** that such a principle hold everywhere as a law of nature. For, a will that decided this would conflict with itself, since many cases could occur in which one would need the love and sympathy[4] of others and in which, by such a law of nature arisen from his own will, he would rob himself of all hope of the assistance he wishes for himself.

These are a few of the many actual duties, or at least of what we take to be such, whose derivation[5] from the one principle cited above is clear. We must *be able to will* that a maxim of our action become a universal law: this is the canon of moral appraisal of action in general. Some actions are so constituted that their maxim cannot even be *thought* without contradiction as a universal law of nature, far less could one *will* that it *should* become such. In the case of others that inner impossibility is indeed not to be found, but it is still impossible to *will* that their maxim be raised to the universality of a law of nature because such a will would contradict itself. It is easy to see that the first is opposed to strict or narrower (unremitting)[6] duty, the second only to wide (meritorious) duty; and so all duties, as far as the kind of obligation (not the object of their action) is concerned, have by these examples been set out completely in their dependence upon the one principle.

If we now attend to ourselves in any transgression of a duty, we find that we do not really will that our maxim should become a universal law, since that is impossible for us, but that the opposite of our maxim should instead remain a universal law, only we take the liberty of making an *exception* to it for ourselves (or just for this once) to the advantage of our inclination. Consequently, if we weighed all cases from one and the same point of view, namely that of reason, we would find a contradiction in our own will, namely that a certain principle be objectively necessary as a universal law and yet subjectively not hold universally but allow exceptions. Since, however, we at one time regard our action from the point of view of a will wholly conformed with reason but then regard the very same action from the point of view of a will affected by inclination, there is really no contradiction here but instead a resistance[7] of inclination to the precept of reason (*antagonismus*), through which the universality of the principle (*universalitas*) is changed into mere generality (*generalitas*) and the practical rational principle is to meet the maxim half way. Now, even though this cannot be justified in our own impartially rendered judgment, it still shows that we really acknowledge the validity of the categorical imperative and permit ourselves (with all respect for it) only a few exceptions that, as it seems to us, are inconsiderable and wrung from us.

We have therefore shown at least this much: that if duty is a concept that is to contain significance and real lawgiving for our actions it can be expressed only in categorical imperatives and by no means in hypothetical ones; we have also – and this is already a great deal – set forth distinctly and as determined for every use the content of the categorical imperative, which must contain the principle of all duty (if there is such a thing at all). But we have not yet advanced so far as to prove a priori that there really is such an imperative, that there is a practical law, which commands absolutely of itself and without any incentives, and that the observance of this law is duty.

For the purpose of achieving this it is of the utmost importance to take warning that we must not let ourselves think of wanting to derive the reality of this principle from the *special property of human nature*. For, duty is to be practical unconditional necessity of action and it must therefore hold for all rational beings (to which alone an imperative can apply at all) and *only because of this* be also a law for all human wills. On the other hand, what is derived from the special natural constitution of humanity – what is derived from certain feelings and propensities and even, if possible, from a special tendency that would be peculiar to human reason and would not have to hold necessarily for the will of every rational being – that can indeed yield a maxim for us but not a law; it can yield a subjective principle on which we might act if we have the propensity and inclination,[8] but not an objective principle on which we would be *directed* to act even though every propensity, inclination, and natural tendency of ours were against it – so much so that the sublimity and inner dignity of the command in a duty is all the more manifest the fewer are the subjective causes in favor of it and the more there are against it, without thereby weakening in the least the necessitation by the law or taking anything away from its validity.

Here, then, we see philosophy put in fact in a precarious position, which is to be firm even though there is nothing in heaven or on earth from which it depends or on which it is based. Here philosophy is to manifest its purity as sustainer of its own laws, not as herald of laws that an implanted sense or who knows what tutelary nature whispers to it, all of which – though they may always be better than nothing at all – can still never yield basic principles that reason dictates and that must have their source entirely and completely a priori and, at the same time, must have their commanding authority from this: that they expect nothing from the inclination of human beings but everything from the supremacy of the law and the respect owed it or, failing this, condemn the human being to contempt for himself and inner abhorrence.

Hence everything empirical, as an addition[9] to the principle of morality, is not only quite inept for this; it is also highly prejudicial to the purity of morals, where the proper worth of an absolutely good will – a worth raised above all price – consists just in the principle of action being free from all influences of contingent grounds, which only experience can furnish. One cannot give too many or too frequent warnings against this laxity, or even mean cast of mind, which seeks its principle among empirical motives and laws; for, human reason in its weariness gladly rests on this pillow and in a dream of sweet illusions (which allow it to embrace a cloud instead of Juno) it substitutes for morality a bastard patched up from limbs of quite diverse ancestry, which looks like whatever one wants to see in it but not like virtue for him who has once seen virtue in her true form.*

The question is therefore this: is it a necessary law *for all rational beings* always to appraise their actions in accordance with such maxims as they themselves could will to serve as universal laws? If there is such a law, then it must already be connected (completely a priori) with the concept of the will of a rational being as such. But in order to discover this connection we must, however reluctantly, step forth, namely into metaphysics, although into a domain[10] of it that is distinct from speculative philosophy, namely into metaphysics of morals. In a practical philosophy, where we have to do not with assuming[11] grounds for what *happens* but rather laws for what *ought to happen* even if it never does, that is, objective practical laws, we do not need to undertake an investigation into the grounds on account of which something pleases or displeases; how the satisfaction of mere sensation differs from taste, and whether the latter differs from a general satisfaction of reason; upon what the feeling of pleasure or displeasure rests, and how from it desires and inclinations arise, and from them, with the cooperation of reason, maxims; for all that belongs to an empirical doctrine of the soul,[12] which would constitute the second part of the doctrine of nature when this is regarded as *philosophy of nature* insofar as it is based *on empirical laws*. Here, however, it is a question of objective practical laws and hence of the relation of a will to itself insofar as it determines itself only by reason; for then everything that has reference to the empirical falls away of itself, since if reason entirely by itself determines conduct (and the possibility of this is just what we want now to investigate), it must necessarily do so a priori.

The will is thought as a capacity to determine itself to acting in conformity with the *representation of certain laws*. And such a capacity can be found only in rational beings. Now, what serves the will as the objective ground of its self-determination is an end, and this, if it is given by reason alone, must hold equally for all rational beings. What, on the other hand, contains merely the ground of the possibility of an action the effect of which is an end is called a *means*. The subjective ground of desire is an

---

* To behold virtue in her proper form is nothing other than to present morality stripped of any admixture of the sensible and of any spurious adornments of reward or self-love. By means of the least effort of his reason everyone can easily become aware of how much virtue then eclipses everything else that appears charming to the inclinations, provided his reason is not altogether spoiled for abstraction.

incentive; the objective ground of volition is a *motive*; hence the distinction between subjective ends, which rest on incentives, and objective ends, which depend on motives, which hold for every rational being. Practical principles are *formal* if they abstract from all subjective ends, whereas they are *material* if they have put these, and consequently certain incentives, at their basis. The ends that a rational being proposes at his discretion as *effects* of his actions (material ends) are all only relative; for only their mere relation to a specially constituted[13] faculty of desire on the part of the subject gives them their worth, which can therefore furnish no universal principles, no principles valid and necessary for all rational beings and also for every volition, that is, no practical laws. Hence all these relative ends are only the ground of hypothetical imperatives.

But suppose there were something the *existence of which in itself* has an absolute worth, something which as *an end in itself* could be a ground of determinate laws; then in it, and in it alone, would lie the ground of a possible categorical imperative, that is, of a practical law.

Now I say that the human being and in general every rational being *exists* as an end in itself, *not merely as a means* to be used by this or that will at its discretion; instead he must in all his actions, whether directed to himself or also to other rational beings, always be regarded *at the same time as an end*. All objects of the inclinations have only a conditional worth; for, if there were not inclinations and the needs based on them, their object would be without worth. But the inclinations themselves, as sources of needs, are so far from having an absolute worth, so as to make one wish to have them,[14] that it must instead be the universal wish of every rational being to be altogether free from them. Thus the worth of any object *to be acquired* by our action is always conditional. Beings the existence of which rests not on our will but on nature, if they are beings without reason, still have only a relative worth, as means, and are therefore called *things*,[15] whereas rational beings are called *persons* because their nature already marks them out as an end in itself, that is, as something that may not be used merely as a means, and hence so far limits all choice (and is an object of respect). These, therefore, are not merely subjective ends, the existence of which as an effect of our action has a worth *for us*, but rather *objective ends*, that is, beings[16] the existence of which is in itself an end, and indeed one such that no other end, to which they would serve *merely* as means, can be put in its place, since without it nothing of *absolute worth* would be found anywhere; but if all worth were conditional and therefore contingent, then no supreme practical principle for reason could be found anywhere.

If, then, there is to be a supreme practical principle and, with respect to the human will, a categorical imperative, it must be one such that, from the representation of what is necessarily an end for everyone because it is an *end in itself*, it constitutes an *objective* principle of the will and thus can serve as a universal practical law.[17] The ground of this principle is: *rational nature exists as an end in itself*. The human being necessarily represents his own existence in this way; so far it is thus a *subjective* principle of human actions. But every other rational being also represents his existence in this way consequent on[18] just the same rational ground that also holds for me;* thus it is at the same time an *objective* principle from which, as a supreme practical ground, it must be possible to derive all laws of the will. The practical imperative will therefore be the following: *So act that you use humanity, whether in your own person or in the person of any other, always at the same time as an end, never merely as a means.* . . . .

This principle of humanity, and in general of every rational nature, *as an end in itself* (which is the supreme limiting condition of the freedom of action of every human being) is not borrowed from experience; first because of its universality, since it applies to all rational beings as such and no experience is sufficient to determine anything about them; second because in it humanity is represented not as an end of human beings (subjectively), that is, not as an object that we of ourselves actually make our end, but as an objective end that, whatever ends we may have, ought as law to constitute the supreme limiting condition of all subjective ends, so that the principle must arise from pure reason. That is to say, the ground of all practical lawgiving lies (in accordance with the first principle) *objectively in the rule* and the form of universality which makes it fit to be a law (possibly[19] a law of nature); *subjectively*, however, it lies in the *end*; but the subject of all ends is every rational being as an end in itself (in accordance with the second principle); from this there follows now the third practical principle of the will, as supreme condition of its harmony with universal practical reason, the idea *of the will of every rational being as a will giving universal law.*

In accordance with this principle all maxims are repudiated that are inconsistent with the will's own giving of universal law. Hence the will is not merely subject to the law but subject to it in such a way that it must be viewed as also giving the law to itself[20] and just because of this as first subject to the law (of which it can regard itself as the author).[21]

---

* Here I put forward this proposition as a postulate. The grounds for it will be found in the last Section.

Notes

1   *Bestimmung.*
2   *bestehen.*
3   *Naturanlagen.*
4   *Teilnehmung.*
5   reading *Ableitung* instead of *Abteilung*, "classification."
6   *unnachlaßlich.*
7   *Widerstand.*
8   *nach welchem wir handeln zu dürfen Hang und Neigung haben.*
9   *Zutat*, literally "an ornament."
10   *Gebiet.*
11   *anzunehmen.*
12   *Seelenlehre.*
13   *geartetes.*
14   *um sie selbst zu wünschen.*
15   *Sachen.*
16   *Dinge.* Although both *Sache* and *Ding* would usually be translated as "thing," *Sache* has the technical sense of something usable that does not have free choice, i.e., "*Sache ist ein Ding*" to which nothing can be imputed (*The Metaphysics of Morals* 6:223).
17   *ausmacht, mithin zum allgemeinen praktischen Gesetz dienen kann.* It is not clear, grammatically, whether the subject of "can serve" is "end in itself" or "objective principle."
18   *zufolge.*
19   *allenfalls.*
20   Or "as itself lawgiving," *als selbstgesetzgebend.*
21   *Urheber.*

2

From *The Metaphysics of Morals*

Immanuel Kant

Introduction, Section III

The following concepts are common to both parts of *The Metaphysics of Morals*.

Obligation is the necessity of a free action under a categorical imperative of reason.

An imperative is a practical rule by which an action in itself contingent is *made* necessary. An imperative differs from a practical law in that a law indeed represents an action as necessary but takes no account of whether this action already inheres by an *inner* necessity in the acting subject (as in a holy being) or whether it is contingent (as in the human being); for where the former is the case there is no imperative. Hence an imperative is a rule the representation of which *makes* necessary an action that is subjectively contingent and thus represents the subject as one that must be *constrained* (necessitated)[1] to conform with the rule. – A categorical (unconditional) imperative is one that represents an action as objectively necessary and makes it necessary not indirectly, through the representation of some *end* that can be attained by the action, but through the mere representation of this action itself (its form), and hence directly. No other practical doctrine can furnish instances of such imperatives than that which prescribes obligation (the doctrine of morals). All

Immanuel Kant, *Practical Philosophy* (Cambridge: Cambridge University Press, 1996), pp. 377–9, 552–4.

other imperatives are *technical* and are, one and all, conditional. The ground of the possibility of categorical imperatives is this: that they refer to no other property of choice (by which some purpose can be ascribed to it) than simply to its *freedom*.

That action is *permitted* (*licitum*) which is not contrary to obligation; and this freedom which is not limited by any opposing imperative, is called an authorization (*facultas moralis*). Hence it is obvious what is meant by *forbidden* (*illicitum*).

Duty is that action to which someone is bound. It is therefore the matter of obligation, and there can be one and the same duty (as to the action) although we can be bound to it in different ways.

A categorical imperative, because it asserts an obligation with respect to certain actions, is a morally practical *law*. But since obligation involves not merely practical necessity (such as a law in general asserts) but also *necessitation*, a categorical imperative is a law that either commands or prohibits, depending upon whether it represents as a duty the commission or omission of an action. An action that is neither commanded nor prohibited is merely *permitted*, since there is no law limiting one's freedom (one's authorization) with regard to it and so too no duty. Such an action is called morally indifferent (*indifferens, adiaphoron, res merae facultatis*). The question can be raised whether there are such actions and, if there are, whether there must be permissive laws (*lex permissiva*), in addition to laws that command and prohibit (*lex praeceptiva, lex mandati* and *lex prohibitiva, lex vetiti*), in order to account for someone's being free to do or not to do something as he pleases. If so, the authorization would not always have to do with an indifferent action (*adiaphoron*); for, considering the action in terms of moral laws, no special law would be required for it.

An action is called a *deed* insofar as it comes under obligatory laws and hence insofar as the subject, in doing it, is considered in terms of the freedom of his choice. By such an action the agent is regarded as the *author* of its effect, and this, together with the action itself, can be *imputed* to him, if one is previously acquainted with the law by virtue of which an obligation rests on these.

A *person* is a subject whose actions can be *imputed* to him. *Moral* personality is therefore nothing other than the freedom of a rational being under moral laws (whereas psychological personality is merely the ability[2] to be conscious of one's identity in different conditions of one's existence). From this it follows that a person is subject to no other laws than those he gives to himself (either alone or at least along with others).

A *thing* is that to which[3] nothing can be imputed. Any object of free choice which itself lacks freedom is therefore called a thing (*res corporalis*).

A deed is *right* or *wrong* (*rectum aut minus rectum*)[4] in general insofar as it conforms with duty or is contrary to it (*factum licitum aut illicitum*);[5] the duty itself, in terms of its content or origin, may be of any kind. A deed contrary to duty is called a *transgression* (*reatus*).

An *unintentional* transgression which can still be imputed to the agent is called a mere *fault* (*culpa*). An *intentional* transgression (i.e., one accompanied by consciousness of its being a transgression) is called a *crime* (*dolus*). What is right in accordance with external laws is called *just* (*iustum*); what is not, *unjust* (*iniustum*).[6]

A *conflict of duties* (*collisio officiourum s. obligationum*)[7] would be a relation between them in which one of them would cancel the other (wholly or in part). – But since duty and obligation are concepts that express the objective practical *necessity* of certain actions and two rules opposed to each other cannot be necessary at the same time, if it is a duty to act in accordance with one rule, to act in accordance with the opposite rule is not a duty but even contrary to duty; so a *collision of duties* and obligations is inconceivable (*obligationes non colliduntur*).[8] However, a subject may have, in a rule he prescribes to himself, two *grounds* of obligation (*rationes obligandi*), one or the other of which is not sufficient to put him under obligation[9] (*rationes obligandi non obligantes*), so that one of them is not a duty. – When two such grounds conflict with each other, practical philosophy says, not that the stronger obligation takes precedence (*fortior obligatio vincit*)[10] but that the stronger *ground of obligation* prevails (*fortior obligandi ratio vincit*).[11]

Notes

1 *genötigt* (*necessitiert*). Kant repeatedly gives *Zwang* (constraint) and *Nötigung* (necessitation) as synonyms. Although *Nötigung* is perhaps his favored term, I have often translated *Nötigung* by the more common English word "constraint."

2 *Vermögen*.

3 *Sache ist ein Ding*.

4   right or less right.
5   licit or illicit deed.
6   *gerecht . . . ungerecht.*
7   collision of duties or obligations.
8   obligations do not conflict.
9   *zur Verpflichtung nicht zureichend ist.* Although Kant apparently uses both *Verbindlichkeit* and *Verpflichtung* for "obligation," the latter seems at times to have the sense of "put under obligation" and to be closely related to *verbinden,* which I often translate as "to bind."
10   the stronger obligation wins.
11   the stronger ground of obligation wins.

Chapter II.
The Human Being's Duty to Himself Merely as a Moral Being

This duty is opposed to the vices of *lying, avarice* and *false humility* (servility).

I.
ON LYING

§ 9

The greatest violation of a human being's duty to himself regarded merely as a moral being (the humanity in his own person) is the contrary of truthfulness, *lying (aliud lingua promptum, aliud pectore inclusum gerere).*[1] In the doctrine of right an intentional untruth is called a lie only if it violates another's right; but in ethics, where no authorization is derived from harmlessness, it is clear of itself that no intentional untruth in the expression of one's thoughts can refuse this harsh name. For, the dishonor (being an object of moral contempt) that accompanies a lie also accompanies a liar like his shadow. A lie can be an external lie (*mendacium externum*) or also an internal lie. – By an external lie a human being makes himself an object of contempt in the eyes of others; by an internal lie he does what is still worse: he makes himself contemptible in his own eyes and violates the dignity of humanity in his own person. And so, since the harm that can come to others from lying is not what distinguishes this vice (for if it were, the vice would consist only in violating one's duty to others), this harm is not taken into account here. Neither is the harm that a liar brings upon himself; for then a lie, as a mere error in prudence, would conflict with the pragmatic maxim, not the moral maxim, and it could not be considered a violation of duty at all. – By a lie a human being throws away and, as it were, annihilates his dignity as a human being. A human being who does not himself believe what he tells another (even if the other is a merely ideal person) has even less worth than if he were a mere thing; for a thing, because it is something real and given, has the property of being serviceable so that another can put it to some use. But communication of one's thoughts to someone through words that yet (intentionally) contain the contrary of what the speaker thinks on the subject is an end that is directly opposed to the natural purposiveness of the speaker's capacity to communicate his thoughts, and is thus a renunciation by the speaker of his personality, and such a speaker is a mere deceptive appearance of a human being, not a human being himself. – *Truthfulness* in one's declarations is also called *honesty*[2] and, if the declarations are promises, *sincerity*;[3] but, more generally, truthfulness is called *rectitude*.[4]

Lying (in the ethical sense of the word), intentional untruth as such, need not be *harmful* to others in order to be repudiated; for it would then be a violation of the rights of others. It may be done merely out of frivolity or even good nature;[5] the speaker may even intend to achieve a really good end by it. But his way of pursuing this end is, by its mere form, a crime of a human being against his own person and a worthlessness that must make him contemptible in his own eyes.

It is easy to show that the human being is actually guilty of many **inner** lies, but it seems more difficult to explain how they are possible; for a lie requires a second person whom one intends to deceive, whereas to deceive oneself on purpose seems to contain a contradiction.

The human being as a moral being (*homo noumenon*) cannot use himself as a natural being (*homo phaenomenon*) as a mere means (a speaking machine), as if his natural being were not bound to the inner end (of communicating thoughts), but is bound to the condition of using himself as a natural being in agreement with the declaration (*declaratio*) of his moral being and is under obligation to himself to *truthfulness*. – Someone tells an inner lie, for example, if he professes belief in a future judge of the world, although he really finds no such belief within himself but persuades himself that it could do no harm and might even be useful to profess in his thoughts to one who scrutinizes hearts a belief in such a judge, in order to win his favor in case he should exist. Someone also lies if, having no doubt about the existence of this future judge, he still flatters himself that he inwardly reveres his law, though the only incentive he feels is fear of punishment.

Insincerity is mere lack of *conscientiousness*, that is, of purity in one's professions before one's *inner* judge, who is thought of as another person when conscientiousness is taken quite strictly; then if someone, from self-love, takes a wish for the deed because he has a really good end in mind, his inner lie, although it is indeed contrary to his duty to himself, gets the name of a frailty, as when a lover's wish to find only good qualities in his beloved blinds him to her obvious faults. – But such insincerity in his declarations, which a human being perpetrates upon himself, still deserves the strongest censure, since it is from such a rotten spot (falsity, which seems to be rooted in human nature itself) that the ill of untruthfulness spreads into his relations with other human beings as well, once the highest principle of truthfulness has been violated.

Remark

It is noteworthy that the Bible dates the first crime, through which evil entered the world, not from *fratricide* (Cain's) but from the first *lie* (for even nature rises up against fratricide), and calls the author of all evil a liar from the beginning and the father of lies. However, reason can assign no further ground for the human propensity to *hypocrisy*[6] (*esprit fourbe*), although this propensity must have been present before the lie; for, an act of freedom cannot (like a natural effect) be deduced and explained in accordance with the natural law of the connection of effects with their causes, all of which are appearances.

Casuistical questions

Can an untruth from mere politeness (e.g., the "your obedient servant" at the end of a letter) be considered a lie? No one is deceived by it. – An author asks one of his readers "How do you like my work?" One could merely seem to give an answer, by joking about the impropriety of such a question. But who has his wit always ready? The author will take the slightest hesitation in answering as an insult. May one, then, say what is expected of one?

If I say something untrue in more serious matters,[7] having to do with what is mine or yours, must I answer for all the consequences it might have? For example, a householder has ordered his servant to say "not at home" if a certain human being asks for him. The servant does this and, as a result, the master slips away and commits a serious crime, which would otherwise have been prevented by the guard sent to arrest him. Who (in accordance with ethical principles) is guilty in this case? Surely the servant, too, who violated a duty to himself by his lie, the results of which his own conscience imputes to him.

Notes

1 To have one thing shut up in the heart and another ready on the tongue. Sallust *The War with Catiline* 10.5.
2 *Ehrlichkeit.*
3 *Redlichkeit.*
4 *Aufrichtigkeit.*
5 *Gutmütigkeit,* perhaps "kindness."
6 *Gleisnerei.*
7 *in wirklichen Geschäften.*

3

On a Supposed Right to Lie from Philanthropy[1]

Immanuel Kant

In the journal *Frankreich im Jahr* 1797, Part VI, No. 1, "On Political Reactions" by Benjamin Constant contains the following (p. 123).

"The moral principle 'it is a duty to tell the truth' would, if taken unconditionally and singly, make any society impossible. We have proof of this in the very direct consequences drawn from this principle by a German philosopher, who goes so far as to maintain that it would be a crime to lie to a murderer who asked us whether a friend of ours whom he is pursuing has taken refuge in our house."*

The French philosopher rebuts this principle as follows (p. 124): "It is a duty to tell the truth. The concept of duty is inseparable from the concept of right. A duty is that on the part of one being which corresponds to the rights of another. Where there are no rights, there are no duties. To tell the truth is therefore a duty, but only to one who has a right to the truth. But no one has a right to a truth that harms others."

The πρῶτον ψεῦδος[2] here lies in the proposition *"To tell the truth is a duty, but only to one who has a right to the truth."*

It is to be noted, first, that the expression "to have a right to the truth" is meaningless. One must instead say one has a right to his own *truthfulness (veracitas)*, that is, to the subjective truth in his person. For to have a right to a truth objectively would be tantamount to saying that, as in the case with what is yours or mine generally, it is a matter of one's *will*

Immanuel Kant, *Practical Philosophy* (Cambridge: Cambridge University Press, 1996), pp. 611–15.
* "J. D. Michaelis of Göttingen put forward this extraordinary opinion earlier than Kant. The author of this paper himself told me that the philosopher spoken of in this passage is Kant." K. F. Cramer (I hereby grant that I actually said this somewhere or other, though I cannot now recall where.)

whether a given proposition is to be true or false; and this would give rise to an extraordinary logic.

Now the *first question* is whether someone, in cases where he cannot evade an answer of "yes" or "no," has the *authorization* (the right) to be untruthful. The *second question* is whether he is not, indeed, bound to be untruthful in a certain statement which he is compelled[3] to make by an unjust constraint,[4] in order to prevent a threatened misdeed to himself or to another.

Truthfulness in statements that one cannot avoid is a human being's duty to everyone,* however great the disadvantage to him or to another that may result from it; and although I indeed do no wrong to him who unjustly compels me to make the statement if I falsify it, I nevertheless do wrong in the most essential part of duty *in general* by such falsification, which can therefore be called a lie (though not in a jurist's sense); that is, I bring it about, as far as I can, that statements (declarations) in general are not believed, and so too that all rights which are based on contracts come to nothing and lose their force; and this is a wrong inflicted upon humanity generally.

Thus a lie, defined merely as an intentionally untrue declaration to another, does not require what jurists insist upon adding for their definition, that it must harm another (*mendacium est falsiloquium in praeiudicium alterius*).[5] For it always harms another, even if not another individual, nevertheless humanity generally, inasmuch as it makes the source of right unusable.

Such a well-meant lie *can*, however, also become by an *accident* (*casus*) punishable in accordance with civil laws; but what escapes being punishable merely by accident can be condemned as wrong even in accordance with external laws. That is to say, if you have *by a lie* prevented someone just now bent on murder from committing the deed, then you are legally[6] accountable for all the consequences that might arise from it. But if you have kept strictly to the truth, then public justice can hold nothing against you, whatever the unforeseen consequences might be. It is still possible that, after you have honestly answered "yes" to the murderer's question as to whether his enemy is at home, the latter has nevertheless gone out unnoticed, so that he would not meet the murderer and the deed would not be done; but if you had lied and said that he is not

---

*   I here prefer not to sharpen this principle to the point of saying: "Untruthfulness is a violation of duty to oneself." For this belongs to ethics, but what is under discussion here is a duty of right. The doctrine of virtue looks, in this transgression, only to *worthlessness*, reproach for which a liar draws upon himself.

at home, and he has actually gone out (though you are not aware of it), so that the murderer encounters him while going away and perpetrates his deed on him, then you can by right[7] be prosecuted as the author[8] of his death. For if you had told the truth to the best of your knowledge, then neighbors might have come and apprehended the murderer while he was searching the house for his enemy and the deed would have been prevented. Thus one *who tells a lie*, howèver well disposed he may be, must be responsible for its consequences even before a civil court and must pay the penalty for them, however unforeseen they may have been; for truthfulness is a duty that must be regarded as the basis of all duties to be grounded on contract, the law of which is made uncertain and useless if even the least exception to it is admitted.

To be *truthful* (honest) in all declarations is therefore a sacred command of reason prescribing unconditionally, one not to be restricted by any conveniences.[9]

In this connection Constant makes a well-considered and also correct remark about the decrying of principles so strict that they allegedly lose themselves in impracticable ideas and are thus to be repudiated. "Every time," he says (at the bottom of p. 123), "that a principle proved to be true seems inapplicable, this is because we do not know the *intermediary principle*,[10] which contains the means of application." He adduces (p. 121) the doctrine of *equality* as the first link in the formation of the social chain: "namely, (p. 122) that no human being can be bound except through laws to the formation of which he has contributed. In a very closely knit society this principle can be applied in an immediate way and needs no intermediary principle in order to become a common one. But in a very large society one must add a new principle to the principle that we have here put forward. This intermediary principle is that individuals can contribute to the formation of laws either in their own person or through *representatives*. One who wanted to apply the *first* principle to a large society without adopting the intermediary one in order to do so would inevitably bring about its ruin. But this circumstance, which would only testify to the ignorance or incompetence[11] of the legislator, would prove nothing against the principle." He concludes (p. 125) with these words: "A principle recognized as true must therefore never be abandoned, however apparent is the danger present in it."[12] (And yet the good man himself had abandoned the unconditional principle of truthfulness because of the danger to society it brought with it, since he could discover no intermediary principle that would serve to prevent this danger, and here there is actually no such principle to be inserted.)

If we are going to keep the names of persons as they were specified here, "the French philosopher" confused an action by which someone *harms* (*nocet*) another by telling a truth he cannot avoid admitting with an action by which he *wrongs* (*laedit*) another. It was merely an *accident* (*casus*) that the truthfulness of the statement harmed the resident of the house, not a free *deed* (in the juridical sense). For, from one's right to require another to lie to one's advantage would follow a claim opposed to all lawfulness. Every individual, however, has not only a right but even the strictest duty to truthfulness in statements that he cannot avoid, though they may harm himself or others. Thus in telling the truth he himself does not, strictly speaking, *do* the harm to the one who suffers by it; instead, an accident *causes* the harm. For he is not at all free to choose[13] in the matter, because truthfulness (if he must speak) is an unconditional duty. The "German philosopher" will therefore not take as his principle the proposition (p. 124), "To tell the truth is a duty but only to someone who *has a right to the truth*," first because the principle is not clearly formulated, inasmuch as truth is not a possession the right to which could be granted to one but denied to another; but he will not do so mainly because the duty of truthfulness (the only matter under discussion here) makes no distinction between persons to whom one has this duty and those to whom one can exempt oneself from it, since it is, instead, an *unconditional duty*, which holds in all relations.

Now, in order to progress from a *metaphysics* of right (which abstracts from all conditions of experience) to a principle of *politics* (which applies these concepts to cases of experience) and, by means of this, to the solution of a problem of politics in keeping with the universal principle of right, a philosopher will give 1) an *axiom*, that is, an apodictically certain proposition that issues immediately from the definition of external right (consistency of the *freedom* of each with the freedom of everyone in accordance with a universal law); 2) a *postulate* (of external public *law*, as the united will of all in accordance with the principle of *equality*, without which there would be no freedom of everyone); 3) a *problem* of how it is to be arranged that in a society, however large, harmony in accordance with the principles of freedom and equality is maintained (namely, by means of a representative system); this will then be a principle of *politics*, the arrangement and organization of which will contain decrees, drawn from experiential cognition of human beings, that have in view only the mechanism for administering right and how this can be managed appropriately.[14] Right must never be accommodated to politics, but politics must always be accommodated to right.

The author says, "A proposition recognized as true (to which I add, recognized a priori, hence apodictically) must never be abandoned, however apparent is the danger present in it." But here one must understand not the danger of *harming* (contingently) but of *doing wrong* generally, as would happen if I make the duty of truthfulness, which is altogether unconditional and constitutes the supreme rightful condition in statements, into a conditional duty subordinate to other considerations and, though by a certain lie I in fact[15] wrong no one, I nevertheless violate the principle of right with respect to all unavoidable necessary statements *in general* (I do wrong formally though not materially); and this is much worse than committing an injustice to someone or other, since such a deed does not always presuppose in the subject a principle of doing so.[16]

Someone who is not indignant at another's question as to whether he is going to be truthful in the statement he is about to make – indignant at the suspicion it expresses that he might be a liar – but asks permission to think about possible exceptions is already a liar (*in potentia*); for he shows that he does not recognize truthfulness as a duty in itself but reserves for himself exceptions to a rule that by its essence does not admit of exceptions, since in doing so it would directly contradict itself.

All practical principles of right[17] must contain strict truth, and here the so-called intermediary principles can contain only the closer determination of their application to cases that come up (in accordance with rules of politics), but never exceptions from those principles; for exceptions would nullify the universality on account of which alone they are called principles.

Notes

1 *aus Menschenliebe.*
2 original falsity.
3 *nötigt.*
4 *ungerechter Zwang.*
5 a lie is speaking falsely in prejudice to another.
6 *auf rechtliche Art.*
7 *mit Recht.*
8 *Urheber.*
9 *Convenienzen.*
10 *mittlern Grundsatz.*
11 *Ungeschicklichkeit.*
12 *wie anscheinend auch Gefahr dabei sich bafindet.*

13 *wählen.*
14 *zweckmäßig.*
15 *in der Tat.*
16 *einen Grundsatz dazu.*
17 *rechtlich-praktische Grundsätze.*

4

From *A Review of the Principal Questions in Morals*

Richard Price

CHAPTER I Of the Origin of our Ideas of Moral Right and Wrong

Let us now return to our first enquiry, and apply the foregoing observations to our ideas of *right* and *wrong* in particular.

'Tis a very necessary previous observation, that our ideas of *right* and *wrong* are simple ideas, and must therefore be ascribed to some power of *immediate* perception in the human mind. He that doubts this, need only try to give definitions of them, which shall amount to more than synonymous expressions. Most of the confusion in which the question concerning the foundation of morals has been involved has proceeded from inattention to this remark. There are, undoubtedly, some actions that are *ultimately* approved, and for justifying which no reason can be assigned; as there are some ends, which are *ultimately* desired, and for chusing which no reason can be given. Were not this true; there would be an infinite progression of reasons and ends, and therefore nothing could be at all approved or desired.

Supposing then, that we have a power *immediately* perceiving right and wrong: the point I am now to endeavour to prove, is, that this power is the *Understanding*, agreeably to the assertion at the end of the *first* section. I cannot but flatter myself, that the main obstacle to the acknowledgment of this, has been already removed, by the observations made in the preceding section, to shew that the understanding is a power of immediate perception, which gives rise to new original ideas; nor do I think it

Richard Price, *A Review of the Principal Questions in Morals*, ed. D. D. Raphael (Oxford: Clarendon Press, 1974), pp. 40–4, 50–5, 131–9, 148–9, 151, 152, 153, 154–7, 164–5, 166–70.

possible that there should have been many disputes on this subject had this been properly considered.

But, in order more explicitly and distinctly to evince what I have asserted (in the only way the nature of the question seems capable of) let me,

First, Observe, that it implies no absurdity, but evidently *may* be true. It is undeniable, that many of our ideas are derived from our INTUITION of truth, or the discernment of the natures of things by the understanding. This therefore *may* be the source of our moral ideas. It is at least *possible*, that *right* and *wrong* may denote what we *understand* and *know* concerning certain objects, in like manner with proportion and disproportion, connexion and repugnancy, contingency and necessity, and the other ideas before-mentioned. – I will add, that nothing has been offered which has any tendency to prove the contrary. All that can appear, from the objections and reasonings of the Author[1] of the *Enquiry into the original of our ideas of beauty and virtue*, is only, what has been already observed, and what does not in the least affect the point in debate: Namely, that the words *right* and *wrong*, *fit* and *unfit*, express simple and undefinable ideas. But that the power perceiving them is properly a *sense* and not *reason*; that these ideas denote nothing *true* of actions, nothing in the *nature* of actions; this, he has left entirely without proof. He appears, indeed, to have taken for granted, that if virtue and vice are *immediately* perceived, they must be perceptions of an *implanted* sense. But no conclusion could have been more hasty. For will any one take upon him to say, that all powers of immediate perception must be arbitrary and implanted; or that there can be no simple ideas denoting any thing besides the qualities and passions of the mind? – In short. Whatever some writers have said to the contrary, it is certainly a point not yet decided, that virtue is wholly factitious, and to be *felt* not *understood*.

As there are some propositions, which, when attended to, necessarily determine all minds to *believe* them: And as (which will be shewn hereafter) there are some ends, whose natures are such, that, when perceived, all beings immediately and necessarily *desire* them: So is it very credible, that, in like manner, there are some actions whose natures are such, that, when observed, all rational beings immediately and necessarily *approve* them.

I do not at all care what follows from Mr. *Hume*'s assertion, that all our ideas are either *impressions, or *copies of impressions*; or from Mr. *Locke*'s

* See Mr. *Hume*'s *Treatise of Human Nature*, and *Philosophical Essays*.

assertion that they are all *deducible from* SENSATION *and* REFLEXION. – The first of these assertions is, I think, destitute of all proof; supposes, when applied in this as well as many other cases, the point in question; and, when pursued to its consequences, ends in the destruction of all truth and the subversion of our intellectual faculties. – The other wants much explication to render it consistent with any tolerable account of the original of our moral ideas: Nor does there seem to be any thing necessary to convince a person, that all our ideas are not deducible from sensation and reflexion, except taken in a very large and comprehensive sense, besides considering how Mr. *Locke* derives from them our *moral ideas*. He places them among our ideas of relations, and represents *rectitude* as signifying the conformity of actions to some rules or laws; which rules or laws, he says, are either *the will of God*, the *decrees of the magistrate, or the fashion of the country*: From whence it follows, that it is an absurdity to apply *rectitude* to rules and laws themselves; to suppose the *divine* will to be directed by it; or to consider it as *itself* a rule and law. But, it is undoubted, that this great man would have detested these consequences; and, indeed, it is sufficiently evident, that he was strangely embarrassed in his notions on this, as well as some other subjects. But,

Secondly, I know of no better way of determining this point, than by referring those who doubt about it to common sense, and putting them upon considering the nature of their own perceptions. – Could we suppose a person, who, when he perceived an external object, was at a loss to determine whether he perceived it by means of his organs of sight or touch; what better method could be taken to satisfy him? There is no possibility of doubting in any such cases. And it seems not more difficult to determine in the present case.

Were the question; what that perception is, which we have of number, diversity, causation or proportion; and whether our ideas of them signify truth and reality perceived by the understanding, or impressions made by the objects to which we ascribe them, on our minds; were, I say, this the question; would it not be sufficient to appeal to every man's consciousness? – These perceptions seem to me to have no greater pretence to be denominated perceptions of the understanding, than *right* and *wrong*.

The following important corollary arises from these arguments:

That morality is *eternal and immutable*.

Right and wrong, it appears, denote what actions *are*. Now whatever any thing *is*, that it is, not by will, or decree, or power, but by *nature and necessity.* Whatever a triangle or circle is, that it is unchangeably and eternally. It depends upon no will or power, whether the three angles of a triangle and two right ones shall be *equal*; whether the periphery of a circle and its diameter shall be *incommensurable*; or whether matter shall be *divisible, moveable, passive,* and *inert.* Every object of the under- standing has an indivisible and invariable essence; from whence arise its properties, and numberless truths concerning it. Omnipotence does not consist in a power to alter the nature of things, and to destroy necessary truth (for this is contradictory, and would infer the destruction of all wisdom, and knowledge) but in an absolute command over all *particular, external* existences, to create or destroy them, or produce any possible changes among them. – The natures of things then being immutable; whatever we suppose the natures of actions to be, they must be immutably. If they are indifferent, this indifference is itself immutable, and there neither is nor can be any one thing that, *in reality,* we *ought* to do rather than another. The same is to be said of right and wrong, of moral good and evil, as far as they express *real characters* of actions. They must immutably and necessarily belong to those actions of which they are *truly* affirmed.

No will, therefore, can render *any thing* good and obligatory, which was not so antecedently, and from eternity; or any action right, that is not so in itself; meaning by *action,* not the bare external effect produced, but the ultimate principle of conduct, or the determination of a reasonable being, considered as arising from the perception of some motives and reasons and intended for some end. According to this sense of the word *action,* whenever the principle from which we act is different, the action is different, though the external effects produced, may be the same. If we attend to this, the meaning and truth of what I have just observed, will be easily seen. – Put the case of any action, the performance of which is *indifferent,* or attended with no circumstances of the agent that render it better or fitter to be done than omitted. Is it not plain that, *while all things continue the same,* it is as impossible for any will or power to make acting obligatory here, as it is for them to make two equal things unequal without producing any change in either? It is true, the doing of any indif- ferent thing may become obligatory, in consequence of a command from a being possessed of rightful authority over us: But it is obvious, that in this case, the command produces a change in the circumstances of the agent, and that what, in consequence of it, becomes obligatory, is not the same with what *before* was indifferent. The external effect, that is, the *matter of the action* is indeed the same; but nothing is plainer, than that actions in this sense the same, may in a moral view be totally different according to the ends aimed at by them, and the principles of morality under which they fall.

When an action, otherwise indifferent, becomes obligatory, by being made the subject of a *promise*; we are not to imagine, that our own will or breath alters the nature of things by making what is indifferent not so. But what was indifferent *before* the promise is still so; and it cannot be supposed, that, *after* the promise, it becomes obligatory, without a contradiction. All that the promise does, is, to alter the connexion of a particular effect; or to cause that to be an *instance* of right conduct which was not so before. There are no effects producible by us, which may not, in this manner, fall under different principles of morality; acquire connexions sometimes with happiness, and sometimes with misery; and thus stand in different relations to the eternal rules of duty.

The objection, therefore, to what is here asserted, taken from the effects of positive laws and promises, has no weight. It appears, that when an obligation to particular indifferent actions arises from the command of the Deity, or positive laws; it is by no means to be inferred from hence, that obligation is the creature of will, or that the nature of what is indifferent is changed: nothing then becoming obligatory, which was not so from eternity; that is, *obeying the divine will, and just authority*. And had there been nothing right in this, had there been no reason from the natures of things for obeying God's will; it is certain, it could have induced no obligation, nor at all influenced an intellectual nature as such. – Will and laws signify nothing, abstracted from something previous to them, in the character of the law-giver and the relations of beings to one another, to give them force and render disobedience a crime. If mere will ever obliged, what reason can be given, why the will of one being should oblige, and of another not; why it should not oblige alike to every thing it requires; and why there should be any difference between *power* and *authority*? It is truth and reason, then, that, in all cases, oblige, and not mere will. So far, we see, is it from being possible, that any will or laws should *create* right; that they can have no effect, but in virtue of natural and antecedent right.

Thus, then, is morality fixed on an immoveable *basis*, and appears not to be, in any sense, *factitious*; or the *arbitrary production* of any power human or divine; but *equally everlasting* and *necessary* with all *truth* and *reason*. And this we find to be as evident, as that right and wrong signify a *reality* in what is so denominated.

I shall conclude this chapter, with observing; that the opinion of those, who maintain that our ideas of morality are derived from sense, is far from being entirely modern. There were among the antients, philosophers, (*Protagoras*, in particular, and his followers) who entertained a like opinion; but extended it much further; that is, to *all science*; denied all absolute and immutable truth; and asserted every thing to be relative to perception. And indeed it seems not a very unnatural transition, from denying absolute *moral* truth, to denying *all truth*; from making right and wrong, just and unjust, dependent on perception, to asserting the same of whatever we commonly rank among the objects of the understanding. Why may not he who rejects the reality of rightness in beneficence, and of wrong in producing needless misery, be led, by the same steps, to deny the certainty of other self-evident principles? Why may he not as well deny the reality, for example, of *straitness* in a line drawn the shortest way between two points; or of aptness and unaptness, of connexion and proportion between certain objects and quantities? He that distrusts his reason in the one case, why should he not also in the other? He that refers the former perceptions to a sense; why should he not, with the before-mentioned philosopher, make *all knowledge to be sense*? – Consequences much worse cannot follow from making all the principles of knowledge arbitrary and factitious, than from making morality so; from supposing all we perceive of the natures and relations of things, to denote modes of sensation in our minds, than from supposing this of the objects of our moral discernment. If the one overthrows *all* truth, the other overthrows that *part* of truth which is most important and interesting. If the one destroys the necessary wisdom and intelligence of the Deity (the very idea of a mind and of knowledge, being impossible, if there is nothing permanent in the nature of things, nothing *necessarily* true, and therefore nothing to be *known*) the other equally destroys his moral perfections.

One argument which, it seems, *Protagoras* made great use of in maintaining his opinions, was, that colours, tastes, and sounds, and the other sensible qualities of bodies exist only when perceived, and therefore are not qualities inherent in bodies, but sensations ever-varying, begot between the sensible object and organ, and produced by the action of the one on the other; the same object, as he reasoned, often appearing to have different qualities to different persons; and no two persons having exactly the same ideas of any one sensible quality of any object. From hence, and from a notion, not very consistent with it, that consciousness and understanding were to be resolved into matter and motion; he concluded, that all things are in a perpetual flux; and that nothing is true or false (any more than sweet or sour) in itself, but relatively to the perceiving mind. That he applied this particularly to moral good and evil, appears from several passages in *Plato's Theætetus*, where these notions of *Protagoras's* are at large explained and confuted. – He that would have a fuller view of what is here said, may consult this Dialogue of *Plato's* or Dr. *Cudworth's Treatise* of *Immutable and Eternal Morality*.

Note

1   Hutcheson.

CHAPTER VII Of the Subject-matter of Virtue, or its principal Heads and Divisions

There remain yet three questions to be considered in relation to virtue.

First, To what particular course of action we give this name, or what are the chief *heads* of virtue.

Secondly, What is the *principle* or *motive,* from which a virtuous agent, as such, acts.

Thirdly, What is meant by the different *degrees* of virtue, in different actions and characters, and how we estimate them. – Each of these questions shall be examined in the order in which they are here proposed.

There would be less occasion for the first of these enquiries, if several writers had not maintained, that the *whole* of virtue consists in BENEVOLENCE. Nothing better can be offered on this point, than what is said under the fifth observation in the *Dissertation on the Nature of Virtue,* annexed to Bishop *Butler's Analogy.* – From hence, therefore, I shall borrow the following passage: – 'Benevolence and the want of it, singly considered, are in no sort the whole of virtue and vice; for, if this were the case, in the review of one's own character, or that of others, our moral understanding and moral sense, would be indifferent to every thing, but the degrees in which benevolence prevailed, and the degrees in which it was wanting: That is, we should neither approve of benevolence to some persons rather than to others, nor disapprove injustice and falshood upon any other account, than merely as an over-balance of happiness was foreseen likely to be produced by the first, and of misery by the last. But now, on the contrary, suppose two men competitors for any thing whatever, which would be of equal advantage to either of them. Though nothing indeed would be more impertinent, than for a stranger to busy himself to get one of them preferred to the other, yet such endeavour would be virtue in behalf of a friend, or benefactor, abstracted from all consideration of distant consequences; as, that examples of gratitude, and the cultivation of friendship, would be of general good to the world. – Again, suppose one man should by fraud or violence, take from another the fruit of his labour, with intent to give it to a third, who, he thought, would have as much pleasure from it, as would balance the pleasure which the first possessor would have had in the enjoyment, and his vexation in the loss of it; suppose again, that no bad consequences would follow, yet such an action would surely be vicious.'

The cases here put are clear and decisive, nor is it easy to conceive what can be said in reply to them. Many other cases and observations, to the same purpose, might be mentioned. – It cannot be true, for instance, that promises and engagements are not in any case binding upon any one, any further than he thinks the observance of them will be productive of good upon the whole to society; or, that we are released from all obligation to regard them, as soon as we believe, that violating them will not hurt the person to whom they have been made, or that, if detrimental to him, it will be equally beneficial to ourselves, or, in any other way, will be attended with advantages equivalent to the foreseen harm. He would be looked upon by all, as having acted basely, who, having any advantage to bestow which he had engaged to give to one person, should give it another; nor would it be regarded as any vindication of his conduct to alledge, that he knew this other would reap equal profit from it. Many particular actions, and omissions of action, become, in consequence of promises and engagements, highly evil, which otherwise would have been entirely innocent; and the degree of vice in any harm done, is always greatly increased, when done by means of deceit and treachery. – To treat a party of rebels, after they had surrendered themselves upon certain terms stipulated with them, in the same manner as if they had been reduced by force, would be generally disapproved: And yet it might be hard to shew, that the consequences of not keeping faith with them would have been very detrimental to the publick. – A general would be universally condemned, who, by means of any treacherous contrivance should engage his enemies to trust themselves in his power, and then destroy them. How different are our ideas of such conduct from those we have of the same end gained by open and fair conquest?

Would it be indifferent whether a person, supposed to be just returned from some unknown country or new world, gave a true or false account of what he had seen? Is there a man in the world who, in such a case, would not think it better to tell truth than needlessly and wantonly to deceive? Is it possible any one can think he may innocently (to save himself or another from some small inconvenience, which he can full as well prevent by other means) tell any lies or make any false protestations, if he *knows* they will never be found out? If he may thus impose upon his fellow-creatures by declaring one falsehood, why may he not in like circumstances declare any number of falsehoods, and with any possible circumstances of solemnity? Why is he not at liberty to make any declarations, however deceitful, to practise any kinds of dissimulation and commit perjuries, whenever he believes they are likely to hurt no one, and will be the means of introducing him to any degree of greater ease or usefulness in life? – Can we, when we consider these things, avoid pronouncing, that there is *intrinsick rectitude* in keeping faith and in sincerity, and *intrinsick evil* in the contrary; and that it is by no means true, that veracity and falshood appear *in themselves*, and *exclusive* of *their consequences*, wholly indifferent to our moral judgment? Is it a notion capable of being seriously defended, or even endured by an ingenuous mind, that the goodness of the end always consecrates the means; or that, *cæteris paribus*, it is as innocent and laudable to accomplish our purposes by lies, prevarication and perjury, as by faithful and open dealing and honest labour? wherein, upon such sentiments, would consist the wickedness of pious frauds; and why are they condemned and detested?

No worse mistake, indeed, can be well conceived than this; for, as the excellent author before-cited observes, 'it is certain, that some of the most shocking instances of injustice,* adultery, murder, perjury, and even persecution, may, in many supposable cases, not have the appearance of being likely to produce an overbalance of misery in the present state; perhaps, sometimes, may have a contrary appearance.'

A disapprobation in the human mind of ingratitude, injustice, and deceit, none deny. The point under examination is, the *ground* of this

---

* Is a man warranted to destroy himself, as soon as he believes his life is become useless or burthensome to those about him, and miserable to himself? How shocking in many circumstances would the most private assassination be of a person whose death all may wish for, and consider as a benefit to himself and to the world? Who would not severely reproach himself for reserving to himself the property of another which had been lost, and which he had accidentally found, however secretly he might do this, and whatever reason he might have for thinking that it would be of greater use to him than to the proprietor? There would be no end of mentioning cases of this sort, but I have chosen to instance particularly in veracity.

disapprobation; whether it arises solely from views of inconvenience to others and confusion in society occasioned by them; or whether there be not also *immediate wrong* apprehended in them, independently of their effects. The instances and considerations here produced seem sufficiently to determine this. It appears, that they are disapproved when productive of no harm, and even when in some degree beneficial.

'Shall it be still urged that, in cases of this kind, our disapprobation is owing to the idea of a plan or system of common utility established by custom in the mind with which these vices are apprehended to be inconsistent; or to a habit acquired of considering them as of general pernicious tendency, by which we are insensibly influenced, whenever, in any particular circumstances or instances, we contemplate them?' – But why must we have recourse to the influence of habits and associations in this case? This has been the refuge of those, who would resolve all our moral perceptions into views of private advantage, and may serve to evade almost any evidence which can be derived from the experience we have of the workings of our minds and the motives of our actions. In the cases which have been mentioned, we may remove entirely the idea of a publick, and suppose no persons existing whose state they can at all influence; or, we may suppose all memory of the action to be for ever lost as soon as done, and the agent to foresee this; and yet, the same ideas of the ingratitude, injustice, or violation of truth will remain. – If the whole reason for regarding truth arose from its influence on society, a primitive Christian would not have been blame-worthy for renouncing his religion, blaspheming Christ, and worshipping the Pagan gods (all which is no more than denying truth) whenever he could purchase his life by these means, and at the same time avoid a discovery, and thus prevent the prejudice to Christians and Pagans that might arise from his conduct? – *Peter* would not have been innocent in denying his Master with oaths and imprecations, though he had known that he should never be detected. A stranger, in a Pagan country, would not do right to comply with its superstitions, to worship and profess contrary to his sentiments, and abjure his faith, in order to secure his quiet or life, provided he judged the deceit would not be known, that he could do no good by a different conduct, or that his hypocrisy had no tendency to establish and perpetuate idolatry.

It is further to be observed on this argument, that in these cases it does not appear that mankind in general much attended to distant consequences. Children, particularly, cannot be supposed to consider consequences, or to have any fixed ideas of a public or a community; and yet, we observe in them the same aversion to falshood and relish for truth, as in the rest of mankind. There is indeed no less evidence, that, in the cases specified, we approve and disapprove *immediately*, than there is that we do so, when we consider benevolence or cruelty. It has been urged against those who derive all our desires and actions from self-love, that they find out views and reasonings for men, which never entered the minds of most of them; and which, in all probability, none attended to in the common course of their thoughts and pursuits. – The same may be urged against those, who derive all our sentiments of moral good and evil from our approbation of benevolence and disapprobation of the want of it; and both, in my opinion, have undertaken tasks almost equally impracticable. Any person, one would imagine, who will impartially examine his own mind, may feel, in his dislike of several vices, something different from the apprehension of their diminishing happiness or producing misery, and easily observe that it is not merely under these notions that he always censures and condemns. It is true, this apprehension, when it occurs, always heightens our disapprobation. Falshood, ingratitude, and injustice undermine the foundations of all social intercourse and happiness, and the consequences of them, were they to become universal, would be terrible. – For this reason, supposing morality founded on an arbitrary structure of our minds, there would be a necessity for distinct senses immediately condemning and forbidding them. Leaving them to the influence of a general disapprobation of all actions evidencing a neglect of publick good, or without any particular determination against them any farther than by every man they should be thought likely to produce more misery than happiness, would be attended with the worst effects. It would not, in all likelihood, by any means, be sufficient to secure tolerably the order of human society; especially, considering how many amongst mankind there are, who are incapable of enlarged reflexions, and whose thoughts are confined within the narrowest limits; and how little prone all men naturally are to be affected with or to regard remote events, as well as how liable they are to take up the wrongest opinions of the tendencies of their actions, and the good or ill to the world which they may occasion.

Perhaps, he who should maintain, that we have no affection properly resting in *ourselves*, but that all our desires and aversions arise from a prospect of advantage or detriment to *others*, would not assert what would be much less defensible that what those assert who maintain the reverse of this, and deny all *disinterested benevolence*. – In like manner, to assert that our approbation of *beneficence* is to be resolved into our approbation of *veracity*, or that the whole of morality consists in *signifying and denying truth*, would not be much more unreasonable than the contrary assertion, that our approbation of *veracity* and of all that is denominated virtue, is resolvable into the approbation of *beneficence*. But why must there be in the human mind approbation only of one sort of actions? Why must all moral good be reduced to one particular species of it, and kind affections, with the actions flowing from them, be represented, as alone capable of appearing to our moral faculty *virtuous*? Why may we not as well have an immediate relish also for truth, for candour, sincerity, piety, gratitude, and many other modes and principles of conduct? – Admitting all our ideas of morality to be derived from implanted determinations; the latter of these determinations is equally possible with the other; and what has been above hinted shews that there is the greatest occasion for them to secure the general welfare, and that therefore it might antecedently be expected that a good Being would give them to us.

How unreasonable is that love of uniformity and simplicity which inclines men thus to seek them where it is so difficult to find them? It is this that, on other subjects, has often led men astray. What mistakes and extravagances in natural philosophy have been produced, by the desire of discovering *one* principle which shall account for all effects? I deny not but that in the human mind, as well as in the material world, the most wonderful simplicity takes place; but we ought to learn to wait, till we can, by careful observation and enquiry, find out wherein it consists; and not suffer ourselves rashly to determine any thing concerning it, or to receive any general causes and principles which cannot be proved by experience.

If the account of morality I have given is just, it is not to be conceived, that promoting the happiness of others should comprehend the whole of our duty, or that the consideration of publick good should be that alone in *all* circumstances which can have any concern in determining what is right or wrong. It has been observed, that every different situation of a reasonable creature requires a different manner of acting, and that concerning all that can be proposed to be done, something is to be affirmed or denied, which, when known, necessarily implies a *direction* to the agent in regard to his behaviour.

Having premised these observations, I shall now proceed to enumerate some of the most important *Branches of virtue*, or *heads of rectitude and duty*.

What requires the first place is our DUTY TO GOD, or the whole of that regard, subjection and homage we owe him. These seem unquestionably objects of moral approbation, independently of all considerations of utility. They are considered as indispensably obligatory, and yet the principle upon which they are practised cannot be an intention, in any manner, to be useful or profitable to the object of them. Those persons must be uncommonly weak and ignorant who mean, by their religious services, to make an addition to the happiness of the Deity, or who entertain any apprehensions, that it is on his own account, and to advance his own good, he expects their gratitude and prayers. I know, indeed, that some writers of great worth have expressed themselves, as if they doubted, whether the secret spring of all obedience to him, and concurrence with his ends, is not some desire of contributing to his satisfaction and delight. It would be trifling with most of my readers, to employ much time, in representing the prodigious absurdity of such an opinion. . . .

The *second* branch of virtue, which we may take notice of, is that which has *ourselves* for its object. There is, undoubtedly, a certain manner of conduct terminating in ourselves, which is properly matter of *duty* to us. It is too absurd to be maintained by any one, that no relation which an action may have to our own happiness or misery, can (supposing other beings unconcerned) have any influence in determining, whether it is or is not to be done, or make it appear to rational and calm reflexion otherwise than *morally indifferent.* – It is contradictory to suppose, that the same necessity which makes an end to us, and determines us to the choice and desire of it, should be unaccompanied with an approbation of using the means of attaining it. It is, in reality, no more morally indifferent, how we employ our faculties, and what we do relating to our own interest, than it is how we behave to our fellow-creatures. If it is my duty to promote the good of *another*, and to abstain from hurting him; the same, most certainly, must be my duty with regard to *myself.* It would be contrary to all reason to deny this; or to assert that I *ought* to consult the good of another, but not my own; or that the advantage an action will produce to another makes it right to be done, but that an equal advantage to myself leaves me at liberty to do or omit it. – So far is this from being true, that it will be strange, if any one can avoid acknowledging that it is right and fit that a being should, when all circumstances on both sides are equal, *prefer* himself to another; reserve, for example, to *himself*, a certain means of enjoyment he possesses rather than part with it to a *stranger*, to whom it will not be *more* beneficial. . . .

Thirdly, Another part of rectitude is BENEFICENCE, or the study of the good of others. Publick happiness is an object that must necessarily determine all minds to prefer and desire it. It is of essential and unchangeable value and importance; and there is not any thing which appears to our thoughts with greater light and evidence, or of which we have more undeniably an intuitive perception, than that it is *right* to promote and pursue it. – So important a part of virtue is this, and so universally acknowledged, that it is become a considerable subject of debate, whether it be not the *whole* of virtue.

As, under the preceding head, it has been observed, that it would be strange that the good of another should make an action fit to be performed, but our own good not; the contrary observation may be here made; namely, that it cannot be consistently supposed that our own good should make an action fit to be performed, but that of others not.

All rational beings ought to have a share in our kind wishes and affections: But we are surrounded with *fellow-men*, beings of the same nature, in the same circumstances, and having the same wants with ourselves; to whom therefore we are in a peculiar manner linked and related, and whose happiness and misery depend very much on our behaviour to them. These considerations ought to engage us to labour to be useful to mankind, and to cultivate to the utmost the principle of benevolence to them. And how amiable does the man appear in whose breast this divine principle reigns; who studies to make all with whom he has any connexion easy and happy; who loves others as he desires others to love him; whose joy is their joy, and misery their misery; who is humane, patient, humble, and generous; never gives the least indulgence to any harsh or unfriendly dispositions, and comprehends in what he counts *himself* his relations, friends, neighbours, country, and species?

Fourthly, The next head of virtue proper to be mentioned is GRATITUDE. The consideration that we have received benefits, lays us under *peculiar* obligations to the persons who have conferred them; and renders that behaviour, which to others may be innocent, to them criminal. . . .

Fifthly, VERACITY is a most important part of virtue. Of this a good deal has been already said. . . .

Truth then, necessarily recommends itself to our preference. And the essence of *lying* consisting in using established signs in order to *deceive*, it must be disapproved by all rational beings upon the same grounds with those on which truth and knowledge are desired by them, and right judgment preferred to mistake and ignorance. – No beings, supposed alike indifferent to truth and falshood and careless which they embrace, can be conceived to take offence at any imposition upon themselves or others; and he who will not say, that, consequences apart, (which is all along supposed) to *know* is not better than to *err*, or that there is nothing to determine any being *as rational*, to chuse wisdom rather than folly, just apprehensions rather than wrong, to be awake and actually to see rather than to be in a continual delirium: He, I say, who will not maintain this, will scarcely be unwilling to acknowledge an *immediate rectitude* in *veracity*.

Under this head, I would comprehend impartiality and honesty of mind in our enquiries after truth, as well as a sacred regard to it in all we say; fair and ingenuous dealing; such an openness and simplicity of temper as exclude guile and prevarication, and all the contemptible arts of craft, equivocation and hypocrisy; fidelity to our engagements; sincerity and uprightness in our transactions with ourselves as well as others; and the careful avoiding of all secret attempts to deceive ourselves, and to evade or disguise the truth in examining our own characters.

Some of these particulars, though they belong to the division of rectitude I have now in view, and which has truth for its object; yet are not properly included in the signification of *veracity*. – But it requires our notice, that fidelity to promises is *properly* a branch or instance of *veracity*. – *The nature and obligation of *promises* have been said to be attended with great difficulties; which makes it necessary to desire this observation may be particularly considered.

By a *promise* some declaration is made, or assurance given to another, which brings us under an obligation to act or not to act, from which we should have been otherwise free. Such an obligation never flows merely from declaring a *resolution* or *intention*; and therefore a promise must mean more than this; and the whole difference is, that the one relates to the *present*, the other to *future* time. – When I say I *intend* to do an action, I affirm only a present fact. – But to *promise*, is to declare that such a thing *shall* be done, or that such and such events *shall* happen. In this case, it is not enough to acquit me from the charge of falshood, that I *intend* to do what I promise, but it must be actually done, agreeably to the assurances given. After declaring a *resolution* to do an action, a man is under no obligation actually to do it, because he did not say he would; his word and veracity are not engaged; and the non-performance cannot infer the guilt of violating truth. On the contrary, when a person declares he *will* do any action, he becomes obliged to do it, and cannot afterwards omit it, without incurring the imputation of declaring falshood, as really as if he had

---

*   See *Treatise of Human Nature*, Vol. III, Book III, part II, Sect. V.

declared what he knew to be a false past or present fact; and in much the same manner as he would have done, if he had pretended to know, and had accordingly asserted, that a certain event would happen at a certain time which yet did not then happen. There is, however, a considerable difference between this last case, and the falshood implied in breaking promises and engagements; for the object of these is something, the existence of which depends on ourselves, and which we have in our power to bring to pass; and therefore here the falshood must be known and wilful, and entirely imputable to our own neglect and guilt. But in the case of events predicted which are not subject to our dominion, the blame, as far as there may be any, must arise from pretending to knowledge which we really want, and asserting absolutely what we are not sure of.

To *promise* then, being to assert a fact dependent on ourselves, with an intention to produce faith in it and reliance upon it, as certainly to happen; the obligation to keep a promise is the same with the obligation to regard truth; and the intention of it cannot be, in the sense some have asserted, to will or create a new obligation; unless it can be pretended that the obligation to veracity is *created* by the mere breath of men every time they speak, or make any professions. If indeed we mean by creating a new obligation, that the producing a particular effect or performance of an external action becomes fit, in consequence of some new situation of a person (or some preceding acts of his own) which was not fit before; it may be very well acknowledged; nor is there any thing in the least mysterious in it. Thus, performance becomes our duty after a promise, in the same sense that repentance becomes our duty in consequence of doing wrong, reparation of an injury, in consequence of committing it, or a particular manner of conduct, in consequence of placing ourselves in particular circumstances and relations of life.

As a confirmation of this account, if any confirmation was necessary, it might be observed, that false declarations in general, and violations of engagements admit of the same extenuations or aggravations according to the different degrees of solemnity with which they are made, and the different importance of the subjects of them.

The last part of virtue, I shall mention, is JUSTICE: Meaning by this word, that part of virtue which regards *property* and *commerce*.

The origin of the idea of *property* is the same with that of right and wrong in general. It denotes such a relation of a particular object to a particular person, as infers or implies, that it is fit he should have the disposal of it rather than others, and wrong to deprive him of it. This is what every one means by calling a thing his *right*, or saying that it is *his own*.

Upon this there are two questions that may be asked. *First*, How an object obtains that relation to a person? – *Secondly*, Into what we are to resolve, and how we are to account for, the right and wrong we perceive in these instances?

The writers of *Ethicks* are very well agreed in their answers to the first of these questions. An object, it is obvious, will acquire the relation to a person which has been mentioned, in consequence of first possession; in consequence of its being the fruit of his labour; by donation, succession, and many other ways not necessary to be here enumerated. . . .

These then are the main and leading branches of Virtue. It may not be possible properly to comprehend all the particular instances of it under any number of heads. It is by attending to the different relations, circumstances, and qualifications of beings, and the natures and tendencies of objects, and by examining into the whole truth of every case, that we judge what *is* or *is not to be* done. And as there is an endless variety of cases, and the situations of agents and objects are ever changing; the universal law of rectitude, though in the abstract idea of it always invariably the same, must be continually varying in its *particular* demands and obligations. . . .

There is another coincidence between the foregoing heads of virtue worth our notice. I mean, their agreeing very often in requiring the same actions. An act of *justice* may be also an act of *gratitude* and *beneficence;* and whatever any of these oblige us to, that also *piety* to God requires. Were *injustice, fraud, falshood,* and a *neglect* of *private* good universally prevalent, what a dreadful state would the world be in? and how would the ends of *benevolence* be defeated? – No one of the several virtues can be annihilated without the most pernicious consequences to all the rest. This, in a good measure, appears from what happens in the present state of things; but, in the final issue of things, the harmony between them will be found much more strict. Whatever exceptions may now happen, if we will look forwards to the whole of our existence, the three great principles of the love of God, the love of man, and true self-love, will always draw us the same way; and we have the utmost reason to assure ourselves, that at last no one will be able to say he has bettered himself by *any* unjust action, or that, though *less scrupulous* than others, he has been *more successful and happy.*

But though the heads of virtue before-mentioned agree thus far in requiring the same course of action, yet they often also interfere. Though upon the whole, or when considered as making one *general system or plan of conduct*, there is a strict coincidence between them, yet in examining *single acts* and *particular cases*, we find that they lead us contrary ways. – This perhaps has not been enough attended to, and therefore I shall particularly insist upon it.

What creates the difficulty in morals of determining what is right or wrong, in many particular cases, is chiefly the interference now mentioned in such cases between the different general principles of virtue. – Thus, the pursuit of the happiness of others is a duty, and so is the pursuit of private happiness; and though, on the whole, these are inseparably connected, in many particular instances, one of them cannot be pursued without giving up the other. When the publick happiness is very great, and the private very inconsiderable, no difficulties appear. We pronounce as confidently, that the one ought to give way to the other, as we do, that either alone ought to be pursued. But when the former is diminished, and the latter increased to a certain degree, doubt arises; and we may thus be rendered entirely incapable of determining what we ought to chuse. We have the most satisfactory perception, that we ought to study our own good, and, within certain limits, prefer it to that of another; but who can say how far, mark precisely these limits, and inform us in all cases of opposition between them, where right and wrong and indifference take place? – In like manner; the nearer attachments of nature or friendship, the obligations to veracity, fidelity, gratitude, or justice, may interfere with private and publick good, and it is not possible for us to judge always and accurately, what degrees or circumstances of any one of these compared with the others, will or will not cancel its obligation, and justify the violation of it. – It is thus likewise, that the different foundations of property give rise to contrary claims, and that sometimes it becomes very hard to say which of different titles to an object is the best. – If we examine the various intricate and disputed cases in morality, we shall, I believe, find that it is always some interference of this kind that produces the obscurity. Truth and right in all circumstances, require one determinate way of acting; but so variously may different obligations combine with or oppose each other in particular cases, and so imperfect are our discerning faculties, that it cannot but happen, that we should be frequently in the dark, and that different persons should judge differently, according to the different views they have of the several moral principles. Nor is this less unavoidable, or more to be wondered at, than that in matters of mere speculation, we should be at a loss to know what is true, when the arguments for and against a proposition appear nearly equal.

The principles themselves, it should be remembered, are self-evident; and to conclude the contrary, or to assert that there are no moral distinctions, because of the obscurity attending several cases wherein a competition arises between the several principles of morality, is very unreasonable. It is not unlike concluding, that, because in some circumstances we cannot, by their appearance to the eye, judge of the distances and magnitude of bodies, therefore we never can; because undeniable principles may be used in proving and opposing particular doctrines, therefore these principles are not undeniable; or because it may not in some instances be easy to determine what will be the effect of different forces, variously compounded and acting contrary to each other; therefore we can have no assurance what any of them acting separately will produce, or so much as know that there is any such thing as force.*

These observations may be of some use in helping us to determine, how far and in what sense, morality is capable of demonstration. There are undoubtedly a variety of moral principles and maxims, which, to gain assent, need only to be understood: And I see not why such propositions as these, 'gratitude is due to benefactors; reverence is due to our Creator; it is right to study our own happiness; an innocent being ought not to be absolutely miserable; it is wrong to take from another the fruit of his labour,' and others of the like kind, may not be laid down and used as axioms, the truth of which appears as irresistibly as the truth of those which are the foundation of Geometry. But the case is very different when we come to consider *particular* effects. What is meant by demonstrating morality, can only be reducing these under the general self-evident principles of morality, or making out with certainty their relation to them. It would be happy for us were this always possible. We should then be eased of many painful doubts, know universally and infallibly what we should

---

*   How unreasonable would it be to conclude from the difficulty there often is to determine the bounds of *equality* and *inequality* between quantities, or from its appearing doubtful to us in some instances, whether quantities are the *same* or *different*, that such quantities are in reality neither equal nor unequal, neither the same nor different, or that in such instances *equality* and *inequality*, *sameness* and *difference* run into one another? Just as unreasonable would it be to conclude, from its being often difficult to define the bounds of right and wrong, or from its appearing doubtful to us in some nice cases what way of acting is *right* or *wrong*, that in such cases, there is no particular way of acting truly and certainly right or wrong, or that *right* and *wrong* in these cases lose their distinction. The weakness of our discerning faculties cannot in any case affect truth. Things themselves continue invariably the same, however different our opinions of them may be, or whatever doubts or difficulties may perplex us.

do and avoid, and have nothing to attend to besides conforming our practice to our knowledge. How impracticable this is every one must see. – Were benevolence the only virtuous principle, we could by no means apply it always without any danger of mistake to action; because we cannot be more sure, a particular external action is an instance of beneficence, than we are of the tendencies and consequences of that action. The same holds true upon the supposition that self-love is the only principle of virtue. Until we can in every particular know what is good or bad for ourselves and others, and discover the powers and qualities of objects, and what will result from any application of them to one another, we cannot always demonstrate what either of these principles requires, but must continue liable to frequent and unavoidable errors in our moral judgment. – In like manner, what our duty to God, the regard due to the properties and rights of others, and gratitude require, we must be at a loss about, as far as in any circumstances we cannot be sure what the will of God is, where property is lodged, or who our benefactors are and what are our obligations to them. – Thus, if we consider the several moral principles singly (or as liable to no limitations from one another) we find that we must frequently be very uncertain how it is best to act.

But if we further recollect, that in order to discover what is right in a case, we ought to extend our views to all the different *heads* of virtue, to examine how far each is concerned, and compare their respective influence and demands; and that at the same time (as just now explained) they often interfere; a second source of insuperable difficulties will appear. It is not alone sufficient to satisfy us that an action is to be done, that we know it will be the means of good to others: we are also to consider how it affects ourselves, what it is in regard to justice, and all the other circumstances the case may involve must be taken in, and weighed, if we would form a true judgment concerning it. In reality, before we can be capable of deducing demonstrably, accurately and particularly, the whole rule of *right* in every instance, we must possess universal and unerring knowledge. It must be above the power of any finite understanding to do this. He only who knows all truth, is acquainted with the whole law of truth in all its importance, perfection and extent.

Once more; we may, by considerations of this kind, be helped in forming a judgment of the different sentiments and practices in several points of morality, which have obtained in different countries and ages. The foregoing general principles all men at all times have agreed in. It cannot be shewn that there have ever been any human beings who have had no ideas of property and justice, of the rectitude of veracity, gratitude, benevolence, prudence, and religious worship. All the difference has been about particular usages and practices, of which it is impossible but different persons must have different ideas, according to the various opinions they entertain of their relation to the universally acknowledged moral principles, or of their ends, connexions, and tendencies.

5

From *The Right and the Good*

W. D. Ross

What Makes Right Acts Right?

The real point at issue between hedonism and utilitarianism on the one hand and their opponents on the other is not whether "right" means "productive of so and so"; for it cannot with any plausibility be maintained that it does. The point at issue is that to which we now pass, viz. whether there is any general character which makes right acts right, and if so, what it is. Among the main historical attempts to state a single characteristic of all right actions which is the foundation of their rightness are those made by egoism and utilitarianism. But I do not propose to discuss these, not because the subject is unimportant, but because it has been dealt with so often and so well already, and because there has come to be so much agreement among moral philosophers that neither of these theories is satisfactory. A much more attractive theory has been put forward by Professor Moore: that what makes actions right is that they are productive of more *good* than could have been produced by any other action open to the agent.[1]

This theory is in fact the culmination of all the attempts to base rightness on productivity of some sort of result. The first form this attempt takes is the attempt to base rightness on conduciveness to the advantage or pleasure of the agent. This theory comes to grief over the fact, which stares us in the face, that a great part of duty consists in an observance of the rights and a furtherance of the interests of others, whatever the cost to ourselves may be. Plato and others may be right in holding that a regard for the rights of others never in the long run involves a loss of happiness for the agent, that "the just life profits a man". But this, even if true, is

W. D. Ross, *The Right and the Good* (Oxford: Clarendon Press, 1967), pp. 16–47.

irrelevant to the rightness of the act. As soon as a man does an action *because* he thinks he will promote his own interests thereby, he is acting not from a sense of its rightness but from self-interest.

To the egoistic theory hedonistic utilitarianism supplies a much-needed amendment. It points out correctly that the fact that a certain pleasure will be enjoyed by the agent is no reason why he *ought* to bring it into being rather than an equal or greater pleasure to be enjoyed by another, though, human nature being what it is, it makes it not unlikely that he *will* try to bring it into being. But hedonistic utilitarianism in its turn needs a correction. On reflection it seems clear that pleasure is not the only thing in life that we think good in itself, that for instance we think the possession of a good character, or an intelligent understanding of the world, as good or better. A great advance is made by the substitution of "productive of the greatest good" for "productive of the greatest pleasure".

Not only is this theory more attractive than hedonistic utilitarianism, but its logical relation to that theory is such that the latter could not be true unless *it* were true, while it might be true though hedonistic utilitarianism were not. It is in fact one of the logical bases of hedonistic utilitarianism. For the view that what produces the maximum pleasure is right has for its bases the views (1) that what produces the maximum good is right, and (2) that pleasure is the only thing good in itself. If they were not assuming that what produces the maximum *good* is right, the utilitarians' attempt to show that pleasure is the only thing good in itself, which is in fact the point they take most pains to establish, would have been quite irrelevant to their attempt to prove that only what produces the maximum *pleasure* is right. If, therefore, it can be shown that productivity of the maximum good is not what makes all right actions right, we shall *a fortiori* have refuted hedonistic utilitarianism.

When a plain man fulfils a promise because he thinks he ought to do so, it seems clear that he does so with no thought of its total consequences, still less with any opinion that these are likely to be the best possible. He thinks in fact much more of the past than of the future. What makes him think it right to act in a certain way is the fact that he has promised to do so – that and, usually, nothing more. That his act will produce the best possible consequences is not his reason for calling it right. What lends colour to the theory we are examining, then, is not the actions (which form probably a great majority of our actions) in which some such reflection as "I have promised" is the only reason we give ourselves for thinking a certain action right, but the exceptional cases in which the consequences of fulfilling a promise (for instance) would be so disastrous to others that we judge it right not to do so. It must of course be admitted that such cases exist. If I have promised to meet a friend at a particular time for some trivial purpose, I should certainly think myself justified in breaking my engagement if by doing so I could prevent a serious accident or bring relief to the victims of one. And the supporters of the view we are examining hold that my thinking so is due to my thinking that I shall bring more good into existence by the one action than by the other. A different account may, however, be given of the matter, an account which will, I believe, show itself to be the true one. It may be said that besides the duty of fulfilling promises I have and recognize a duty of relieving distress,[2] and that when I think it right to do the latter at the cost of not doing the former, it is not because I think I shall produce more good thereby but because I think it the duty which is in the circumstances more of a duty. This account surely corresponds much more closely with what we really think in such a situation. If, so far as I can see, I could bring equal amounts of good into being by fulfilling my promise and by helping some one to whom I had made no promise, I should not hesitate to regard the former as my duty. Yet on the view that what is right is right because it is productive of the most good I should not so regard it.

There are two theories, each in its way simple, that offer a solution of such cases of conscience. One is the view of Kant, that there are certain duties of perfect obligation, such as those of fulfilling promises, of paying debts, of telling the truth, which admit of no exception whatever in favour of duties of imperfect obligation, such as that of relieving distress. The other is the view of, for instance, Professor Moore and Dr. Rashdall, that there is only the duty of producing good, and that all "conflicts of duties" should be resolved by asking "by which action will most good be produced?" But it is more important that our theory fit the facts than that it be simple, and the account we have given above corresponds (it seems to me) better than either of the simpler theories with what we really think, viz. that normally promise-keeping, for example, should come before benevolence, but that when and only when the good to be produced by the benevolent act is very great and the promise comparatively trivial, the act of benevolence becomes our duty.

In fact the theory of "ideal utilitarianism", if I may for brevity refer so to the theory of Professor Moore, seems to simplify unduly our relations to our fellows. It says, in effect, that the only morally significant relation in which my neighbours stand to me is that of being possible beneficiaries by my action.[3] They do stand in this relation to me, and this relation is morally significant. But they may also stand to me in the relation of promisee to promiser, of creditor to debtor, of wife to husband, of child to parent, of friend to friend, of fellow countryman to fellow countryman, and the like; and each of these relations is the foundation of a *prima facie* duty, which is more or less incumbent on me according to the circumstances of the case. When I am in a situation, as perhaps I always am, in which more than one of these *prima facie* duties is incumbent on me, what I have to do is to study the situation as fully as I can until I form the considered opinion (it is never more) that in the circumstances one of them is more incumbent than any other; then I am bound to think that to do this *prima facie* duty is my duty *sans phrase* in the situation.

I suggest "*prima facie* duty" or "conditional duty" as a brief way of referring to the characteristic (quite distinct from that of being a duty proper) which an act has, in virtue of being of a certain kind (e.g. the keeping of a promise), of being an act which would be a duty proper if it were not at the same time of another kind which is morally significant. Whether an act is a duty proper or actual duty depends on *all* the morally significant kinds it is an instance of. The phrase "*prima facie* duty" must be apologized for, since (1) it suggests that what we are speaking of is a certain kind of duty, whereas it is in fact not a duty, but something related in a special way to duty. Strictly speaking, we want not a phrase in which duty is qualified by an adjective, but a separate noun. (2) "*Prima*" *facie* suggests that one is speaking only of an appearance which a moral situation presents at first sight, and which may turn out to be illusory; whereas what I am speaking of is an objective fact involved in the nature of the situation, or more strictly in an element of its nature, though not, as duty proper does, arising from its *whole* nature. I can, however, think of no term which fully meets the case. "Claim" has been suggested by Professor Prichard. The word "claim" has the advantage of being quite a familiar one in this connexion, and it seems to cover much of the ground. It would be quite natural to say, "a person to whom I have made a promise has a claim on me", and also, "a person whose distress I could relieve (at the cost of breaking the promise) has a claim on me". But (1) while "claim" is appropriate from *their* point of view, we want a word to express the corresponding fact from the agent's point of view – the fact of his being subject to claims that can be made against him; and ordinary language provides us with no such correlative to "claim". And (2) (what is more important) "claim" seems inevitably to suggest two persons, one of whom might make a claim on the other; and while this covers the ground of social duty, it is inappropriate in the case of that important part of duty which is the duty of cultivating a certain kind of character in oneself. It would be artificial, I think, and at any rate metaphorical, to say that one's character has a claim on oneself.

There is nothing arbitrary about these *prima facie* duties. Each rests on a definite circumstance which cannot seriously be held to be without moral significance. Of *prima facie* duties I suggest, without claiming completeness or finality for it, the following division.[4]

(1) Some duties rest on previous acts of my own. These duties seem to include two kinds, (*a*) those resting on a promise or what may fairly be called an implicit promise, such as the implicit undertaking not to tell lies which seems to be implied in the act of entering into conversation (at any rate by civilized men), or of writing books that purport to be history and not fiction. These may be called the duties of fidelity. (*b*) Those resting on a previous wrongful act. These may be called the duties of reparation. (2) Some rest on previous acts of other men, i.e. services done by them to me. These may be loosely described as the duties of gratitude.[5] (3) Some rest on the fact or possibility of a distribution of pleasure or happiness (or of the means thereto) which is not in accordance with the merit of the persons concerned; in such cases there arises a duty to upset or prevent such a distribution. These are the duties of justice. (4) Some rest on the mere fact that there are other beings in the world whose condition we can make better in respect of virtue, or of intelligence, or of pleasure. These are the duties of beneficence. (5) Some rest on the fact that we can improve our own condition in respect of virtue or of intelligence. These are the duties of self-improvement. (6) I think that we should distinguish from (4) the duties that may be summed up under the title of "not injuring others". No doubt to injure others is incidentally to fail to do them good; but it seems to me clear that non-maleficence is apprehended as a duty distinct from that of beneficence, and as a duty of a more stringent character. It will be noticed that this alone among the types of duty has been stated in a negative way. An attempt might no doubt be made to state this duty, like the others, in a positive way. It might be said that it is really the duty to prevent ourselves from acting either from an inclination to harm others or from an inclination to seek our own pleasure, in doing which we should incidentally harm them. But on reflection it seems clear that the primary duty here is the duty not to harm others, this being a duty whether or not we have an inclination that if followed would lead to our harming them; and that when we have such an inclination the primary duty not to harm others gives rise to a consequential duty to resist the inclination. The recognition of this duty of non-maleficence is the first step on the way to the recognition of the duty of beneficence; and that accounts for the prominence of the commands "thou shalt not kill", "thou shalt not commit adultery", "thou shalt not steal", "thou shalt not bear false

witness", in so early a code as the Decalogue. But even when we have come to recognize the duty of beneficence, it appears to me that the duty of non-maleficence is recognized as a distinct one, and as *prima facie* more binding. We should not in general consider it justifiable to kill one person in order to keep another alive, or to steal from one in order to give alms to another.

The essential defect of the "ideal utilitarian" theory is that it ignores, or at least does not do full justice to, the highly personal character of duty. If the only duty is to produce the maximum of good, the question who is to have the good – whether it is myself, or my benefactor, or a person to whom I have made a promise to confer that good on him, or a mere fellow man to whom I stand in no such special relation – should make no difference to my having a duty to produce that good. But we are all in fact sure that it makes a vast difference.

One or two other comments must be made on this provisional list of the divisions of duty. (1) The nomenclature is not strictly correct. For by "fidelity" or "gratitude" we mean, strictly, certain states of motivation; and, as I have urged, it is not our duty to have certain motives, but to do certain acts. By "fidelity", for instance, is meant, strictly, the disposition to fulfil promises and implicit promises *because we have made them*. We have no general word to cover the actual fulfilment of promises and implicit promises *irrespective of motive*; and I use "fidelity", loosely but perhaps conveniently, to fill this gap. So too I use "gratitude" for the returning of services, irrespective of motive. The term "justice" is not so much confined, in ordinary usage, to a certain state of motivation, for we should often talk of a man as acting justly even when we did not think his motive was the wish to do what was just simply for the sake of doing so. Less apology is therefore needed for our use of "justice" in this sense. And I have used the word "beneficence" rather than "benevolence", in order to emphasize the fact that it is our duty to do certain things, and not to do them from certain motives.

(2) If the objection be made, that this catalogue of the main types of duty is an unsystematic one resting on no logical principle, it may be replied, first, that it makes no claim to being ultimate. It is a *prima facie* classification of the duties which reflection on our moral convictions seems actually to reveal. And if these convictions are, as I would claim that they are, of the nature of knowledge, and if I have not misstated them, the list will be a list of authentic conditional duties, correct as far as it goes though not necessarily complete. The list of *goods* put forward by the rival theory is reached by exactly the same method – the only sound one in the circumstances – viz. that of direct reflection on what we really think.

Loyalty to the facts is worth more than a symmetrical architectonic or a hastily reached simplicity. If further reflection discovers a perfect logical basis for this or for a better classification, so much the better.

(3) It may, again, be objected that our theory that there are these various and often conflicting types of *prima facie* duty leaves us with no principle upon which to discern what is our actual duty in particular circumstances. But this objection is not one which the rival theory is in a position to bring forward. For when we have to choose between the production of two heterogeneous goods, say knowledge and pleasure, the "ideal utilitarian" theory can only fall back on an opinion, for which no logical basis can be offered, that one of the goods is the greater; and this is no better than a similar opinion that one of two duties is the more urgent. And again, when we consider the infinite variety of the effects of our actions in the way of pleasure, it must surely be admitted that the claim which *hedonism* sometimes makes, that it offers a readily applicable criterion of right conduct, is quite illusory.

I am unwilling, however, to content myself with an *argumentum ad hominem*, and I would contend that in principle there is no reason to anticipate that every act that is our duty is so for one and the same reason. Why should two sets of circumstances, or one set of circumstances, *not* possess different characteristics, any one of which makes a certain act our *prima facie* duty? When I ask what it is that makes me in certain cases sure that I have a *prima facie* duty to do so and so, I find that it lies in the fact that I have made a promise; when I ask the same question in another case, I find the answer lies in the fact that I have done a wrong. And if on reflection I find (as I think I do) that neither of these reasons is reducible to the other, I must not on any *a priori* ground assume that such a reduction is possible.

An attempt may be made to arrange in a more systematic way the main types of duty which we have indicated. In the first place it seems self-evident that if there are things that are intrinsically good, it is *prima facie* a duty to bring them into existence rather than not to do so, and to bring as much of them into existence as possible. It will be argued in our fifth chapter that there are three main things that are intrinsically good – virtue, knowledge, and, with certain limitations, pleasure. And since a given virtuous disposition, for instance, is equally good whether it is realized in myself or in another, it seems to be my duty to bring it into existence whether in myself or in another. So too with a given piece of knowledge.

The case of pleasure is difficult; for while we clearly recognize a duty to produce pleasure for others, it is by no means so clear that we recognize a duty to produce pleasure for ourselves. This appears to arise from the following facts. The thought of an act as our duty is one that presupposes a certain amount of reflection about the act; and for that reason does not normally arise in connexion with acts towards which we are already impelled by another strong impulse. So far, the cause of our not thinking of the promotion of our own pleasure as a duty is analogous to the cause which usually prevents a highly sympathetic person from thinking of the promotion of the pleasure of others as a duty. He is impelled so strongly by direct interest in the well-being of others towards promoting their pleasure that he does not stop to ask whether it is his duty to promote it; and we are all impelled so strongly towards the promotion of our own pleasure that we do not stop to ask whether it is a duty or not. But there is a further reason why even when we stop to think about the matter it does not usually present itself as a duty: viz. that, since the performance of most of our duties involves the giving up of some pleasure that we desire, the doing of duty and the getting of pleasure for ourselves come by a natural association of ideas to be thought of as incompatible things. This association of ideas is in the main salutary in its operation, since it puts a check on what but for it would be much too strong, the tendency to pursue one's own pleasure without thought of other considerations. Yet if pleasure is good, it seems in the long run clear that it is right to get it for ourselves as well as to produce it for others, when this does not involve the failure to discharge some more stringent *prima facie* duty. The question is a very difficult one, but it seems that this conclusion can be denied only on one or other of three grounds: (1) that pleasure is not *prima facie* good (i.e. good when it is neither the actualization of a bad disposition nor undeserved), (2) that there is no *prima facie* duty to produce as much that is good as we can, or (3) that though there is a *prima facie* duty to produce other things that are good, there is no *prima facie* duty to produce pleasure which will be enjoyed by ourselves. I give reasons later for not accepting the first contention. The second hardly admits of argument but seems to me plainly false. The third seems plausible only if we hold that an act that is pleasant or brings pleasure to ourselves must for that reason not be a duty; and this would lead to paradoxical consequences, such as that if a man enjoys giving pleasure to others or working for their moral improvement, it cannot be his duty to do so. Yet it seems to be a very stubborn fact, that in our ordinary consciousness we are not aware of a duty to get pleasure for ourselves; and by way of partial explanation of this I may add that though, as I think, one's own pleasure is a good and there is a duty to produce it, it is only if we *think* of our own pleasure not as simply our own pleasure, but as an objective good, something that an impartial spectator would approve, that we can think of the getting it as a duty; and we do not habitually think of it in this way.

If these contentions are right, what we have called the duty of beneficence and the duty of self-improvement rest on the same ground. No different principles of duty are involved in the two cases. If we feel a special responsibility for improving our own character rather than that of others, it is not because a special principle is involved, but because we are aware that the one is more under our control than the other. It was on this ground that Kant expressed the practical law of duty in the form "seek to make yourself good and other people happy". He was so persuaded of the internality of virtue that he regarded any attempt by one person to produce virtue in another as bound to produce, at most, only a counterfeit of virtue, the doing of externally right acts not from the true principle of virtuous action but out of regard to another person. It must be admitted that one man cannot compel another to be virtuous; compulsory virtue would just not be virtue. But experience clearly shows that Kant overshoots the mark when he contends that one man cannot do anything to *promote* virtue in another, to bring such influences to bear upon him that his own response to them is more likely to be virtuous than his response to other influences would have been. And our duty to do this is not different in kind from our duty to improve our own characters.

It is equally clear, and clear at an earlier stage of moral development, that if there are things that are bad in themselves we ought, *prima facie*, not to bring them upon others; and on this fact rests the duty of nonmaleficence.

The duty of justice is particularly complicated, and the word is used to cover things which are really very different – things such as the payment of debts, the reparation of injuries done by oneself to another, and the bringing about of a distribution of happiness between other people in proportion to merit. I use the word to denote only the last of these three. [In a later chapter] I shall try to show that besides the three (comparatively) simple goods, virtue, knowledge, and pleasure, there is a more complex good, not reducible to these, consisting in the proportionment of happiness to virtue. The bringing of this about is a duty which we owe to all men alike, though it may be reinforced by special responsibilities that we have undertaken to particular men. This, therefore, with beneficence and self-improvement, comes under the general principle that we should produce as much good as possible, though the good here involved is different in kind from any other.

But besides this general obligation, there are special obligations. These may arise, in the first place, incidentally, from acts which were not essentially meant to create such an obligation, but which nevertheless create it. From the nature of the case such acts may be of two kinds – the infliction of injuries on others, and the acceptance of benefits from them. It seems clear that these put us under a special obligation to other men, and that only these acts can do so incidentally. From these arise the twin duties of reparation and gratitude.

And finally there are special obligations arising from acts the very intention of which, when they were done, was to put us under such an obligation. The name for such acts is "promises"; the name is wide enough if we are willing to include under it implicit promises, i.e. modes of behaviour in which without explicit verbal promise we intentionally create an expectation that we can be counted on to behave in a certain way in the interest of another person.

These seem to be, in principle, all the ways in which *prima facie* duties arise. In actual experience they are compounded together in highly complex ways. Thus, for example, the duty of obeying the laws of one's country arises partly (as Socrates contends in the *Crito*) from the duty of gratitude for the benefits one has received from it; partly from the implicit promise to obey which seems to be involved in permanent residence in a country whose laws we know we are *expected* to obey, and still more clearly involved when we ourselves invoke the protection of its laws (this is the truth underlying the doctrine of the social contract); and partly (if we are fortunate in our country) from the fact that its laws are potent instruments for the general good.

Or again, the sense of a general obligation to bring about (so far as we can) a just apportionment of happiness to merit is often greatly reinforced by the fact that many of the existing injustices are due to a social and economic system which we have, not indeed created, but taken part in and assented to; the duty of justice is then reinforced by the duty of reparation.

It is necessary to say something by way of clearing up the relation between *prima facie* duties and the actual or absolute duty to do one particular act in particular circumstances. If, as almost all moralists except Kant are agreed, and as most plain men think, it is sometimes right to tell a lie or to break a promise, it must be maintained that there is a difference between *prima facie* duty and actual or absolute duty. When we think ourselves justified in breaking, and indeed morally obliged to break, a promise in order to relieve some one's distress, we do not for a moment cease to recognize a *prima facie* duty to keep our promise, and this leads us to feel, not indeed shame or repentance, but certainly compunction, for behaving as we do; we recognize, further, that it is our duty to make up somehow to the promisee for the breaking of the promise. We have to distinguish from the characteristic of being our duty that of tending to be our duty. Any act that we do contains various elements in virtue of which it falls under various categories. In virtue of being the breaking of a promise, for instance, it tends to be wrong; in virtue of being an instance of relieving distress it tends to be right. Tendency to be one's duty may be called a parti-resultant attribute, i.e. one which belongs to an act in virtue of some one component in its nature. *Being* one's duty is a toti-resultant attribute, one which belongs to an act in virtue of its whole nature and of nothing less than this.[6] This distinction between parti-resultant and toti-resultant attributes is one which we shall meet in another context also.

Another instance of the same distinction may be found in the operation of natural laws. *Qua* subject to the force of gravitation towards some other body, each body tends to move in a particular direction with a particular velocity; but its actual movement depends on *all* the forces to which it is subject. It is only by recognizing this distinction that we can preserve the absoluteness of laws of nature, and only by recognizing a corresponding distinction that we can preserve the absoluteness of the general principles of morality. But an important difference between the two cases must be pointed out. When we say that in virtue of gravitation a body tends to move in a certain way, we are referring to a causal influence actually exercised on it by another body or other bodies. When we say that in virtue of being deliberately untrue a certain remark tends to be wrong, we are referring to no causal relation, to no relation that involves succession in time, but to such a relation as connects the various attributes of a mathematical figure. And if the word "tendency" is thought to suggest too much a causal relation, it is better to talk of certain types of act as being *prima facie* right or wrong (or of different persons as having different and possibly conflicting claims upon us), than of their tending to be right or wrong.

Something should be said of the relation between our apprehension of the *prima facie* rightness of certain types of act and our mental attitude towards particular acts. It is proper to use the word "apprehension" in the former case and not in the latter. That an act, *qua* fulfilling a promise, or *qua* effecting a just distribution of good, or *qua* returning services rendered, or *qua* promoting the good of others, or *qua* promoting the virtue or insight of the agent, is *prima facie* right, is self-evident; not in the sense that it is evident from the beginning of our lives, or as soon as we attend to the proposition for the first time, but in the sense that when we have reached sufficient mental maturity and have given sufficient attention to the proposition it is evident without any need of proof, or of evidence beyond itself. It is self-evident just as a mathematical axiom, or the validity of a form of inference, is evident. The moral order expressed in these propositions is just as much part of the fundamental nature of the universe (and, we may add, of any possible universe in which there were moral agents at all) as is the spatial or numerical structure expressed in the axioms of geometry or arithmetic. In our confidence that these propositions are true there is involved the same trust in our reason that is involved in our confidence in mathematics; and we should have no justification for trusting it in the latter sphere and distrusting it in the former. In both cases we are dealing with propositions that cannot be proved, but that just as certainly need no proof.

Some of these general principles of *prima facie* duty may appear to be open to criticism. It may be thought, for example, that the principle of returning good for good is a falling off from the Christian principle, generally and rightly recognized as expressing the highest morality, of returning good for evil. To this it may be replied that I do not suggest that there is a principle commanding us to return good for good and forbidding us to return good for evil, and that I do suggest that there is a positive duty to seek the good of all men. What I maintain is that an act in which good is returned for good is recognized as *specially* binding on us just because it is of that character, and that *ceteris paribus* any one would think it his duty to help his benefactors rather than his enemies, if he could not do both; just as it is generally recognized that *ceteris paribus* we should pay our debts rather than give our money in charity, when we cannot do both. A benefactor is not only a man, calling for our effort on his behalf on that ground, but also our benefactor, calling for our *special* effort on *that* ground.

Our judgements about our actual duty in concrete situations have none of the certainty that attaches to our recognition of the general principles of duty. A statement is certain, i.e. is an expression of knowledge, only in one or other of two cases: when it is either self-evident, or a valid conclusion from self-evident premises. And our judgements about our particular duties have neither of these characters. (1) They are not self-evident. Where a possible act is seen to have two characteristics, in virtue of one of which it is *prima facie* right, and in virtue of the other *prima facie* wrong, we are (I think) well aware that we are not certain whether we ought or ought not to do it; that whether we do it or not, we are taking a moral risk. We come in the long run, after consideration, to think one duty more pressing than the other, but we do not feel certain that it is so. And though we do not always recognize that a possible act has two such characteristics, and though there *may* be cases in which it has not, we are never certain that any particular possible act has not, and therefore never certain that it is right, nor certain that it is wrong. For, to go no further in the analysis, it is enough to point out that any particular act will in all probability in the course of time contribute to the bringing about of good or of evil for many human beings, and thus have a *prima facie* rightness or wrongness of which we know nothing. (2) Again, our judgements about our particular duties are not logical conclusions from self-evident premisses. The only possible premisses would be the general principles stating their *prima facie* rightness or wrongness *qua* having the different characteristics they do have; and even if we could (as we cannot) apprehend the extent to which an act will tend on the one hand, for example, to bring about advantages for our benefactors, and on the other hand to bring about disadvantages for fellow men who are not our benefactors, there is no principle by which we can draw the conclusion that it is on the whole right or on the whole wrong. In this respect the judgement as to the rightness of a particular act is just like the judgement as to the beauty of a particular natural object or work of art. A poem is, for instance, in respect of certain qualities beautiful and in respect of certain others not beautiful; and our judgement as to the degree of beauty it possesses on the whole is never reached by logical reasoning from the apprehension of its particular beauties or particular defects. Both in this and in the moral case we have more or less probable opinions which are not logically justified conclusions from the general principles that are recognized as self-evident.

There is therefore much truth in the description of the right act as a fortunate act. If we cannot be certain that it is right, it is our good fortune if the act we do is the right act. This consideration does not, however, make the doing of our duty a mere matter of chance. There is a parallel here between the doing of duty and the doing of what will be to our personal advantage. We never *know* what act will in the long run be to our advantage. Yet it is certain that we are more likely in general to secure our advantage if we estimate to the best of our ability the probable tendencies of our actions in this respect, than if we act on caprice. And similarly we are more likely to do our duty if we reflect to the best of our ability on the *prima facie* rightness or wrongness of various possible acts in virtue of the characteristics we perceive them to have, than if we act without reflection. With this greater likelihood we must be content.

Many people would be inclined to say that the right act for me is not that whose general nature I have been describing, viz. that which if I were omniscient I should see to be my duty, but that which on all the evidence available to me I should think to be my duty. But suppose that from the state of partial knowledge in which I think act A to be my duty, I could pass to a state of perfect knowledge in which I saw act B to be my duty, should I not say "act B was the right act for me to do"? I should no doubt add "though I am not to be blamed for doing act A". But in adding this, am I not passing from the question "what is right" to the question "what is morally good"? At the same time I am not making the *full* passage from the one notion to the other; for in order that the act should be morally good, or an act I am not to be blamed for doing, it must not merely be the act which it is reasonable for me to think my duty; it must also be done for that reason, or from some other morally good motive. Thus the conception of the right act as the act which it is reasonable for me to think my duty is an unsatisfactory compromise between the true notion of the right act and the notion of the morally good action.

The general principles of duty are obviously not self-evident from the beginning of our lives. How do they come to be so? The answer is, that they come to be self-evident to us just as mathematical axioms do. We find by experience that this couple of matches and that couple make four matches, that this couple of balls on a wire and that couple make four balls: and by reflection on these and similar discoveries we come to see that it is of the nature of two and two to make four. In a precisely similar way, we see the *prima facie* rightness of an act which would be the fulfilment of a particular promise, and of another which would be the fulfilment of another promise, and when we have reached sufficient maturity to think in general terms, we apprehend *prima facie* rightness to belong to the nature of any fulfilment of promise. What comes first in time is the apprehension of the self-evident *prima facie* rightness of an individual act of a particular type. From this we come by reflection to apprehend the self-evident general principle of *prima facie* duty. From this, too, perhaps along with the apprehension of the self-evident *prima facie* rightness of the same act in virtue of its having another characteristic as well, and perhaps in spite of the apprehension of its *prima facie* wrongness in virtue of its having some third characteristic, we come to believe something not self-evident at all, but an object of probable opinion, viz. that this particular act is (not *prima facie* but) actually right.

In this respect there is an important difference between rightness and mathematical properties. A triangle which is isosceles necessarily has two of its angles equal, whatever other characteristics the triangle may have – whatever, for instance, be its area, or the size of its third angle. The equality of the two angles is a parti-resultant attribute.[7] And the same is true of all mathematical attributes. It is true, I may add, of *prima facie* rightness. But no act is ever, in virtue of falling under some general description, necessarily actually right; its rightness depends on its whole nature[8] and not on any element in it. The reason is that no mathematical object (no figure, for instance, or angle) ever has two characteristics that tend to give it opposite resultant characteristics, while moral acts often (as every one knows) and indeed always (as on reflection we must admit) have different characteristics that tend to make them at the same time *prima facie* right and *prima facie* wrong; there is probably no act, for instance, which does good to any one without doing harm to some one else, and *vice versa*.

Supposing it to be agreed, as I think on reflection it must, that no one *means* by "right" just "productive of the best possible consequences", or "optimific", the attributes "right" and "optimific" might stand in either of two kinds of relation to each other. (1) They might be so related that we could apprehend *a priori*, either immediately or deductively, that any act that is optimific is right and any act that is right is optimific, as we can apprehend that any triangle that is equilateral is equiangular and *vice versa*. Professor Moore's view is, I think, that the coextensiveness of "right" and "optimific" is apprehended immediately.[9] He rejects the possibility of any proof of it. Or (2) the two attributes might be such that the question whether they are invariably connected had to be answered by means of an inductive inquiry. Now at first sight it might seem as if the constant connexion of the two attributes could be immediately apprehended. It might seem absurd to suggest that it could be right for any one to do an act which would produce consequences less good than those which would be produced by some other act in his power. Yet a little thought will convince us that this is not absurd. The type of case in which it is easiest to see that this is so is, perhaps, that in which one has made a promise. In such a case we all think that *prima facie* it is our duty to fulfil the promise irrespective of the precise goodness of the total consequences. And though we do not think it is necessarily our actual or absolute duty to do so, we are far from thinking that any, even the slightest, gain in the value of the total consequences will necessarily justify us in doing something else instead. Suppose, to simplify the case by abstraction, that the fulfilment of a promise to *A* would produce 1,000 units of good[10] for him, but that by doing some other act I could produce, 1,001 units of good for *B*, to whom I have made no promise, the other consequences of the two acts being of equal value; should we really think it self-evident that it was our duty to do the second act and not the first? I think not. We should, I fancy, hold that only a much greater disparity of value between the total consequences would justify us in failing to discharge our *prima facie* duty to *A*. After all, a promise is a promise, and is not to be treated so lightly as the theory we are examining would imply. What, exactly, a promise is, is not so easy to determine, but we are surely agreed that it constitutes a serious moral limitation to our freedom of action. To produce the 1,001 units of good for *B* rather than fulfil our promise to *A* would be to take, not perhaps our duty as philanthropists too seriously, but certainly our duty as makers of promises too lightly.

Or consider another phase of the same problem. If I have promised to confer on *A* a particular benefit containing 1,000 units of good, is it self-evident that if by doing some different act I could produce 1,001 units of good for *A* himself (the other consequences of the two acts being supposed equal in value), it would be right for me to do so? Again, I think not. Apart from my general *prima facie* duty to do *A* what good I can, I have another *prima facie* duty to do him the particular service I have promised to do him, and this is not to be set aside in consequence of a disparity of good of the order of 1,001 to 1,000, though a much greater disparity might justify me in so doing.

Or again, suppose that *A* is a very good and *B* a very bad man, should I then, even when I have made no promise, think it self-evidently right to produce 1,001 units of good for *B* rather than 1,000 for *A*? Surely not. I should be sensible of a *prima facie* duty of justice, i.e. of producing a distribution of goods in proportion to merit, which is not outweighed by such a slight disparity in the total goods to be produced.

Such instances – and they might easily be added to – make it clear that there is no self-evident connexion between the attributes "right" and "optimific". The theory we are examining has a certain attractiveness when applied to our decision that a particular act is our duty (though I have tried to show that it does not agree with our actual moral judgements even here). But it is not even plausible when applied to our recognition of *prima facie* duty. For if it were self-evident that the right coincides with the optimific, it should be self-evident that what is *prima facie* right is *prima facie* optimific. But whereas we are certain that keeping a promise is *prima facie* right, we are not certain that it is *prima facie* optimific (though we are perhaps certain that it is *prima facie* bonific). Our certainty that it is *prima facie* right depends not on its consequences but on its being the fulfilment of a promise. The theory we are examining involves too much difference between the evident ground of our conviction about *prima facie* duty and the alleged ground of our conviction about actual duty.

The coextensiveness of the right and the optimific is, then, not self-evident. And I can see no way of proving it deductively; nor, so far as I know, has any one tried to do so. There remains the question whether it can be established inductively. Such an inquiry, to be conclusive, would have to be very thorough and extensive. We should have to take a large variety of the acts which we, to the best of our ability, judge to be right. We should have to trace as far as possible their consequences, not only for the persons directly affected but also for those indirectly affected, and to these no limit can be set. To make our inquiry thoroughly conclusive, we should have to do what we cannot do, viz. trace these consequences into an unending future. And even to make it reasonably conclusive, we should have to trace them far into the future. It is clear that the most we could possibly say is that a large variety of typical acts that are judged right appear, so far as we can trace their consequences, to produce more good than any other acts possible to the agents in the circumstances. And such a result falls far short of proving the constant connexion of the two attributes. But it is surely clear that no inductive inquiry justifying even this result has ever been carried through. The advocates of utilitarian systems have been so much persuaded either of the identity or of the self-evident connexion of the attributes "right" and "optimific" (or "felicific") that they have not attempted even such an inductive inquiry as is possible. And in view of the enormous complexity of the task and the inevitable inconclusiveness of the result, it is worth no one's while to make the attempt. What, after all, would be gained by it? If, as I have tried to show, for an act to be right and to be optimific are not the same thing, and an act's being optimific is not even the ground of its being right, then if we could ask ourselves (though the question is really unmeaning) which we ought to do, right acts because they are right or optimific acts because they are optimific, our answer must be "the former". If they are optimific as well as right, that is interesting but not morally important; if not, we still ought to do them (which is only another way of saying that they *are* the right acts), and the question whether they are optimific has no importance for moral theory.

There is one direction in which a fairly serious attempt has been made to show the connexion of the attributes "right" and "optimific". One of the most evident facts of our moral consciousness is the sense which we have of the sanctity of promises, a sense which does not, on the face of it, involve the thought that one will be bringing more good into existence by fulfilling the promise than by breaking it. It is plain, I think, that in our normal thought we consider that the fact that we have made a promise is in itself sufficient to create a duty of keeping it, the sense of duty resting on remembrance of the past promise and not on thoughts of the future consequences of its fulfilment. Utilitarianism tries to show that this is not so, that the sanctity of promises rests on the good consequences of the fulfilment of them and the bad consequences of their non-fulfilment. It does so in this way: it points out that when you break a promise you not only fail to confer a certain advantage on your promisee but you diminish his confidence, and indirectly the confidence of others, in the fulfilment of promises. You thus strike a blow at one of the devices that have been found most useful in the relations between man and man – the device on which, for example, the whole system of commercial credit rests – and you tend to bring about a state of things wherein each man, being entirely unable to rely on the keeping of promises by others, will have to do everything for himself, to the enormous impoverishment of human well-being.

To put the matter otherwise, utilitarians say that when a promise ought to be kept it is because the total good to be produced by keeping it is greater than the total good to be produced by breaking it, the former including as its main element the maintenance and strengthening of general mutual confidence, and the latter being greatly diminished by a weakening of this confidence. They say, in fact, that the case I put some pages back[11] never arises – the case in which by fulfilling a promise I shall bring into being 1,000 units of good for my promisee, and by breaking it 1,001 units of good for some one else, the other effects of the two acts being of equal value. The other effects, they say, never are of equal value. By keeping my promise I am helping to strengthen the system of mutual confidence; by breaking it I am helping to weaken this; so that really the first act produces $1,000 + x$ units of good, and the second $1,001 - y$ units, and the difference between $+x$ and $-y$ is enough to outweigh the slight superiority in the *immediate* effects of the second act. In answer to this it may be pointed out that there must be *some* amount of good that exceeds the difference between $+x$ and $-y$ (i.e. exceeds $x + y$); say, $x + y + z$. Let us suppose the *immediate* good effects of the second act to be assessed not at 1,001 but at $1,000 + x + y + z$. Then its *net* good effects are $1,000 + x + z$, i.e. greater than those of the fulfilment of the promise; and the utilitarian is bound to say forthwith that the promise should be broken. Now, we may ask whether that is really the way we think about promises? Do we really think that the production of the slightest balance of good, no matter who will enjoy it, by the breach of a promise frees us from the obligation to keep our promise? We need not doubt that a system by which promises are made and kept is one that has great advantages for the general well-being. But that is not the whole truth. To make a promise is not merely to adapt an ingenious device for promoting the general well-being; it is to put oneself in a new relation to one person in particular, a relation which creates a specifically new *prima facie* duty to him, not reducible to the duty of promoting the general well-being of society. By all means let us try to foresee the net good effects of keeping one's promise and the net good effects of breaking it, but even if we assess the first at $1,000 + x$ and the second at $1,000 + x + z$, the question still remains whether it is not our duty to fulfil the promise. It may be suspected, too, that the effect of a single keeping or breaking of a promise in strengthening or weakening the fabric of mutual confidence is greatly exaggerated by the theory we are examining. And if we suppose two men dying together alone, do we think that the duty of one to fulfil before he dies a promise he has made to the other would be extinguished by the fact that neither act would have any effect on the general confidence? Any one who holds this may be suspected of not having reflected on what a promise is.

I conclude that the attributes "right" and "optimific" are not identical, and that we do not know either by intuition, by deduction, or by induction that they coincide in their application, still less that the latter is the foundation of the former. It must be added, however, that if we are ever under no special obligation such as that of fidelity to a promisee or of gratitude to a benefactor, we ought to do what will produce most good; and that even when we are under a special obligation the tendency of acts to promote general good is one of the main factors in determining whether they are right.

In what has preceded, a good deal of use has been made of "what we really think" about moral questions; a certain theory has been rejected because it does not agree with what we really think. It might be said that this is in principle wrong; that we should not be content to expound what our present moral consciousness tells us but should aim at a criticism of our existing moral consciousness in the light of theory. Now I do not doubt that the moral consciousness of men has in detail undergone a good deal of modification as regards the things we think right, at the hands of moral theory. But if we are told, for instance, that we should give up our view that there is a special obligatoriness attaching to the keeping of promises because it is self-evident that the only duty is to produce as much good as possible, we have to ask ourselves whether we really, when we reflect, *are* convinced that this is self-evident, and whether we really *can* get rid of our view that promise-keeping has a bindingness independent of productiveness of maximum good. In my own experience I find that I cannot, in spite of a very genuine attempt to do so; and I venture to think that most people will find the same, and that just because they cannot lose the sense of special obligation, they cannot accept as self-evident, or even as true, the theory which would require them to do so. In fact it seems, on reflection, self-evident that a promise, simply as such, is something that *prima facie* ought to be kept, and it does *not*, on reflection, seem self-evident that production of maximum good is the only thing that makes an act obligatory. And to ask us to give up at the bidding of a theory our actual apprehension of what is right and what is wrong seems like asking people to repudiate their actual experience of beauty, at the bidding of a theory which says "only that which satisfies" such and such conditions can be beautiful". If what I have called our actual apprehension is (as I would maintain that it is) truly an apprehension, i.e. an instance of knowledge, the request is nothing less than absurd.

I would maintain, in fact, that what we are apt to describe as "what we think" about moral questions contains a considerable amount that we do not think but know, and that this forms the standard by reference to which the truth of any moral theory has to be tested, instead of having itself to be tested by reference to any theory. I hope that I have in what precedes indicated what in my view these elements of knowledge are that are involved in our ordinary moral consciousness.

It would be a mistake to found a natural science on "what we really think", i.e. on what reasonably thoughtful and well-educated people think about the subjects of the science before they have studied them scientifically. For such opinions are interpretations, and often misinterpretations, of sense-experience; and the man of science must appeal from these to sense-experience itself, which furnishes his real data. In ethics no such appeal is possible. We have no more direct way of access to the facts about rightness and goodness and about what things are right or good, than by thinking about them; the moral convictions of thoughtful and well-educated people are the data of ethics just as sense-perceptions are the data of a natural science. Just as some of the latter have to be rejected as illusory, so have some of the former; but as the latter are rejected only when they are in conflict with other more accurate sense-perceptions, the former are rejected only when they are in conflict with other convictions which stand better the test of reflection. The existing body of moral convictions of the best people is the cumulative product of the moral reflection of many generations, which has developed an extremely delicate power of appreciation of moral distinctions; and this the theorist cannot afford to treat with anything other than the greatest respect. The verdicts of the moral consciousness of the best people are the foundation on which he must build; though he must first compare them with one another and eliminate any contradictions they may contain.

It is worth while to try to state more definitely the nature of the acts that are right. We may try to state first what (if anything) is the universal nature of *all* acts that are right. It is obvious that any of the acts that we do has countless effects, directly or indirectly, on countless people, and the probability is that any act, however right it be, will have adverse effects (though these may be very trivial) on some innocent people. Similarly, any wrong act will probably have beneficial effects on some deserving people. Every act therefore, viewed in some aspects, will be *prima facie* right, and viewed in others, *prima facie* wrong, and right acts can be distinguished from wrong acts only as being those which, of all those possible for the agent in the circumstances, have the greatest balance of *prima facie* rightness, in those respects in which they are *prima facie* right, over their *prima facie* wrongness, in those respects in which they are *prima facie* wrong – *prima facie* rightness and wrongness being understood in the sense previously explained. For the estimation of the comparative stringency of these *prima facie* obligations no general rules can, so far as I can see, be laid down. We can only say that a great deal of stringency belongs to the duties of "perfect obligation" – the duties of keeping our promises, of repairing wrongs we have done, and of returning the equivalent of services we have received. For the rest, ἐν τῇ αἰσθήσει ἡ κρίσις.[12] This sense of our particular duty in particular circumstances, preceded and informed by the fullest reflection we can bestow on the act in all its bearings, is highly fallible, but it is the only guide we have to our duty.

When we turn to consider the nature of individual right acts, the first point to which attention should be called is that any act may be correctly described in an indefinite, and in principle infinite, number of ways. An act is the production of a change in the state of affairs (if we ignore, for simplicity's sake, the comparatively few cases in which it is the maintenance of an existing state of affairs; cases which, I think, raise no special difficulty). Now the only changes we can *directly* produce are changes in our own bodies or in our own minds. But these are not, as such, what as a rule we think it our duty to produce. Consider some comparatively simple act, such as telling the truth or fulfilling a promise. In the first case what I produce directly is movements of my vocal organs. But what I think it my duty to produce is a true view in some one else's mind about some fact, and between my movement of my vocal organs and this result there intervenes a series of physical events and events in his mind. Again, in the second case, I may have promised, for instance, to return a book to a friend. I may be able, by a series of movements of my legs and hands, to place it in his hands. But what I am just as likely to do, and to think I have done my duty in doing, is to send it by a messenger or to hand it to his servant or to send it by post; and in each of these cases what I *do* directly is worthless in itself and is connected by a series of intermediate links with what I do think it is my duty to bring about, viz. his receiving what I have promised to return to him. This being so, it *seems* as if what I *do* has no obligatoriness in itself and as if one or other of three accounts should be given of the matter, each of which makes rightness not belong to what I do, considered in its own nature.

(1) One of them would be that what is obligatory is not *doing* anything in the natural sense of producing any change in the state of affairs, but *aiming at* something – at, for instance, my friend's reception of the book. But this account will not do. For (*a*) to aim at something is to act from a motive consisting of the wish to bring that thing about. But we have seen that motive never forms part of the content of our duty; if anything is certain about morals, that, I think, is certain. And (*b*) if I have promised to return the book to my friend, I obviously do not fulfil my promise and do my duty merely by aiming at his receiving the book; I must see that he actually receives it. (2) A more plausible account is that which says I must do that which is likely to produce the result. But this account is open to the second of these objections, and probably also to the first. For in the first place, however likely my act may seem, even on careful consideration, and even however likely it may in fact be, to produce the result, if it does not produce it I have not done what I promised to do, i.e. have not done my duty. And secondly, when it is said that I ought to do what is likely to produce the result, what is *probably* meant is that I ought to do a certain thing as a result of the wish to produce a certain result, and of the thought that my act is likely to produce it; and this again introduces motive into the content of duty. (3) Much the most plausible of the three accounts is that which says, "I ought to do that which will actually produce a certain result." This escapes objection (*b*). Whether it escapes objection (*a*) or not depends on what exactly is meant. If it is meant that I ought to do a certain thing from the wish to produce a certain result and the thought that it will do so, the account is still open to objection (*a*). But if it is meant simply that I ought to do a certain thing, and that the reason why I ought to do it is that it will produce a certain result, objection (*a*) is avoided. Now this account in its second form is that which utilitarianism gives. It says what is right is certain acts, not certain acts motivated in a certain way; and it says that acts are never right by their own nature but by virtue of the goodness of their actual results. And this account is, I think, clearly nearer the truth than one which makes the rightness of an act depend on the goodness of either the *intended* or the *likely* results.

Nevertheless, this account appears not to be the true one. For it implies that what we consider right or our duty is what we do *directly*. It is this, e.g. the packing up and posting of the book, that derives its moral significance not from its own nature but from its consequences. But this is *not* what we should describe, strictly, as our duty; our duty is to fulfil our promise, i.e. to put the book into our friend's possession. This we consider obligatory in its own nature, just because it is a fulfilment of promise, and not because of *its* consequences. But, it might be replied by the utilitarian, I do not do this; I only do something that leads up to this, and what I do has no moral significance in itself but only because of its consequences. In answer to this, however, we may point out that a cause produces not only its immediate, but also its remote consequences, and the latter no less than the former. I, therefore, not only produce the immediate movements of parts of my body but also my friend's reception of the book, which results from these. Or, if this be objected to on the grounds that I can hardly be said to have produced my friend's reception of the book when I have packed and posted it, owing to the time that has still to elapse before he receives it, and that to say I have produced the result hardly does justice to the part played by the Post Office, we may at least say that I have *secured* my friend's reception of the book. What I do is as truly describable in this way as by saying that it is the packing and posting of a book. (It is equally truly describable in many other ways; e.g. I have provided a few moments' employment for Post Office officials. But this is irrelevant to the argument.) And if we ask ourselves whether it is *qua* the packing and posting of a book, or *qua* the securing of my friend's getting what I have promised to return to him, that my action is right, it is clear that it is in the second capacity that it is right; and in this capacity, the only capacity in which it is right, it is right by its own nature and not because of its consequences.

This account may no doubt be objected to, on the ground that we are ignoring the freedom of will of the other agents – the sorter and the postman, for instance – who are equally responsible for the result. Society, it may be said, is not like a machine, in which event follows event by rigorous necessity. Some one may, for instance, in the exercise of his freedom of will, steal the book on the way. But it is to be observed that I have excluded that case, and any similar case. I am dealing with the case in which I secure my friend's receiving the book; and if he does not receive it I have not secured his receiving it. If on the other hand the book reaches its destination, that alone shows that, the system of things being what it is, the trains by which the book travels and the railway lines along which it travels being such as they are and subject to the laws they are subject to, the postal officials who handle it being such as they are, having the motives they have and being subject to the psychological laws they are subject to, my posting the book was the one further thing which was sufficient to procure my friend's receiving it. If it had not been sufficient, the result would not have followed. The attainment of the result proves the sufficiency of the means. The objection in fact rests on the supposition that there can be unmotived action, i.e. an event without a cause, and may be refuted by reflection on the universality of the law of causation.

It is equally true that non-attainment of the result proves the insufficiency of the means. If the book had been destroyed in a railway accident or stolen by a dishonest postman, that would prove that my immediate act was not sufficient to produce the desired result. We get the curious consequence that however carelessly I pack or dispatch the book, if it comes to hand I have done my duty, and however carefully I have acted, if the book does not come to hand I have not done my duty. Success and failure are the only test, and a sufficient test, of the performance of duty. Of course, I should deserve more praise in the second case than in the first; but that is an entirely different question; we must not mix up the question of right and wrong with that of the morally good and the morally bad. And that our conclusion is not as strange as at first sight it might seem is shown by the fact that if the carelessly dispatched book comes to hand, it is not my duty to send another copy, while if the carefully dispatched book does not come to hand I must send another copy to replace it. In the first case I have not my duty still to do, which shows that I have done it; in the second I have it still to do, which shows that I have not done it.

We have reached the result that my act is right *qua* being an ensuring of one of the particular states of affairs of which it is an ensuring, viz., in the case we have taken, of my friend's receiving the book I have promised to return to him. But this answer requires some correction; for it refers only to the *prima facie* rightness of my act. If to be a fulfilment of promise were a sufficient ground of the rightness of an act, all fulfilments of promises would be right, whereas it seems clear that there are cases in which some other *prima facie* duty overrides the *prima facie* duty of fulfilling a promise. The more correct answer would be that the ground of the actual rightness of the act is that, of all acts possible for the agent in the circumstances, it is that whose *prima facie* rightness in the respects in which it is *prima facie* right most outweighs its *prima facie* wrongness in any respects in which it is *prima facie* wrong. But since its *prima facie* rightness is mainly due to its being a fulfilment of promise, we may call its being so the salient element in the ground of its rightness.

Subject to this qualification, then, it is as being the production (or if we prefer the word, the securing or ensuring) of the reception by my friend of what I have promised him (or in other words as the fulfilment of my promise) that my act is right. It is not right as a packing and posting of a book. The packing and posting of the book is only incidentally right, right only because it is a fulfilment of promise, which is what is directly or essentially right.

Our duty, then, is not to do certain things which will produce certain results. Our acts, at any rate our acts of special obligation, are not right because they will produce certain results – which is the view common to all forms of utilitarianism. To say that is to say that in the case in question what is essentially right is to pack and post a book, whereas what is essentially right is to secure the possession by my friend of what I have promised to return to him. An act is not right because it, being one thing, produces good results different from itself; it is right because it is itself the production of a certain state of affairs. Such production is right in itself, apart from any consequence.

But, it might be said, this analysis applies only to acts of special obligation; the utilitarian account still holds good for the acts in which we are not under a special obligation to any person or set of persons but only under that of augmenting the general good. Now merely to have established that there *are* special obligations to do certain things irrespective of their consequences would be already to have made a considerable breach in the utilitarian walls; for according to utilitarianism there is no such thing, there is only the single obligation to promote the general good. But, further, on reflection it is clear that just as (in the case we have taken) my act is not only the packing and posting of a book but the fulfilling of a promise, and just as it is in the latter capacity and not in the former that it is my duty, so an act whereby I augment the general good is not only, let us say, the writing of a begging letter on behalf of a hospital, but the producing (or ensuring) of whatever good ensues therefrom, and it is in the latter capacity and not in the former that it is right, if it *is* right. That which is right is right not because it is an act, one thing, which will produce another thing, an increase of the general welfare, but because it is itself the producing of an increase in the general welfare. Or, to qualify this in the necessary way, its being the production of an increase in the general welfare is the salient element in the ground of its rightness. Just as before we were led to recognize the *prima facie* rightness of the fulfilment of promises, we are now led to recognize the *prima facie* rightness of promoting the general welfare. In both cases we have to recognize the *intrinsic* rightness of a certain type of act, not depending on its consequences but on its own nature.

Notes

1   I take the theory which, as I have tried to show, seems to be put forward in *Ethics* rather than the earlier and less plausible theory put forward in *Principia Ethica*.

2   These are not strictly speaking duties, but things that tend to be our duty, or *prima facie* duties. Cf. pp. 58–60.

3   Some will think it, apart from other considerations, a sufficient refutation of this view to point out that I also stand in that relation to myself, so that for this view the distinction of oneself from others is morally insignificant.

4   I should make it plain at this stage that I am *assuming* the correctness of some of our main convictions as to *prima facie* duties, or, more strictly, am claiming that we *know* them to be true. To me it seems as self-evident as anything could be, that to make a promise, for instance, is to create a moral claim on us in someone else. Many readers will perhaps say that they do *not* know this to be true. If so, I certainly cannot prove it to them; I can only ask them to reflect again, in the hope that they will ultimately agree that they also know it to be true. The main moral convictions of the plain man seem to me to be, not opinions which it is for philosophy to prove or disprove, but knowledge from the start; and in my own case I seem to find little difficulty in distinguishing these essential convictions from other moral convictions which I also have, which are merely fallible opinions based on an imperfect study of the working for good or evil of certain institutions or types of action.

5   For a needed correction of this statement, cf. p. 60.

6   But cf. the qualification in note 9.

7   Cf. pp. 64–5.

8   To avoid complicating unduly the statement of the general view I am putting forward, I have here rather overstated it. Any act is the origination of a great variety of things many of which make no difference to its rightness or wrongness. But there are always many elements in its nature (i.e. in what it is the origination of) that make a difference to its rightness or wrongness, and no element in its nature can be dismissed without consideration as indifferent.

9   *Ethics*, 181.

10   I am assuming that good is objectively quantitative, but not that we can accurately assign an exact quantitative measure to it. Since it is of a definite amount, we can make the *supposition* that its amount is so-and-so, though we cannot with any confidence *assert* that it is.

11   p. 69.

12   "The decision rests with perception". Arist. *Nic. Eth.* 1109 b 23, 1126 b 4.

Part II

Contemporary Expressions

6

Moral Constraints and Moral Goals

Robert Nozick

A moral concern [need not] function only as a moral *goal* [this question was posed by Chapter 3, "Moral Constraints and the State"], as an end state for some activities to achieve as their result. It may, indeed, seem to be a necessary truth that "right," "ought," "should," and so on, are to be explained in terms of what is, or is intended to be, productive of the greatest good, with all goals built into the good. Thus it is often thought that what is wrong with utilitarianism (which *is* of this form) is its too narrow conception of good. Utilitarianism doesn't, it is said, properly take rights and their nonviolation into account; it instead leaves them a derivative status. Many of the counterexample cases to utilitarianism fit under this objection, for example, punishing an innocent man to save a neighborhood from a vengeful rampage. But a theory may include in a primary way the nonviolation of rights, yet include it in the wrong place and the wrong manner. For suppose some condition about minimizing the total (weighted) amount of violations of rights is built into the desirable end state to be achieved. We then would have something like a "utilitarianism of rights"; violations of rights (to be *minimized*) merely would replace the total happiness as the relevant end state in the utilitarian structure. (Note that we do not hold the nonviolation of our rights as our sole greatest good or even rank it first lexicographically to exclude trade-offs, if there is some desirable society we would choose to inhabit even though in it some rights of ours sometimes are violated, rather than move to a desert island where we could survive alone.) This still would require us to violate someone's rights when doing so minimizes the total (weighted)

Robert Nozick, "Moral Constraints and Moral Goals," *Anarchy, State, and Utopia* (New York: Basic Books, 1974), pp. 28–35.

amount of the violation of rights in the society. For example, violating someone's rights might deflect others from *their* intended action of gravely violating rights, or might remove their motive for doing so, or might divert their attention, and so on. A mob rampaging through a part of town killing and burning *will* violate the rights of those living there. Therefore, someone might try to justify his punishing another *he* knows to be innocent of a crime that enraged a mob, on the grounds that punishing this innocent person would help to avoid even greater violations of rights by others, and so would lead to a minimum weighted score for rights violations in the society.

In contrast to incorporating rights into the end state to be achieved, one might place them as side constraints upon the actions to be done: don't violate constraints C. The rights of others determine the constraints upon your actions. (A *goal-directed* view with constraints added would be: among those acts available to you that don't violate constraints C, act so as to maximize goal G. Here, the rights of others would constrain your goal-directed behavior. I do not mean to imply that the correct moral view includes mandatory goals that must be pursued, even within the constraints.) This view differs from one that tries to build the side constraints C *into* the goal G. The side-constraint view forbids you to violate these moral constraints in the pursuit of your goals; whereas the view whose objective is to minimize the violation of these rights allows you to violate the rights (the constraints) in order to lessen their total violation in the society.*

---

* Unfortunately, too few models of the structure of moral views have been specified heretofore, though there are surely other interesting structures. Hence an argument for a side-constraint structure that consists largely in arguing against an end-state maximization structure is inconclusive, for these alternatives are not exhaustive. An array of structures must be precisely formulated and investigated; perhaps some novel structure then will seem most appropriate.

The issue of whether a side-constraint view can be put in the form of the goal-without-side-constraint view is a tricky one. One might think, for example, that each person could distinguish in his goal between *his* violating rights and someone else's doing it. Give the former infinite (negative) weight in his goal, and no amount of stopping others from violating rights can outweigh his violating someone's rights. In addition to a component of a goal receiving infinite weight, indexical expressions also appear, for example, "*my* doing something." A careful statement delimiting "constraint views" would exclude these gimmicky ways of transforming side constraints into the form of an end-state view as sufficient to constitute a view as end state. Mathematical methods of transforming a con-

The claim that the proponent of the ultraminimal state is inconsistent, we now can see, assumes that he is a "utilitarian of rights." It assumes that his goal is, for example, to minimize the weighted amount of the violation of rights in the society, and that he should pursue this goal even through means that themselves violate people's rights. Instead, he may place the nonviolation of rights as a constraint upon action, rather than (or in addition to) building it into the end state to be realized. The position held by this proponent of the ultraminimal state will be a consistent one if his conception of rights holds that your being *forced* to contribute to another's welfare violates your rights, whereas someone else's not providing you with things you need greatly, including things essential to the protection of your rights, does not *itself* violate your rights, even though it avoids making it more difficult for someone else to violate them. (That conception will be consistent provided it does not construe the monopoly element of the ultraminimal state as itself a violation of rights.) That it is a consistent position does not, of course, show that it is an acceptable one.

Why Side Constraints?

Isn't it *irrational* to accept a side constraint C, rather than a view that directs minimizing the violations of C? (The latter view treats C as a condition rather than a constraint.) If nonviolation of C is so important, shouldn't that be the goal? How can a concern for the nonviolation of C lead to the refusal to violate C even when this would prevent other more extensive violations of C? What is the rationale for placing the nonviolation of rights as a side constraint upon action instead of including it solely as a goal of one's actions?

strained minimization problem into a sequence of unconstrained minimizations of an auxiliary function are presented in Anthony Fiacco and Garth McCormick, *Nonlinear Programming: Sequential Unconstrained Minimization Techniques* (New York: Wiley, 1968). The book is interesting both for its methods and for their limitations in illuminating our area of concern; note the way in which the penalty functions include the constraints, the variation in weights of penalty functions (sec. 7.1), and so on.

The question of whether these side constraints are absolute, or whether they may be violated in order to avoid catastrophic moral horror, and if the latter, what the resulting structure might look like, is one I hope largely to avoid.

Side constraints upon action reflect the underlying Kantian principle that individuals are ends and not merely means; they may not be sacrificed or used for the achieving of other ends without their consent. Individuals are inviolable. More should be said to illuminate this talk of ends and means. Consider a prime example of a means, a tool. There is no side constraint on how we may use a tool, other than the moral constraints on how we may use it upon others. There are procedures to be followed to preserve it for future use ("don't leave it out in the rain"), and there are more and less efficient ways of using it. But there is no limit on what we may do to it to best achieve our goals. Now imagine that there was an overrideable constraint C on some tool's use. For example, the tool might have been lent to you only on the condition that C not be violated unless the gain from doing so was above a certain specified amount, or unless it was necessary to achieve a certain specified goal. Here the object is not *completely* your tool, for use according to your wish or whim. But it is a tool nevertheless, even with regard to the overrideable constraint. If we add constraints on its use that may not be overridden, then the object may not be used as a tool *in those ways. In those respects*, it is not a tool at all. Can one add enough constraints so that an object cannot be used as a tool at all, in *any* respect?

Can behavior toward a person be constrained so that he is not to be used for any end except as he chooses? This is an impossibly stringent condition if it requires everyone who provides us with a good to approve positively of every use to which we wish to put it. Even the requirement that he merely should not object to any use we plan would seriously curtail bilateral exchange, not to mention sequences of such exchanges. It is sufficient that the other party stands to gain enough from the exchange so that he is willing to go through with it, even though he objects to one or more of the uses to which you shall put the good. Under such conditions, the other party is not being used solely as a means, in that respect. Another party, however, who would not choose to interact with you if he knew of the uses to which you *intend* to put his actions or good, *is* being used as a means, even if he receives enough to choose (in his ignorance) to interact with you. ("All along, you were just *using* me" can be said by someone who chose to interact only because he was ignorant of another's goals and of the uses to which he himself would be put.) Is it morally incumbent upon someone to reveal his intended uses of an interaction if he has good reason to believe the other would refuse to interact if he knew? Is he *using* the other person, if he does not reveal this? And what of the cases where the other does not choose to be of use at all? In getting pleasure from seeing an attractive person go by, does one use the other solely as a means? Does someone so use an object of sexual fantasies? These and related questions raise very interesting issues for moral philosophy; but not, I think, for political philosophy.

Political philosophy is concerned only with *certain* ways that persons may not use others; primarily, physically aggressing against them. A specific side constraint upon action toward others expresses the fact that others may not be used in the specific ways the side constraint excludes. Side constraints express the inviolability of others, in the ways they specify. These modes of inviolability are expressed by the following injunction: "Don't use people in specified ways." An end-state view, on the other hand, would express the view that people are ends and not merely means (if it chooses to express this view at all), by a different injunction: "Minimize the use in specified ways of persons as means." Following this precept itself may involve using someone as a means in one of the ways specified. Had Kant held this view, he would have given the second formula of the categorical imperative as, "So act as to minimize the use of humanity simply as a means," rather than the one he actually used: "Act in such a way that you always treat humanity, whether in your own person or in the person of any other, never simply as a means, but always at the same time as an end."

Side constraints express the inviolability of other persons. But why may not one violate persons for the greater social good? Individually, we each sometimes choose to undergo some pain or sacrifice for a greater benefit or to avoid a greater harm: we go to the dentist to avoid worse suffering later; we do some unpleasant work for its results; some persons diet to improve their health or looks; some save money to support themselves when they are older. In each case, some cost is borne for the sake of the greater overall good. Why not, *similarly*, hold that some persons have to bear some costs that benefit other persons more, for the sake of the overall social good? But there is no *social entity* with a good that undergoes some sacrifice for its own good. There are only individual people, different individual people, with their own individual lives. Using one of these people for the benefit of others, uses him and benefits the others. Nothing more. What happens is that something is done to him for the sake of others. Talk of an overall social good covers this up. (Intentionally?) To use a person in this way does not sufficiently respect and take account of the fact that he is a separate person, that his is the only life he has. *He* does not get some overbalancing good from his sacrifice, and no one is entitled to force this upon him – least of all a state or government that claims his allegiance (as other individuals do not) and that therefore scrupulously must be *neutral* between its citizens.

Libertarian Constraints

The moral side constraints upon what we may do, I claim, reflect the fact of our separate existences. They reflect the fact that no moral balancing act can take place among us; there is no moral outweighing of one of our lives by others so as to lead to a greater overall *social* good. There is no justified sacrifice of some of us for others. This root idea, namely, that there are different individuals with separate lives and so no one may be sacrificed for others, underlies the existence of moral side constraints, but it also, I believe, leads to a libertarian side constraint that prohibits aggression against another.

The stronger the force of an end-state maximizing view, the more powerful must be the root idea capable of resisting it that underlies the existence of moral side constraints. Hence the more seriously must be taken the existence of distinct individuals who are not resources for others. An underlying notion sufficiently powerful to support moral side constraints against the powerful intuitive force of the end-state maximizing view will suffice to derive a libertarian constraint on aggression against another. Anyone who rejects *that particular* side constraints has three alternatives: (1) he must reject *all* side constraints; (2) he must produce a different explanation of why there are moral side constraints rather than simply a goal-directed maximizing structure, an explanation that doesn't itself entail the libertarian side constraint; or (3) he must accept the strongly put root idea about the separateness of individuals and yet claim that initiating aggression against another is compatible with this root idea. Thus we have a promising sketch of an argument from moral form to moral content: the form of morality includes F (moral side constraints); the best explanation of morality's being F is p (a strong statement of the distinctness of individuals); and from p follows a particular moral content, namely, the libertarian constraint. The particular moral content gotten by this argument, which focuses upon the fact that there are distinct individuals each with his *own* life to lead, will not be the *full* libertarian constraint. It will prohibit sacrificing one person to benefit another. Further steps would be needed to reach a prohibition on paternalistic aggression: using or threatening force for the benefit of the person against whom it is wielded. For this, one must focus upon the fact that there are distinct individuals, each with his own life *to lead*.

A nonaggression principle is often held to be an appropriate principle to govern relations among nations. What difference is there supposed to be between sovereign individuals and sovereign nations that makes aggression permissible among individuals? Why may individuals jointly, through their government, do to someone what no nation may do to another? If anything, there is a stronger case for nonaggression among individuals; unlike nations, they do not contain as parts individuals that others legitimately might intervene to protect or defend.

I shall not pursue here the details of a principle that prohibits physical aggression, except to note that it does not prohibit the use of force in defense against another party who is a threat, even though he is innocent and deserves no retribution. An *innocent threat* is someone who innocently is a causal agent in a process such that he would be an aggressor had he chosen to become such an agent. If someone picks up a third party and throws him at you down at the bottom of a deep well, the third party is innocent and a threat; had he chosen to launch himself at you in that trajectory he would be an aggressor. Even though the falling person would survive his fall onto you, may you use your ray gun to disintegrate the falling body before it crushes and kills you? Libertarian prohibitions are usually formulated so as to forbid using violence on innocent persons. But innocent threats, I think, are another matter to which different principles must apply. Thus, a full theory in this area also must formulate the *different* constraints on response to innocent threats. Further complications concern *innocent shields of threats*, those innocent persons who themselves are nonthreats but who are so situated that they will be damaged by the only means available for stopping the threat. Innocent persons strapped onto the front of the tanks of aggressors so that the tanks cannot be hit without also hitting them are innocent shields of threats. (Some uses of force on people to get at an aggressor do not act upon innocent shields of threats; for example, an aggressor's innocent child who is tortured in order to get the aggressor to stop wasn't *shielding* the parent.) May one knowingly injure innocent shields? *If* one may attack an aggressor and injure an innocent shield, may the innocent shield fight back in self-defense (supposing that he cannot move against or fight the aggressor)? Do we get two persons battling each other in self-defense? Similarly, if you use force against an innocent threat to you, do you thereby become an innocent threat to him, so that he may now justifiably use additional force against you (supposing that he can do this, yet cannot prevent his original threateningness)? I tiptoe around these incredibly difficult issues here, merely noting that a view that says it makes nonaggression central must resolve them explicitly at some point.

7

Agent-Relativity and Deontology

Thomas Nagel

1. Three Kinds of Agent-relativity

In this chapter I want to take up some of the problems that must be faced by any defender of the objectivity of ethics who wishes to make sense of the actual complexity of the subject. The treatment will be general and very incomplete. Essentially I shall discuss some examples in order to suggest that the enterprise is not hopeless.

The discussion will revolve around the distinction between agent-relative and agent-neutral values. I won't try to set forth a full ethical theory, even in outline, but I will try to say something in this chapter and the next about the central problem of ethics: how the lives, interests, and welfare of others make claims on us and how these claims, of various forms, are to be reconciled with the aim of living our own lives. My assumption is that the shape of a moral theory depends on the interplay of forces in the psychic economy of complex rational beings. (I shall not say anything about aesthetic values, whose relation to human interests is obscure, though they are revealed to us by the capacity of certain things outside us to command our interest and respect.)

There is one important component of ethics that is consequentialist and impersonal. [S]ome kind of hedonistic, agent-neutral consequentialism describes a significant form of concern that we owe to others. Life is filled with basic pleasures and pains, and they matter. Perhaps other basic human goods, such as health and survival, have the same status, but let me put that aside for the moment. I want now to examine other sorts of

Thomas Nagel, "Agent-Relativity and Deontology," *The View From Nowhere* (New York: Oxford University Press, 1986), pp. 164–85.

objective reasons that complicate the picture. Ethics is concerned not only with what should happen, but also independently with what people should or may *do*. Neutral reasons underlie the former; but relative reasons can affect the latter. In philosophical discussion, the hegemony of neutral reasons and impersonal values is typically challenged by three broad types of reasons that are relative in form, and whose existence seems to be independent of impersonal values.

The first type of reason stems from the desires, projects, commitments, and personal ties of the individual agent, all of which give him reasons to act in the pursuit of ends that are his own. These I shall collect under the general heading of reasons of autonomy (not to be confused with the autonomy of free will).

The second type of reason stems from the claims of other persons not to be maltreated in certain ways. What I have in mind are not neutral reasons for everyone to bring it about that no one is maltreated, but relative reasons for each individual not to maltreat others himself, in his dealings with them (for example by violating their rights, breaking his promises to them, etc.). These I shall collect under the general, ugly, and familiar heading of deontology. Autonomous reasons would limit what we are obliged to do in the service of impersonal values. Deontological reasons would limit what we are *permitted* to do in the service of either impersonal or autonomous ones.

The third type of reason stems from the special obligations we have toward those to whom we are closely related: parents, children, spouses, siblings, fellow members of a community or even a nation. Most people would acknowledge a noncontractual obligation to show special concern for some of these others – though there would be disagreement about the strength of the reasons and the width of the net. I'll refer to them as reasons of obligation, even though they don't include a great many obligations that are voluntarily undertaken. I mention them here only for completeness and won't discuss them in detail. I have less confidence here than with regard to the other two categories that in ordinary thought they resist agent-neutral justification.

I am not sure whether all these agent-relative reasons actually exist. The autonomous ones and perhaps the obligatory ones are fairly intelligible; but while the idea behind the deontological ones can I think be explained, it is an explanation which throws some doubt on their validity. The only way to find out what limits there are to what we may or must do in the service of impersonal values is to see what sense can be made of the apparent limits, and to accept or reject them according to whether the maximum sense is good enough.

Taken together, autonomous, obligatory, neutral, and deontological reasons cover much of the territory of unreflective bourgeois morality. Common sense suggests that each of us should live his own life (autonomy), give special consideration to certain others (obligation), have some significant concern for the general good (neutral values), and treat the people he deals with decently (deontology). It also suggests that these aims may produce serious inner conflict. Common sense doesn't have the last word in ethics or anywhere else, but it has, as J. L. Austin said about ordinary language, the first word: it should be examined before it is discarded.

Attempts have been made to find room for some version of all three types of apparent exception to impersonal ethics in a more complex impersonal system, using developments of consequentialism like rule-utilitarianism and motive-utilitarianism. A recent example is Hare's two-level version of utilitarianism in *Moral Thinking*. And T. M. Scanlon offers a consequentialist but nonutilitarian justification of deontological rights in "Rights, Goals, and Fairness." I shall not try to show that these reductions of the agent-relative to the agent-neutral fail, since I believe they are partly correct. They just aren't the whole truth. I shall try to present an alternative account of how the exceptions might make sense independently. My aim is to explain what it is that eludes justification in neutral terms. Since this is most conspicuous with regard to autonomy and deontology, I shall concentrate on them. The account in both cases depends on certain discrepancies between what can be valued from an objective standpoint and what can be seen from an objective standpoint to have value from a less objective standpoint.

2. Reasons of Autonomy

Not all the sources of subjective reasons are as simple as sensory pleasure and pain. I believe that the most reasonable objectification of the value that we all recognize in our own encounter with these experiences is an impersonal one. Difficult as it may be to carry out, each of us has reason to give significant weight to the simple sensory pleasure or pain of others as well as to his own. When these values occur in isolation, the results can be demanding. If you and a stranger have both been injured, you have one dose of painkiller, and his pain is much more severe than yours, you should give him the painkiller – not for any complicated reasons, but simply because of the relative severity of the two pains, which provides a neutral reason to prefer the relief of the more severe. The same may be said of other basic elements of human good and ill.

But many values are not like this. Though some human interests (and not only pleasure and pain) give rise to impersonal values, I now want to argue that not all of them do. If I have a bad headache, anyone has a reason to want it to stop. But if I badly want to climb to the top of Mount Kilimanjaro, not everyone has a reason to want me to succeed. I have a reason to try to get to the top, and it may be much stronger than my reason for wanting a headache to go away, but other people have very little reason, if any, to care whether I climb the mountain or not. Or suppose I want to become a pianist. Then I have a reason to practice, but other people have little or no reason to care if I practice or not. Why is this?

Why shouldn't the satisfaction of my desire to climb the mountain have impersonal value comparable to the value it has for me – just like the elimination of my headache? As it happens, you may have to put up with severe altitude headaches and nausea to get to the top of a mountain that high: it has to be worth it to you. Why doesn't the objectification of these values preserve the relation among them that exists in the perspective of the climber? This problem was originally formulated by Scanlon. He makes a strong case against the view that the satisfaction of preferences as such provides the raw material for ethics – the basis of our claims to the concern of others. The impersonal value of things that matter to an individual need not correspond to their personal value to him. "The fact that someone would be willing to forgo a decent diet in order to build a monument to his god does not mean that his claim on others for aid in his project has the same strength as a claim for aid in obtaining enough to eat" (Scanlon (1), pp. 659–60).

There are two ways in which a value may be conditional on a desire: the value may lie either outside or inside the conditional, so to speak. In the former case, a person's having X if he desires X has neutral value: satisfaction of the desire has objective utility that everyone has reason to promote. In the latter case, if a person desires X, his having X has relative value for him: susceptibility to the value is conditional on having the desire, and satisfaction of the desire does not have impersonal utility.

It isn't easy to state a general rule for assigning desires to one category or the other. I have claimed that sensory experiences which we strongly like or dislike simply in themselves have agent-neutral value because of those desires. Such immediate likes and dislikes, not resulting from any choice or underlying reason, are very different from the desires that define our broader aims and ambitions. The former result in mental states that are transparently good or bad, because the attitude of the subject is decisive. The latter require more complicated evaluation.

Most of the things we pursue, if not most of the things we avoid, are optional. Their value to us depends on our individual aims, projects, and concerns, including particular concerns for other people that reflect our relations with them; they acquire value only because of the interest we develop in them and the place this gives them in our lives, rather than evoking interest because of their value. When we look at such desires objectively, from outside, we can acknowledge the validity of the reasons they give for action without judging that there is a neutral reason for any of those things to be done. That is because when we move to the objective standpoint, we leave behind the perspective from which the values have to be accepted.

The crucial question is how far the authority of each individual runs in determining the objective value of the satisfaction of his own desires and preferences. From the objective standpoint we see a world which contains multiple individual perspectives. Some of the appearances of value from within those perspectives can just be taken over by the objective self. But I believe that others must remain essentially perspectival – appearances of value only *to the subject*, and valid only from within his life. Their value is not impersonally detachable, because it is too bound up with the idiosyncratic attitudes and aims of the subject, and can't be subsumed under a more universal value of comparable importance, like that of pleasure and pain.

Anyone may of course make the ends of another person his own, but that is a different matter: a matter of personal sympathy rather than of objective acknowledgment. So long as I truly occupy the objective standpoint, I can recognize the value of one of these optional ends only vicariously, through the perspective of the person who has chosen it, and not in its own right.

This is true even if the person is myself. When I regard my life from outside, integration of the two standpoints cannot overcome a certain form of detachment. I can't directly appreciate the value of my climbing Mount Kilimanjaro just because I want to, as I appreciate the value of my being adequately fed and clothed. The *fact* that I want to, viewed from outside, has none of the importance of *wanting to*, experienced from within. I can see a reason here only through the perspective of TN [Thomas Nagel], who has chosen an optional goal which adds to the values operating within his life something beyond the reasons that simply come at him independently of his choices. I cannot see it except as a value for him, and I cannot therefore take it on without qualification as an impersonal value.

While this seems to me true, there is a natural way to dispute it. I have acknowledged that in the case of sensations, a strong desire or aversion can confer agent-neutral value, and it doesn't require that I have the desire or even fully understand it. Even if, for example, I don't mind the sound of squeaking chalk, I can acknowledge that it is impersonally bad for someone who hates it to be subjected to that sound. The impersonal badness attaches not to the experience conceived merely as a certain sound, but to someone's *having an experience he hates*. The evident awfulness is enough. Now someone might ask, why shouldn't a comparable impersonal value attach to someone's *having (or doing) something he wants* – whatever the desire is? Even if I can't objectively identify with the desire, and therefore can't assign any value to the achievement as such, why can't I judge it to have impersonal value under this more complex description? This would be the universal value under which one could objectively favor all preference-satisfaction.

It isn't easy to make the case convincingly, but I don't believe there is such a universal value. One reason is that the personal projects we are talking about generally involve things happening in the world outside our minds. It seems too much to allow an individual's desires to confer impersonal value on something outside himself, even if he is to some extent involved in it. The impersonal authority of the individual's values diminishes with distance from his inner condition. We can see this clearly, I think, in the limiting case of a personal desire for something which will never impinge on his consciousness: posthumous fame, for example. If someone wants posthumous fame, he may have a reason to do what he thinks will achieve it but one cannot see it as anything but a good *for him*. There is no agent-neutral value whatever in the realization of his hope: the only reason anyone else could have for caring about it would be a specific personal concern for him and his ambitions.

On the other hand, the more a desire has as its object the quality of the subject's experience, and the more immediate and independent of his other values it is, the more it will tend to generate impersonal as well as personal reasons. But to the extent that it transcends his own experience, the achievement of a typical personal project or ambition has no value except from the perspective of its subject – at least none in any way comparable to the value reasonably placed on it by the person whose ambition it is. (I am assuming here that we can abstract from any intrinsic value the achievement may have which does not depend on his interest at all – or else that we are dealing with projects whose actual value, whatever it is, derives entirely from the interest of the subject.) Whereas one clearly can find value in the occurrence/nonoccurrence of a sensory experience that is strongly liked/disliked for itself, whether or not one has or even empathizes with the reaction. To put it in a way that sounds paradoxical: the more subjective the object of the desire, the more impersonal the value of its satisfaction.

If this is right, then a certain amount of dissociation is inevitable when we bring the two standpoints together. From within I am directly subject to certain agent-relative reasons. From without all I can do is to acknowledge the reasonableness for the person I am of being motivated by those reasons – without being motivated by them myself, qua objective self. My objectivity shows up in the acknowledgment that these relative reasons are examples of something general, and could arise for any other agent with optional goals of his own. From a point of view outside the perspective of the ambition to climb Kilimanjaro or become a pianist, it is possible to recognize and understand that perspective and so to acknowledge the reasons that arise inside it; but it is not possible to accept those reasons as one's own, unless one occupies the perspective rather than merely recognizing it.

There is nothing incoherent in wanting to be able to climb Kilimanjaro or play all the Beethoven piano sonatas, while thinking that impersonally it doesn't matter whether one can do this. In fact one would have to be dotty to think it did matter impersonally. It doesn't even matter much impersonally that *if* someone wants to play all the Beethoven sonatas by heart, he should be able to. It matters a little, so that if he is incapable of achieving it, it might be better if he didn't want to – leaving aside whatever value there may be in the ambition itself. The neutral values of pleasure and pain come into effect here. But even that is a rather weak neutral value, since it is not the neutral correlate of the agent-relative reasons deriving directly from the ambition, whose object is not pleasure. If an interest is developed by the agent himself through his choices and actions, then the objective reasons it provides are primarily relative.

Any neutral reasons stemming from it must express values that are independent of the particular perspective and system of preferences of the agent. The general values of pleasure and pain, satisfaction and frustration, fill this role to some extent, as I have said, though only to the extent that they can be detached from the value of the object of desire whose acquisition or loss produces the feeling. (This, incidentally, explains the appeal of hedonism to consequentialists: it reduces all value to the impersonal common denominator of pleasure and pain.) But what there is not, I believe, is a completely general impersonal value of the satisfaction of desires and preferences. The strength of an individual's personal preferences in general determines what they give him reason to do, but it does not determine the impersonal value of his getting what he wants. There is no independent value of preference-satisfaction per se, which preserves its force even from an impersonal standpoint.

3. Personal Values and Impartiality

This may seem harsh, and if we left it at that, it would be. For if agent-neutral reasons derived only from pleasure and pain, we would have no reason to care about many fundamental aspects of other people's welfare which cannot easily be given a hedonistic interpretation – their freedom, their self-respect, their access to opportunities and resources that enable them to live fulfilling lives.

But I believe there is another way in which these things can be seen as having impersonal value – without giving carte blanche to individual preferences. These very general human goods share with the much more specific goods of pleasure and freedom from pain a characteristic that generates neutral reasons. Their value does not have to be seen through the particular values of the individual who has or lacks them, or through the particular preferences or projects he has formed.[1] Also, though they do not involve solely the contents of consciousness, such goods are very "close to home": they determine the character of life from the inside, and this lends authority to the value placed on them by the subject. For both these reasons, when we contemplate our own lives and those of others from outside, the most plausible objectification of these very general goods is not agent-relative.

From the objective standpoint, the fundamental thing leading to the recognition of agent-neutral reasons is a sense that no one is more important than anyone else. The question then is whether we are all equally unimportant or all equally important, and the answer, I think, is somewhere in between. The areas in which we must continue to be concerned about ourselves and others from outside are those whose value comes as close as possible to being universal. If impersonal value is going to be admitted at all, it will naturally attach to liberty, general opportunities, and the basic resources of life, as well as to pleasure and the absence of suffering. This is not equivalent to assigning impersonal value to each person's getting whatever he wants.

The hypothesis of two levels of objectification implies that there is not a significant reason for something to happen corresponding to every reason for someone to do something. Each person has reasons stemming from the perspective of his own life which, though they can be publicly recognized, do not in general provide reasons for others and do not correspond to reasons that the interests of others provide for him. Since the relative reasons are general and not purely subjective, he must acknowledge that the same is true of others with respect to him. A certain objective distance from his own aims is unavoidable; there will be some dissociation of the two standpoints with respect to his individual concerns. The ethical results will depend on the size of the impersonal demands made on him and others by the actual circumstances, and how strongly they weigh against more personal reasons.

One difficult question is whether such a two-tier system implies a significant limit to the degree to which ethics requires us to be impartial between ourselves and others.[2] It would imply this if the agent-relative reasons coming from our personal aims were simply added on to the neutral reasons derived from more universal values. For then I would be permitted to pursue my personal projects in preference to the impersonal good of others just as I can pursue those projects in preference to my own health, comfort, etc.; and I wouldn't have to sacrifice myself in return for the furtherance of *their* personal projects – only for their impersonal good. So it looks as though each person's agent-relative reasons would give him a margin of protection against the claims of others – though of course it could be overridden by sufficiently strong impersonal reasons.

However, there is some reason to doubt that the result will be this straightforward. In weighing our agent-relative reasons against the impersonal claims of others, we may not be able to use the same standards we use within our own lives. To take Scanlon's example again: just as we have more reason to help someone get enough to eat than to help him build a monument to his god – even if he is willing to forgo the food for the monument – so he may have more reason to help feed others than to build the monument, even if he cannot be faulted for starving himself. In other words, we have to give basic impersonal goods more weight when they come from other people's needs than when they compete with personal reasons within our own lives.

I am not sure of the best account of this, or how far it would go toward requiring impartiality. Full impartiality would seem to demand that any tendency toward self-favoritism on the basis of personal reasons be offset by a corresponding decrease in the weight given in one's interpersonal decisions to impersonal reasons deriving from one's own basic needs – so that one's total is not increased, so to speak. All reasons would have to be weighted so that everyone was equally important. But I don't know whether a credible system of this kind could be described, at any rate for the purposes of individual decision making. It seems more likely that interpersonal impartiality, both among others and between oneself and others, would have to be defined in terms of agent-neutral values, and that this would leave room for some partiality toward oneself and one's personal concerns and attachments, the extent of it depending on the comparative importance of relative and neutral reasons in the overall system. A stronger form of impartiality, if one is required, would have to appear at a higher level, in the application of practical reason to the social and political institutions that provide a background to individual choice.

There is one objection to this approach which ought to be mentioned, though probably few people would make it. I have claimed that a neutral objectification of the bulk of individualistic subjective reasons does not make sense. But of course that doesn't entail that a relative objectification is correct instead. There is a radical alternative: it could be that these reasons have no objective validity at all, relative or neutral. That is, it might be said by an uncompromising utilitarian that if there isn't a neutral reason for me to climb Kilimanjaro or learn the Beethoven sonatas – if it wouldn't be a good thing in itself, if the world wouldn't be a better place for my getting to the top of the mountain or being able to play the sonatas – then I have no reason of any kind to do those things, and I had better get rid of my desire to do them as soon as possible. I may not, in other words, accord more personal value to anything in my life than is justified by its impersonal value.

That is a logically possible move, but not a plausible one. It results from the aim of eliminating perspective from the domain of real value to the greatest possible extent, and that aim is not required of us by objectivity, so far as I can see. We should certainly try to harmonize our lives to some extent with how we think the world should be. But there is no necessity, I now believe, to abandon all values that do not correspond to anything desirable from an impersonal standpoint, even though this may be possible as a personal choice – a choice of self-transcendence.

If there are, objectively, both relative and neutral reasons, this raises a problem about how life is to be organized so that both can be given their due. One way of dealing with the problem is to put much of the responsibility for securing impersonal values into the hands of an impersonal institution like the state. A well designed set of political and social institutions should function as a moral buffer to protect personal life against the ravenous claims of impersonal good, and vice versa. I shall say a bit more about the relation between ethics and political theory later.

Before leaving the subject of autonomy, let me compare what I have said with another recent treatment of the relation between personal and impersonal values in ethical theory: Samuel Scheffler's *The Rejection of Consequentialism*. He proposes an "agent-centred prerogative," which would permit each individual to accord extra weight to all of his interests in deciding what to do, above that which they contribute to the neutral value of the total outcome of his actions, impersonally viewed.

> More specifically, I believe that a plausible agent-centred prerogative would allow each agent to assign a certain proportionately greater weight to his own interests than to the interests of other people. It would then allow the agent to promote the non-optimal outcome of his own choosing, provided only that the degree of its inferiority to each of the superior outcomes he could instead promote in no case exceeded, by more than the specified proportion, the degree of sacrifice necessary for him to promote the superior outcome. (p. 20)

This proposal is different from mine but not strictly incompatible with it. Scheffler does not make the distinction I have made between those interests and desires that do and those that do not generate impersonal values. He is not committed to a particular method of ranking the impersonal value of states of affairs, but his discussion suggests that he believes the satisfaction of most types of human preferences could be counted in determining whether one state of affairs or outcome was impersonally better than another. But whether or not he would accept my distinction, one could accept it and still formulate the proposal of an agent-centered prerogative; for that proposal describes a limit on the requirement always to produce the impersonally best outcome, which is independent of how the comparative impersonal value of outcomes is determined. It might be determined not by all interests but only by some. Then the prerogative would allow an individual to give those interests extra weight if they were his.

The trouble is that on the autonomy view I have put forward, he may already have some unopposed reasons which favor himself, arising from those desires whose satisfaction yields personal but not impersonal value. Perhaps it's going too far in moral indulgence to add to these a further prerogative of favoring himself with respect to the fundamental goods and evils whose impersonal value is clear.

An alternative position, which combines aspects of Scheffler's and mine, might be this. The division between interests that give rise to impersonal values and interests that don't is not sharp; it is a matter of degree. Some interests generate only relative reasons and no neutral ones; some generate neutral reasons that are just as strong as the relative ones; but some generate both relative reasons and somewhat weaker neutral ones. An individual is permitted to favor himself with respect to an interest to the degree to which the agent-relative reason generated by that interest exceeds the corresponding agent-neutral reason. There is no uniform prerogative of assigning a single proportionately greater weight to the cure of one's headaches, the realization of one's musical or athletic ambitions, and the happiness of one's children.

A variable prerogative of this kind would accord better than a uniform prerogative with Scheffler's account of the motivation behind it: the wish to give moral significance to the personal point of view by permitting morality to reflect the way in which concerns and commitments are naturally generated from within a particular point of view. If some interests are more dependent on a particular normative point of view than others, they will more naturally resist assimilation to the unifying claims of impersonal value in the construction of morality. All this emerges from the attempt to combine subjective and objective standpoints toward action and its motives.

On the other hand, even after such adjustments there will still be claims of impersonal morality that seem from an individual point of view excessive, and it may be that the response to this will have to include a more general agent-centered prerogative.

4. Deontology

Let me turn now to the obscure topic of deontological constraints. These are agent-relative reasons which depend not on the aims or projects of the agent but on the claims of others. Unlike autonomous reasons, they are not optional. If they exist, they restrict what we may do in the service of either relative or neutral goals.

They complicate an already complicated picture. If there are agent-relative reasons of autonomy that do not give rise to agent-neutral interpersonal claims, then the claims of others must compete with these personal reasons in determining what one should do. Deontological constraints add further agent-relative reasons to the system – reasons not to treat others in certain ways. They are not impersonal claims derived from the interests of others, but personal demands governing one's relations with others.

Whatever their explanation, they are conspicuous among the moral appearances. Here is an example to focus your intuitions.

You have an auto accident one winter night on a lonely road. The other passengers are badly injured, the car is out of commission, and the road is deserted, so you run along it till you find an isolated house. The house turns out to be occupied by an old woman who is looking after her small grandchild. There is no phone, but there is a car in the garage, and you ask desperately to borrow it, and explain the situation. She doesn't believe you. Terrified by your desperation she runs upstairs and locks herself in the bathroom, leaving you alone with the child. You pound ineffectively on the door and search without success for the car keys. Then it occurs to you that she might be persuaded to tell you where they are if you were to twist the child's arm outside the bathroom door. Should you do it?

It is difficult not to see this as a dilemma, even though the child's getting its arm twisted is a minor evil compared with your friends' not getting to the hospital. The dilemma must be due to a special reason against *doing* such a thing. Otherwise it would be obvious that you should choose the lesser evil and twist the child's arm.

Common moral intuition recognizes several types of deontological reasons – limits on what one may do to people or how one may treat them. There are the special obligations created by promises and agreements; the restrictions against lying and betrayal; the prohibitions against violating various individual rights, rights not to be killed, injured, imprisoned, threatened, tortured, coerced, robbed; the restrictions against imposing certain sacrifices on someone simply as means to an end; and perhaps the special claim of immediacy, which makes distress at a distance so different from distress in the same room. There may also be a deontological requirement of fairness, of evenhandedness or equality in one's treatment of people. (This is to be distinguished from an impersonal value thought to attach to equality in the distribution of benefits, considered as an aspect of the assessment of states of affairs.)

In all these cases it appears that the special reasons, if they exist, cannot be explained simply in terms of neutral values, because the particular relation of the agent to the outcome is essential. Deontological constraints may be overridden by neutral reasons of sufficient strength, but they are not themselves to be understood as the expression of neutral values of any kind. It is clear from the way such reasons work that they cannot be

explained by the hypothesis that the violation of a deontological constraint has high negative impersonal value. Deontological reasons have
their full force against your doing something – not just against its
happening.

For example, if there really are such constraints, the following things
seem to be true. It seems that you shouldn't break a promise or tell a lie
for the sake of some benefit, even though you would not be required to
forgo a comparable benefit in order to prevent someone else from breaking a promise or telling a lie. And it seems that you shouldn't twist the
arm of a small child to get its grandmother to do something, even something important enough so that you would not be required to forgo a
comparable benefit in order to prevent someone else from twisting a
child's arm. And it may be that you shouldn't engage in certain kinds of
unfair discriminatory treatment (in an official role, for example) even to
produce a good result which you would not be required to forgo in order
to prevent similar unfairness by others.

Some may simply deny the plausibility of such moral intuitions. Others
may say that their plausibility can be subtly accounted for in terms of
impersonal values, and that they appear to involve a fundamentally different type of reason for action only if they are inadequately analyzed. As
I have said, I don't want to take up these alternative accounts here. They
may provide the best hope of rationally justifying something that has the
rough shape of a set of deontological restrictions; but offered as complete
accounts they seem to me essentially revisionist. Even if from that point
of view they contain a good deal of truth, they do not shed light on the
independent deontological conceptions they are intended to replace.
Those conceptions still have to be understood, even if they will eventually be rejected.

Sometimes, particularly when institutions and general practices are
involved in the case, there is a neutral justification for what looks initially
like an agent-relative restriction on action. And it is certainly a help to the
acceptance of deontological constraints that general adherence to them
does not produce disastrous results in the long run. Rules against the
direct infliction of harm and against the violation of widely accepted
rights have considerable social utility, and if it ceased to be so, those rules
would lose much of their moral attractiveness.

But I am convinced that a less indirect, nonstatistical form of evaluation is also at work in support of deontological constraints, and that it
underlies the central, most puzzling intuitions in this area. This is what
would produce a sense of dilemma if it turned out that general adherence
to deontological restrictions worked consistently contrary to impersonal

utility. Right or wrong, it is this type of view that I want to explore and understand. There is no point in trying to show in advance that such dilemmas cannot arise.

One reason for the resistance to deontological constraints is that they are formally puzzling, in a way that the other reasons we have discussed are not. We can understand how autonomous agent-relative reasons might derive from the specific projects and concerns of the agent, and we can understand how neutral reasons might derive from the interests of others, giving each of us reason to take them into account. But how can there be relative reasons to respect the claims of others? How can there be a reason not to twist someone's arm which is not equally a reason to prevent his arm from being twisted by someone else?

The relative character of the reason cannot come simply from the character of the interest that is being respected, for that alone would justify only a neutral reason to protect the interest. And the relative reason does not come from an aim or project of the individual agent, for it is not conditional on what the agent wants. Deontological restrictions, if they exist, apply to everyone: they are mandatory and may not be given up like personal ambitions or commitments.

It is hard to understand how there could be such a thing. One would expect that reasons stemming from the interests of others would be neutral and not relative. How can a claim based on the interests of others apply to those who may infringe it directly or intentionally in a way that it does not apply to those whose actions may damage that same interest just as much indirectly? After all, it is no worse *for the victim* to be killed or injured deliberately than accidentally, or as an unavoidable side-effect of the dangerous rescue operation. In fact the special features of action that bring these reasons into effect may not add to the impersonal badness of the occurrence at all. To use an example of T. M. Scanlon, if you have to choose between saving someone from being murdered and saving someone else from being killed in a similar manner accidentally, and you have no special relation to either of them, it seems that your choice should depend only on which one you're more likely to succeed in saving. Admittedly the wickedness of a murder is in some sense a bad thing; but when it is a matter of deciding which of them there is more reason to prevent, a murder does not seem to be a significantly worse event, impersonally considered, than an accidental or incidental death. Some entirely different kind of value must be brought in to explain the idea that one should not kill one person even to prevent a number of accidental deaths: murder is not just an evil that everyone has reason to prevent, but an act that everyone has reason to *avoid*.

In any case, even if a murder were a worse event, impersonally considered, than an accidental death, this could not be used to explain the deontological constraint against murder. For that constraint prohibits murder even if it is necessary to prevent other *murders* – not only other deaths.

There is no doubt that ideas of this kind form an important part of common moral phenomenology. Yet their paradoxical flavor tempts one to think that the whole thing is a kind of moral illusion resulting either from innate psychological dispositions or from crude but useful moral indoctrination. Before debunking the intuition, however, we ought to have a better grasp of what it is. No doubt it's a good thing for people to have a deep inhibition against torturing children even for very strong reasons, and the same might be said of other deontological constraints. But that does not explain why we find it almost impossible to regard it as a merely useful inhibition. An illusion involves a judgment or a disposition to judge, and not a mere motivational impulse. The phenomenological fact to be accounted for is that we seem to apprehend in each individual case an extremely powerful agent-relative *reason* not to harm an innocent person. This presents itself as the apprehension of a normative truth, not just as a psychological inhibition. It needs to be analyzed and accounted for, and accepted or rejected according to whether the account gives it an adequate justification.

I believe that the traditional principle of double effect, despite problems of application, provides a rough guide to the extension and character of deontological constraints, and that even after the volumes that have been written on the subject in recent years, this remains the right point of convergence for efforts to capture our intuitions.[3] The principle says that to violate deontological constraints one must maltreat someone else intentionally. The maltreatment must be something that one does or chooses, either as an end or as a means, rather than something one's actions merely cause or fail to prevent but that one doesn't aim at.

It is also possible to foresee that one's actions will cause or fail to prevent a harm that one does not intend to bring about or permit. In that case it does not come under a deontological constraint, though it may still be objectionable for neutral reasons. The precise way to draw this distinction has been the subject of extensive debate, sometimes involving ingenious examples of a runaway trolley which will kill five people unless you . . . , where the dots are filled in by different ways of saving the five, all of which in some way involve one other person's death. I won't try to draw the exact boundaries of the principle. Though I say it with trepidation, I believe that for my purposes they don't matter too much, and I suspect they can't be drawn more than roughly: my deontological intuitions, at least, begin to fail above a certain level of complexity. But one point worth mentioning is that the constraints apply to intentionally permitting as well as to intentionally doing harm. Thus in our example there would be the same kind of objection if with the same end in view you permitted someone else to twist the child's arm. You would have let it happen intentionally, and that would be different from a failure to prevent such an occurrence because you were too engaged in doing something else, which was more important.

5. Agents and Victims

So far this is just moral phenomenology: it does not remove the paradox. Why should we consider ourselves far more responsible for what we do (or permit) intentionally than for consequences of action that we foresee and decide to accept but that do not form part of our aims (intermediate or final)? How can the connection of ends and means conduct responsibility so much more effectively than the connection of foresight and avoidability?

It is as if each action produced a unique normative perspective on the world, determined by intention. When I twist the child's arm intentionally I incorporate that evil into what I do: it is my deliberate creation and the reasons stemming from it are magnified and lit up from my point of view. They overshadow reasons stemming from greater evils that are more "faint" from this perspective, because they do not fall within the intensifying beam of my intentions even though they are consequences of what I do.

That is the picture, but can it be correct? Isn't it a normatively distorted picture?

This problem is an instance of the collision between subjective and objective points of view. The issue is whether the special, personal perspective of agency has legitimate significance in determining what people have reason to do – whether, because of this perspective, I can have sufficient reason not to do something which, considered from an external standpoint, it would be better if I did. That is, *things* will be better, what *happens* will be better, if I twist the child's arm than if I do not. But I will have done something worse. If considerations of what I may do, and the correlative claims of my victim against me, can outweigh the substantial impersonal value of what will happen, that can only be because the perspective of the agent has an importance in practical reasoning that resists domination by a conception of the world as a place where good and bad things happen whose value is perspective-free.

I have already claimed that the dominance of this neutral conception of value is not complete. It does not swallow up or overwhelm the relative reasons arising from those individual ambitions, commitments, and attachments that are in some sense chosen. But the admission of what I have called autonomous reasons does not imply the possibility of deontological reasons.[4] The two are very different. The peculiarity of deontological reasons is that although they are agent-relative, they do not express the subjective autonomy of the agent at all. They are demands, not options. The paradox is that this partial, perspectival respect for the interests of others should not give way to an agent-neutral respect free of perspective. The deontological perspective seems primitive, even superstitious, by comparison: merely a stage on the way to full objectivity. How can what we *do* in this narrow sense be so important?

Let me try to say where the strength of the deontological view lies. We may begin by considering a curious feature of deontological reasons on which I have not yet remarked. Intention appears to magnify the importance of evil aims by comparison with evil side-effects in a way that it does not magnify the importance of good aims by comparison with good side-effects. We are supposed to avoid using evil means to produce a good end, even though it would be permissible to produce that good end by neutral means with comparably evil side-effects. On the other hand, given two routes to a legitimate end, one of which involves good means and neutral side-effects and the other of which involves neutral means and equally good side-effects, there is no reason to choose the first route. Deontological reasons tell us only not to aim at evil; they don't tell us to aim at good, as a means. Why should this be? What is the relation between evil and intention, or aiming, that makes them clash with such force?

The answer emerges if we ask ourselves what it is to aim at something, what differentiates it from merely producing the result knowingly.

The difference is that action intentionally aimed at a goal is guided by that goal. Whether the goal is an end in itself or only a means, action aimed at it must follow it and be prepared to adjust its pursuit if deflected by altered circumstances – whereas an act that merely produces an effect does not follow it, is not *guided* by it, even if the effect is foreseen.

What does this mean? It means that to aim at evil, even as a means, is to have one's action guided by evil. One must be prepared to adjust it to insure the production of evil: a falling-off in the level of the desired evil becomes a reason for altering what one does so that the evil is restored and maintained. But the essence of evil is that it should *repel* us. If something is evil, our actions should be guided, if they are guided by it at all, toward its elimination rather than toward its maintenance. That is what evil *means*. So when we aim at evil we are swimming head-on against the normative current. Our action is guided by the goal at every point in the direction diametrically opposite to that in which the value of that goal points. To put it another way, if we aim at evil we make what we do in the first instance a positive rather than a negative function of it. At every point, the intentional function is simply the normative function reversed, and from the point of view of the agent, this produces an acute sense of moral dislocation.

If you twist the child's arm, your aim is to produce pain. So when the child cries, "Stop, it hurts!" his objection corresponds in perfect diametrical opposition to your intention. What he is pleading as your reason to stop is precisely your reason to go on. If it didn't hurt you would twist harder, or try the other arm. There may be cases (e.g. of justified punishment or obloquy) when pain is not intrinsically evil, but this is not one of them: the victim is innocent. You are pushing directly and essentially against the intrinsic normative force of your goal, for it is the production of his pain that guides you. It seems to me that this is the phenomenological nerve of deontological constraints. What feels peculiarly wrong about doing evil intentionally even that good may come of it is the headlong striving against value that is internal to one's aim.

I have discussed a simple case, but naturally there can be complications. One is the possibility of someone volunteering to be subjected to some kind of pain or damage, either for his own good or for some other end which is important to him. In that case the particular evil that you aim at is swallowed up in the larger aim for deontological purposes. So the evil at which we are constrained not to aim is *our victim's* evil, rather than just a particular bad thing, and each individual has considerable authority in defining what will count as harming him for the purpose of this restriction.[5]

All this still leaves unsettled the question of justification. For it will be objected that if one aims at evil as a means only, then even if several people's interests are involved one's action is really being guided not by evil but by overall good, which includes a balance of goods and evils. So when you twist the child's arm, you are guided by the aim of rescuing your injured friends, and the good of that aim dominates the evil of the child's pain. The immediacy of the fact that you must try to produce evil as a subsidiary aim is phenomenologically important, but why should it be morally important? Even though it adds to the personal cost to you, why should it result in a prohibition?

I don't believe there is a decisive answer here. The question is whether to disregard the resistance encountered by my immediate pursuit of what is evil for my victim, in favor of the overall value of the results of what I do. When I view my act from outside and think of it as resulting from a choice of the impersonally considered state of the world in which it occurs, this seems rational. In thinking of the matter this way, I abstract my will and its choices from my person, as it were, and even from my actions, and decide directly among states of the world, as if I were taking a multiple choice test. If the choice is determined by what on balance is impersonally best, then I am guided by good and not by evil.

But the self that is so guided is the objective self, which regards the world impersonally, as a place containing TN and his actions, among other things. It is detached from the perspective of TN, for it views the world from nowhere within it. It chooses, and TN, its instrument, or perhaps one could say its agent, carries out the instructions as best he can. *He* may have to aim at evil, for the impersonally best alternative may involve the production of good ends by evil means. But he is only following orders.

To see the matter in this light is to see both the appeal of agent-neutral, consequentialist ethics and the contrary force of agent-relative, deontological ethics. The detached, objective view takes in everything and provides a standpoint of choice from which all choosers can agree about what should happen. But each of us is not only an objective self but a particular person with a particular perspective; we act in the world from that perspective, and not only from the point of view of a detached will, selecting and rejecting world-states. So our choices are not merely choices of states of the world, but of actions. Every choice is two choices, and from the internal point of view, the pursuit of evil in twisting the child's arm looms large. The production of pain is the immediate aim, and the fact that from an external perspective you are choosing a balance of good over evil does not cover up the fact that this is the intrinsic character of your action.

I have concentrated on the point of view of the agent, as seems suitable in the investigation of an agent-relative constraint. But there is also something to be said about the point of view of the victim. There too we encounter problems having to do with the integration of the two standpoints, and further support for the analysis. Moral principles don't simply tell agents what they may and may not do. They also tell victims what sort of treatment they may and may not object to, resist, or demand.

If I were justified in killing one innocent person to save five others, then he would have no right to object, and on a fully consequentialist view he would have no right to resist. The other five, by contrast, would have the right to object if I *didn't* kill him to save them. A thoroughly impersonal morality would require that victims as well as actors be dominated by impersonal, agent-neutral values in their judgments about how others treat them.

But this seems an excessive demand to make of individuals whose perspective on the world is inherently complex and includes a strong subjective component. Of course none of the six people in this dilemma wants to die, but only one of them is faced with me trying to kill him. This person is not permitted, on a purely agent-neutral consequentialist view, to appeal for his life against my deliberate attempt to take it from him. His special position as my victim doesn't give him any special standing to appeal to me.

Of course the deontological position has a parallel feature. On a deontological view, the five people I could save by killing the one cannot appeal to me for their lives, against my refusal to save them. (They may appeal against *their* killers, if that's the nature of the death threat, but not against me.) But this does not make the two positions symmetrical, for there is a difference. The deontological constraint permits a victim always to object to those who aim at his harm, and this relation has the same special character of normative magnification when seen from the personal perspective of the victim that it has when seen from the personal perspective of the agent. Such a constraint expresses the direct appeal to the point of view of the agent from the point of view of the person on whom he is acting. It operates through that relation. The victim feels outrage when he is deliberately harmed even for the greater good of others, not simply because of the quantity of the harm but because of the assault on his value of having my actions guided by his evil. What I do is immediately directed against his good: it doesn't just in fact harm him.

The five people I could save by killing him can't say the same, if I refrain. They can appeal only to my objective acknowledgment of the impersonal value of their lives. That is not trivial, of course, but it still seems less pressing than the protest available to my victim – a protest he can make not to them but to me, as the possessor of the life I am aiming to destroy.

This merely corroborates the importance of the internal perspective in accounting for the content of deontological intuitions. It does not prove the correctness of those intuitions. But it confirms that a purely impersonal morality requires the general suppression of the personal perspective in moral motivation, not only in its rejection of relative reasons of autonomy but also in its refusal to accept agent-relative deontological restrictions. Such restrictions need not be absolute: they can be thought of as relative reasons with a certain weight, that are among the sources of morality but do not exhaust it. When we regard human relations objectively, it does not seem irrational to admit such reasons at the basic level into the perspective of both agents and victims.

Notes

1 This is the rationale behind the choice of primary goods as the common measure of welfare for distributive justice in Rawls (1). See Rawls (2) for a much fuller treatment. That essay, Scanlon, and the present discussion are all treatments of the "deep problem" described in Rawls (1), pp. 173–5. Dworkin's defense of resources rather than welfare as the correct measure of equality is also in part a response to this problem.

2 Impartiality should not be confused with equality. Nothing I say here bears on the question of how much equality is required in the allocation of what has impersonal value. Absolute impartiality is consistent with a denial that equality should be an independent factor at all in settling distributive questions.

3 A good statement of a view of this type is found in Fried.

4 This is emphasized by Scheffler, who has a cautiously skeptical discussion of deontological constraints under the heading of "agent-centred restrictions."

5 The same seems to apply even when informed consent is impossible, as when we cause suffering or damage to a young child for its own greater good – though here there may be a residual inhibition: if we imagine in the case described that the *child's* safety depends on getting the car keys, it doesn't altogether remove the revulsion against twisting his arm to get them.

References

Fried, Charles. *Right and Wrong*. Cambridge, MA: Harvard University Press, 1978.
Rawls, John. (1) *A Theory of Justice*. Cambridge, MA: Harvard University Press, 1971.
   (2) "Social Unity and Primary Goods," in A. Sen and B. Williams (eds.) *Utilitarianism and Beyond*. Cambridge University Press, 1982.
Scanlon, T.M. "Preference and Urgency," *Journal of Philosophy*, 1975.
Scheffler, S. *The Rejection of Consequentialism* (Oxford: Oxford University Press, 1982).

8

Agent-Centered Restrictions
From the Inside Out

Stephen Darwall

In what follows I shall be concerned with what might be called "the problem of agent-centered restrictions." Briefly put: How can any restriction on what a person may do to promote the best states of affairs that concerns an act's relation to *himself* (for example, that it would be a breaking by *him* of *his* promise, or that it would be a harming by *him* of *another*) possibly be justified? I shall argue that while any case for agent-centered restrictions remains elusive as long as ethics is approached in one, quite common way, there is another approach, one that begins with the idea of a responsible moral individual, that makes agent-centered restrictions intelligible.

I begin in Section I by sketching a line of thought that puts enormous pressure on agent-centered restrictions in order to set the problem. In Section II I quickly review the earlier history of this problem in Moore, Broad, and Ross. In Section III I discuss a current version of the problem as posed by Samuel Scheffler, and in Section IV I show how some preliminary attempts to advert to individual responsibility to solve it fail. In Section V I show how deeply a theory of right without agent-centered restrictions conflicts with a widely held view about an individual's responsibility for his own moral integrity.

Finally, in Section VI, I sketch an approach to ethical theory, one that can be found in Butler and Kant, that takes this view of responsibility and integrity as fundamental. Apparently no justification for agent-centered restrictions can be found so long as we begin by looking *outside* the moral agent – whether to states of affairs that acts bring about or to the nature of acts themselves considered independently of motivation. If we

Stephen Darwall, "Agent-Centered Restrictions From the Inside Out," *Philosophical Studies* 50 (1986): 291–319.

approach ethics from the outside we are led to consequentialism as a theory of right, unless, like Ross, we simply assert certain agent-centered restrictions as fundamental and underived. The alternative I sketch approaches the theory of right from the direction of an account of responsible moral character. It works, as it were, from the inside-out. My thesis is that this approach is much likelier to provide a rationale for agent-centered restrictions in its theory of right.

I

There is a way of thinking about ethics that makes consequentialism a very appealing position. We begin by thinking of actions as the initiating of changes in the world; actions have consequences. Some of these consequences are causal, but not all are. There is also a sense in which the state of affairs consisting of an act's performance is a consequence of the act: had the act not been performed, the state would not have obtained.

What a person ought to do, what it would be right for her to do, is the best thing she can do. If she does something else she does something worse, and surely there is more justification for doing what is better. We should do the best we can.

One act is better than another if, and only if, the states of affairs brought into existence by the former are better, on the whole, than the states produced by the latter. This may be because the former act has consequences, in the narrow sense, that are better than the latter; its causal consequences may be better. But that will be insufficient by itself. The latter act may partly constitute a state of affairs that is intrinsically better, and its greater intrinsic value may outbalance the greater value of the effects of the first. So if the consequences of one act are better, on the whole, than those of another, then the total value it produces, both the intrinsic value of states it partly constitutes and that of further states it causes, must be greater than that of the other. An act is the best thing one can do just in case the value of its consequences, construed broadly, is greatest. So an act is right just in case it has the best consequences.

Three things should be noted about this line of thought. First, its conclusion is that consequentialism *in the broad sense* is the correct theory of right. Consequentialism has perhaps more usually been associated with theories of the good, such as hedonism, according to which an act's being performed has no value in itself. On these views, there is nothing intrinsically bad about disloyalty, say, or good about distributing resources equally, or in accordance with merit. There is nothing intrinsically good

or bad about any act. Acts, and states of affairs that consist in their performance, can have only extrinsic value.

But there is nothing in the intuitive idea that a right act brings about
the best states that requires this view. A keeping of a promise brings about
a promise's being kept. If that is a good thing in itself, then its value must
be reckoned into a consequentialist calculus. To the extent that consequentialism as a whole has been rejected because consequentialist
theories in the field have had implausibly narrow theories of good, that
rejection must be rethought. What may appear to be arguments against
consequentialism, and for deontology, may actually be arguments for a
more sophisticated consequentialism.

But what, then, is the difference between deontology and consequentialism? If every objection to consequentialism can be absorbed by suitable changes in its theory of good, then is there any remaining difference?
Does the intuitive line of thought just sketched construe consequences so
broadly that the issue is lost? The second thing to notice is that it does
not.

Consequentialism holds that an agent ought to do what will bring
about the best states of affairs. The requisite value of a state of affairs is
fundamentally independent of any relation to the agent – it is "agent-
neutral". Even if the valuable state of affairs essentially includes an action,
its value is independent of being *the agent's* action – of being *his*. For
example, if *S*'s keeping his promise is intrinsically valuable, it is so independently of its being *his* keeping of *his* promise.

Consequentialism is an agent-neutral theory of right. Deontological
theories are not agent-neutral; they often include principles that are agent-
centered.[1] For example, a deontological theory might include a *prima facie*
duty to keep promises. This is different from treating promisekeeping as
intrinsically valuable. A *prima facie* injunction to keep promises is a *prima
facie* injunction to keep *one's* promises, not to bring about the intrinsically
good state of affairs of people keeping their promises.

If the intuitive line of thought sketched at the beginning tells in favor
of consequentialism, it tells against any agent-centered theory. If it is right
to keep my promise, then keeping my promise must be the best thing I
can do. If it is the best thing I can do, then the state of affairs of my keeping
it, together with its further consequences, is best. But whether that *state*
is best in the requisite sense depends in no way on its being *my* keeping
my promise. There can be, consequently, no agent-centered *prima facie*
duty to keep *one's* promises. At best there might be a *prima facie* duty to
promote promisekeeping, if that state of affairs is intrinsically good.

Now it might be thought unreasonably demanding to hold that it is always wrong to do what will have less than optimal consequences. It is one thing to say that the best act brings about the best states of affairs, but quite another to say that anything less than the best is wrong.[2] Thinking along these lines may lead one to conclude with Samuel Scheffler that it is often not wrong for a person to do what is less than optimific when her own projects and commitments would be sufficiently sacrificed by the optimific act. Scheffler proposes an "agent-centered prerogative" according to which a person is permitted to pursue her own projects out of proportion to their agent-neutral value.[3]

Still, even if it is not always wrong not to do what will have the best consequences, it may still never be wrong to do what will. A weaker version of the initial line of thought goes in this direction. Even if it is not always wrong not to do the best act, it can never be wrong to do the best act. After all, how could the best thing one could do be wrong for one to do? If an act is best, then the state of affairs of its being performed is best. If it is never wrong to do what is best, then it is never wrong to bring about the best states.

This, then, is the third thing to notice about the line of thought. While some sort of agent-centered prerogative or permission is compatible with a weaker version, no agent-centered *restriction* or prohibition can be. If the weaker version is correct, it can never be wrong to do what will bring about the best states. If so, there can be no requirement that is agent-centered (say, to keep *one's* promises, or not to harm *others*) that it is wrong to violate even when doing so would produce better consequences.

The plausibility of this line of thought poses an important challenge to deontological theories of right. It is a very common way of thinking about ethics, and it lies behind, I believe, a recent resurgence of support for consequentialist theories.[4] On the one hand, it blunts past criticisms of consequentialism by showing how many can be absorbed within the consequentialist framework. On the other hand, it apparently shows why what is truly distinctive about a deontological theory, agent-centered restrictions, cannot possibly be justified.

The most trenchant version of the challenge can be found in Scheffler's *The Rejection of Consequentialism*. This is ironic in a way since Scheffler's aim is partly to reject consequentialism – or, as he more cautiously puts it, to argue that a rationale exists for an agent-centered prerogative that is independent of consequentialist considerations. He argues that a case for an agent-centered prerogative can be mounted on the basis of two considerations: one, that our motivations naturally arise from our own personal points of view, and, two, that a theory of right that directly "reflects" this with an agent-centered prerogative is a "rational response" to that fact.

Scheffler's challenge to deontology is that the justification for an agent-centered prerogative provides no rationale for any agent-centered restriction (the "independence thesis"), and, moreover, that there is reason to think that no justification of any kind can be given for agent-centered restrictions (the "asymmetry thesis"). He canvasses various proposed justifications and concludes that they all fail.

II

The debate between consequentialism and deontology has been continuous in moral philosophy, in some form or other, since the eighteenth century British moralists. But it is, I believe, only in this century that it has been cast in terms of agent-neutrality versus agent-centeredness in the theory of right. The first place I know this dialectic to have arisen is in connection with the consequentialism, or as he called it "ideal utilitarianism," advanced by G. E. Moore in *Principia Ethica*. Moore's consequentialism is of the sophisticated variety; Ross called it "the culmination of all the attempts to base rightness on productivity of some sort of result."[5] Because of its pluralistic theory of good, Moore's theory of right resists some deontological criticisms of simpler consequentialisms. And, more important for contemporary consequentialists, it shows the resources that a sophisticated consequentialism has available. Moreover, Moore articulated, perhaps more clearly than anyone, the underlying rationale for consequentialism.

Moore's general argument against deontology, as well as his famous "refutation" of egoism, are versions of the intuitive line of thought with which we began. Both egoism and deontology are agent-centered theories. Egoism maintains that each ought to advance his own happiness, and deontology includes duties that are agent-centered. Moore's argument against each was the same. If a person *ought* to do something, then it must be good, indeed *best*, that he so act. The act must promote something with intrinsic value. Perhaps it is the act itself, perhaps some further consequence of the act. In either case, if that state of affairs is good, there will be the same reason for others to produce it as there is for the agent. So, against egoism: there can only be a reason for someone to advance her happiness if her being happy, or acting for the sake of it, is good absolutely. But if that is so, then others will have the same reason to promote that state of affairs, and she will have the same reason to act similarly with respect to others. And against deontology: there can only be a reason for a person to fulfill some (apparently agent-centered) duty if her doing so is good, indeed best. But if it is good that she do so, then others will have the same reason to promote that state of affairs, as will she to promote their so acting. So there is no *agent-centered* duty. At best there are intrinsically good acts the performance of which every agent has a reason to promote.

> It is plain that when we assert that a certain action is our absolute duty, we are asserting that the performance of that action at that time is unique in respect of value. But . . . its value cannot be unique in the sense that it has more intrinsic value than anything else in the world; since *every* act of duty would then be the *best* thing in the world, which is . . . a contradiction. It can, therefore, be unique only in the sense that the whole world will be better, if it be performed, than if any possible alternative were taken.[6]

Although Moore did not put his argument in terms of agent-centeredness and agent-neutrality, C. D. Broad later noted that this was its thrust. He characterized what he called Moore's "ethical neutralism" in this way:

> Ethical neutralism assumes that there is a certain *one* state of affairs – "the sole good" – at which *everyone* ought to aim as an *ultimate* end. Differences in the proximate ends of different persons can be justified only in so far as the one ultimate end is best secured in practice by different persons aiming, not directly at it, but at different proximate ends of a more limited kind.[7]

Actually, since sophisticated consequentialism has a pluralistic theory of good, it would be more correct to say that it provides one *ranking* of states of affairs, and that agents ought to do whatever will bring about the best states of affairs as determined by that ranking.

Broad went on to point out that Moore's argument against egoism, and he could have added, his argument against agent-centered deontology, depended on this commitment to ethical neutralism. But was ethical neutralism a premise or a conclusion for Moore? In *Principia* it is more natural to think of it as a conclusion derived from a deeper premise: namely, that if an act is a duty, if it is right to perform it, then that must be because performing it is "unique in value." If an act is right, then it is best. And "in asserting that the act is *the* best thing to do, we assert that it together with its consequences presents a greater sum of intrinsic value than any possible alternative."[8] For the Moore of *Principia*, there is only one fundamental ethical notion, the *good*, or intrinsic value, and the right can be defined in terms of it.

Ross also noticed the agent-neutrality of Moorean consequentialism, though not in so many words, and pointed out the sharp contrast with his own deontological theory of *prima facie* duties. And recognizing what led Moore in this direction, he steadfastly refused to follow.

Against Moore, Ross argued that the agent's specific context, his relations to others, the history of his past acts and of others' acts towards him, and his special relationship to himself, are all directly relevant to what it would be right for him to do. Moore's theory, he argued,

> seems to simplify unduly our relations to our fellows. It says, in effect, that the only morally significant relation in which my neighbours stand to me is that of being possible beneficiaries by my action. They do stand in this relation to me, and this relation is morally significant. But they may also stand to me in the relation of promisee to promiser, of creditor to debtor, of wife to husband, of child to parent, of friend to friend, of fellow countryman to fellow countryman, and the like.[9]

Strictly speaking, Ross's criticism is a bit wide of the mark. For while Moore called himself an "ideal utilitarian," he did not hold that an act is right only if it maximizes total net *benefit*. A right act maximizes intrinsic value. And Moore held that friendship, or at any rate, personal affection, is among the things that have intrinsic value. So he held that *that* relation does have moral significance. And he *could* have held, and still remained a consequentialist, that all of the relations Ross mentions have intrinsic moral significance. That is, the flourishing of each of these relations might be held to have intrinsic value and to be worth promoting for its own sake.

Ross's criticism becomes clearer when we read the rest of his last sentence.

> and each of these relations is the foundation of a *prima facie* duty, which is more or less incumbent on me according to the circumstances of the case.[10]

Ross's view was not that since these relationships are intrinsically valuable there is moral reason for every person to promote them. Rather, he held that the fact a person is *himself* related to others in various ways creates *prima facie* duties, to care for his children, to be loyal to his friends, to keep his promises, and so on. Moore's view was that *no* relation was relevant in an agent-centered way.

But how did Ross resist the line of thought that led to Moore's neutralist consequentialism – the line from right act, to best available act, to act productive of the most intrinsic value? Ross maintained that "'right' does not stand for a form of value at all."[11] Moore's mistake was to suppose that an act's being the right thing to do *just is* its being productive of the most intrinsic value. As against Moore, Ross argued that the concept of right is no less fundamental to ethics and irreducible than Moore had argued that of intrinsic value to be. Once he had opened a logical space between claims about intrinsic value and claims about what it is right or wrong *to do*, Ross was in a position simply to assert the common sense position that agent-centered characteristics of acts can be right- or wrong-making – that, for example, its being a betrayal of *one's* close friend is directly relevant to whether an act would be right or wrong.

When sophisticated consequentialists objected that a pluralistic theory of right, with no unifying rationale, was arbitrary and unmotivated, Ross replied that he was in no worse a position with respect to the objection than those who generally made it, since they also held pluralistic theories, albeit of the good. This reply is especially strong when made to a sophisticated consequentialist whose theory of the good itself seems formulated expressly to meet deontological criticisms of simpler versions.

III

That agent-centered restrictions have the support of common sense is generally not in dispute. If there is a burden to be carried at the level of considered judgments about specific cases it certainly belongs to the neutral consequentialist. The "problem" of agent-centered restrictions is that there is no apparent rationale for them. The intuitions that support them remain, as Scheffler has put it, "intuition[s] in search of a foundation."(112)

It is at the level of deeper justification that consequentialism appears to be in a stronger position. At least we can identify an intuitive line of thought that underlies it. Like Ross, the deontologist may choose to reject this line of thought. He may urge that an act's being right and the state of affairs of its being performed being best are different things. Being right, he may say, is not a form of value. And he may insist, as did Ross, that there are agent-centered *prima facie* duties. But even if he can defend his position, he may be unable to say what is deeply appealing about it. That is "the problem."

Scheffler puts the problem in this way. He considers a specimen agent-centered restriction, R, against harming innocent others. He then asks us to

> suppose that if Agent A_1 fails to violate ... R by harming some undeserving person P_1, then five other agents, $A_2 ... A_6$, will each violate restriction R by identically harming five other persons, $P_2 ... P_6$ who are just as undeserving as P_1, and whom it would be just as undesirable from an impersonal standpoint to have harmed. (84)

What, he asks, could be the rationale for holding it to be wrong for A_1 to violate R in such a case?

Now it might seem implausible that the debate between consequentialism and deontology should come down to this question. The situation seems contrived, and it may be difficult to see what hangs on it. But there is a point to the question.

The point, to a first approximation, is that unless R has the feature that it is wrong to violate it even if doing so would bring about fewer violations, then R can be fully captured within an agent-neutral consequentialism that holds acting contrary to R to be intrinsically disvaluable. If it is wrong for one to violate R even though that would lead to fewer violations of R, then R is inconsistent even with a neutral consequentialism that holds violations of R to be intrinsically bad.

Two things about the question deserve further comment, however. First, as Scheffler certainly realizes, an agent-centered deontological theory need not be committed to absolutism. That is, it can include agent-centered restrictions that are *prima facie* and that are overridden by other considerations, both agent-centered and agent-neutral. So Ross held, for example, that there is a *prima facie* duty to keep one's promise, but other *prima facie* duties as well that can conflict with it, both agent-centered duties, such as those on one's family, community, and so on, and agent-neutral duties such as the general duty of beneficence.

The point is that there is nothing magic about the number five in Scheffler's question. R might be an agent-centered restriction even if it would not be wrong to violate it to prevent five violations. What matters is that the wrongness of violating R not be reducible to the *disvalue* of its being violated. This could be true even if it would not be wrong to violate it to prevent four violations; or three. In fact, it could be true even if it would not be wrong to violate it to prevent *two* violations. This is so because its being justifiable to violate it in that case need not consist in the violation's producing more value.

This is the second thing to notice. It would be sufficient for R to be an agent-centered restriction, the wrongness of violating which is irreducible to the agent-neutral intrinsic disvalue of its being violated, if it would be wrong to violate R when doing so would promote greater, or equal, value. But this could be true at the same time that it would not be wrong to violate R to prevent two violations. To see this suppose that a violation of R would prevent *one* other violation of R. In this case an agent-neutral consequentialism will hold that, other things equal, there is nothing to choose between abiding by R *oneself*, thereby bringing it about that another person violates R, and violating R oneself, thereby preventing the other from violating R. Each violation would be an equally bad occurrence. From the point of view of an agent-neutral consequentialism it simply does not matter whether the intrinsically bad consequence is one's violation of R or another person's. If a theory holds that that does make a difference, that it matters to what one should do whether it will be one or someone else violating R, then R will be an agent-centered restriction. So it is not necessary for R to be an agent-centered restriction that it be wrong to violate it even to prevent two violations. It is sufficient that it be wrong to violate it to prevent one exactly similar violation by someone else.

That said, I intend to make nothing hang on it. It does seem to make the job of justifying agent-centered restrictions less onerous, but the fundamental problem still remains: if the state of affairs of someone's violating an agent-centered restriction would be better, why would it be wrong for her to violate it?

Scheffler's challenge is that while a justification for an agent-centered prerogative can be identified in the "independence of the personal point of view," none can be identified for any agent-centered restrictions. An agent-centered prerogative does not conflict with the intuitive idea that it cannot be wrong to perform an act when so acting would be part of the best state of affairs that could occur.

IV

As I indicated earlier, my proposal will be that a rationale for some form of agent-centered restrictions is likelier to emerge if we approach ethics from the point of view of individual moral responsibility. In some form or other this suggestion is not new, and Scheffler explicitly considers a version of it. It is instructive to see why various versions are nonstarters.

Bernard Williams pointed out over a decade ago that consequentialism includes a doctrine of *negative responsibility*:

> if I am ever responsible for anything, then I must be just as much responsible for things that I allow or fail to prevent, as I am for things that I myself, in the more everyday restricted sense, bring about.[12]

But, he also noted, common sense recognizes an important difference between consequences that would not have occurred if the agent had acted differently, but whose occurrence is the direct result of some *other* person's action, and direct consequences of the agent's own acts. On a neutral consequentialism, however, all that matters for what a given agent, S, should do in some circumstance are the values of V_i, associated with each possible act A_i, in the conditional: If S had done A_i, then states of affairs with value V_i would have obtained. It is simply irrelevant whether the causal chain goes through other agents' acts.

There is a sense, then, in which on a neutral consequentialism, one is as responsible for bad consequences of others' acts one could have prevented, but did not, as one is for bad consequences resulting directly from acts of one's own. It simply follows from agent-neutrality that whether consequences result directly from *the agent's* act is irrelevant to its being right or wrong. Of course, whether a person should be *held* equally responsible for indirect as for direct consequences will be a different question for the consequentialist. That will depend on the consequences of furthers acts involved in holding people responsible.

Scheffler considers an attempt to motivate agent-centered restrictions by pointing to the common sense idea that one is responsible for the direct effects of one's acts in a way that one simply is not for the effects of the acts of others that one could have prevented. His response is quite reasonable: there is no question that the doctrine of negative responsibility is implausible at the level of common sense, but that is not the issue. The issue is whether there exists some deeper rationale for rejecting it. So far the assertion that people are more responsible for the direct consequences of their acts is no deeper than the assertion that they have no similar duty to prevent the bad consequences that would directly result from the acts of others. To assert the former is virtually to assert the latter; it does not justify it.

A second strategy might be to argue that neutral consequentialism is inconsistent with respect for persons as independent responsible moral agents. Since it holds the consequences of others' acts to be relevant to the rightness of a given act to the extent that the latter can affect the former, neutral consequentialism appears simply to "look through" or disregard the moral agency of any person other than the agent whose act is being evaluated as right or wrong. To the extent that moral agents internalize a neutral consequentialism they will then have a way of regarding others that might be thought morally pernicious. Consequentialism apparently requires that one simply *assume* responsibility for others in an obnoxious way. Even God is thought to do no wrong in leaving us free to act in ways that have ill effects. True, one would not want an ethic to recommend simple quiescence in the face of evil potentially resulting from the acts of others. But the other extreme, that a person regard preventable bad consequences of the acts of others as warranting intervention in every case in which it would be warranted were the consequences the direct result of her own acts, seems unpalatable also. That seems inconsistent with respect for others as independent moral agents.

There is, however, a sort of respect for autonomy that a neutral consequentialism can recognize. A sophisticated consequentialist can hold that autonomy is intrinsically valuable – to respect it is to promote it. If so, neutral consequentialism can hold interference with others' agency to be intrinsically disvaluable, other things equal, thereby avoiding the unpalatable extreme without an agent-centered restriction.

There is justification for an agent-centered restriction only if there is justification not simply for weighing in the intrinsic disvalue of interference, but for a restriction the violation of which is not warranted by an increase in value even when the intrinsic value of autonomy is taken into account. And the intrinsic obnoxiousness of regarding others simply as the conduit of one's own agency does not evidently provide any justification for that. If neutral consequentialism is to be rejected because it conflicts with respect for others as independent responsible agents, therefore, deeper considerations will have to be marshalled.

Finally, one might try to argue against what Scheffler calls the "independence thesis", against, that is, his claim that the rationale he provides for an agent-centered prerogative does not also justify any agent-centered restriction. The prerogative, recall, permits agents to devote energy and attention to their own projects and commitments out of proportion to the (objective) value of their doing so. And its rationale according to Scheffler is that most of our projects and commitments naturally develop from within our own personal points of view. We become committed to particular pursuits, people, communities, and so on, as a result of our own individual personal histories. Scheffler argues that a theory of right should directly reflect that fact with a prerogative. The best that a sophisticated consequentialist can do is a "consequentialist dispensation" that gives intrinsic value to persons' pursuit of their own commitments and projects, but that does not permit them to pursue them when they could promote more self-realization by others by sacrificing their own projects.

When one considers what an ethical theory with an agent-centered prerogative, so justified, but without any agent-centered restrictions, would look like, the result may seem unstable. How can there be a justification for a prerogative, but none for a restriction on interference with its exercise? Won't the theory both permit agent A to pursue a nonoptimific personal commitment but require agent B to prevent A from doing so if that would be optimific, assuming that forbearing interference is not covered by B's prerogative? The idea of a prerogative suggests the idea of a morally protected sphere of personal action, but without an accompanying restriction on the acts of others, the sphere will not be protected against morally sanctioned interference.

The situation is analogous to that considered just above. A neutral consequentialist can treat autonomy, or self-realization, as intrinsically valuable. This value, then, can be weighed in determining whether interference with another's exercise of his prerogative would have the best consequences. Because the value is agent-neutral, however, there will be no case for failing to interfere with A if doing so is necessary to prevent yet greater interference with others. But even if the independence of the personal standpoint justifies an agent-centered prerogative, and not merely a consequentialist dispensation, it is hard to see why it justifies an agent-centered restriction on interference rather than a neutral consequentialism that gives intrinsic value to self-realization and intrinsic disvalue to interference. There is at least some plausibility to the view that the importance of the personal standpoint provides a rationale for persons having some freedom to pursue their own personal projects even when their doing so is at some cost to general self-realization. But when we shift from the agent exercising the prerogative to others, the importance of the personal standpoint provides no apparent rationale for restricting *others* from interfering when doing so would promote greater self-realization. An *agent-centered* restriction on interference seems unmotivated.

V

It seems, then, that no rationale for agent-centered restrictions emerges in any simple and direct way from considerations of responsibility, respect for others as responsible agents, or the independence of the personal standpoint. There is a way of conceiving of each of these within a fundamental rationale that leads to neutral consequentialism and away from any agent-centered restriction. If there is something about responsible moral agency that provides a justification for agent-centered restrictions it will apparently have to be framed within a wholly different line of thought.

In the next section I will sketch a fundamental approach to ethics on which agent-centered restrictions are, as such, unproblematic, and contrast it with the line of thought leading to consequentialism. The latter begins with a view about the intrinsic value of states of affairs conceived independently of any moral evaluation of conduct or character, while the point of departure of the alternative I shall suggest is a fundamental view of character, moral integrity, and of responsibilities relating to these. To put it in a rough and preliminary way, moral integrity involves a person's guiding his life by his own moral judgment, properly understood, and the fundamental responsibility of the moral life is the maintenance of integrity, so conceived. Instead of beginning outside the moral agent with a view about states of affairs that are intrinsically worthy of promotion, the alternative begins inside the moral agent with a view about moral character and integrity. The rationale for agent-centered restrictions is itself agent-centered.

To prepare the way for a discussion of this approach I want first to consider how consequentialists are bound to view the proper relation of integrity and character to what a person ought to do.

To begin with, because on a neutralist view the history of a person's own conduct is not directly relevant to what she should do, there is a sense in which a person bears no direct responsibility for what she has done. Her *own* past conduct leaves no directly relevant trace in determining what she should subsequently do, since were it to do so it would have to be *via* an agent-centered restriction. Neutral consequentialism thus rejects any special duty to try to comprehend, understand, or come to grips with, one's own past conduct, and by doing so to repair moral integrity. Of course, a neutralist can explain why we should do this on many occasions, so that we will be better able to maximize intrinsic value. But we have no special responsibility for our past in the sense that what we should do is intrinsically unaffected by what *we* have done.

Neutral consequentialism does hold that a person has a special responsibility for her acts at the time of their performance, that she does not have for the acts of others, in at least one sense. A theory of right action *just is* a theory of what a person is responsible for *doing* given what, at the time of action, she has it in her power to do. To act contrary to the theory is to do wrong and, in this sense, to fail to discharge one's moral responsibility.

But consequentialism denies that a person has a special responsibility for her character or integrity in the sense that it denies that considerations regarding *her* character and integrity are in any way directly relevant to what she should do. It denies that the consequences of acts for her character are any more relevant in themselves to what she should do than are consequences for the character of others. It denies that an act's constituting a diminishing of her moral integrity, or a violation of her own principles and values, is any more intrinsically relevant to what she should do because it is her own moral integrity that is at stake. And it denies that a person has any but a contingently instrumental obligation to take thought of what she has done and is doing in her life, to "bear [her] own survey," in Hume's phrase, and conduct her life in a way of which she can on honest reflection approve.

A vivid example will be helpful. In a recent essay Tomas E. Hill, Jr. describes "an artist of genius and originality" who "paints a masterwork unappreciated by his contemporaries," but who "cynically, for money and social status," and with some self-disgust, "alters the painting to please the tasteless public and then turns out copies in machine-like fashion."[13] Hill argues that there is a well understood sense in which the artist fails to respect himself: he fails to "live by a set of personal standards by which [he] is prepared to judge [himself]."[14]

Suppose, however, that the story continues. There is another similarly talented artist who is bent on pursuing the same path, but the spectacle of the first artist so sickens him that he decides he cannot do it, and does not. So the consequence of the first artist's conduct is the loss of his integrity, but the prevention of the loss of the other's. A neutral consequentialism will hold that it makes no difference to what the first artist should have done that it violated his integrity. A loss of integrity is a loss of integrity. Other things equal, there was no moral reason for him not to sell out that did not also exist for him to prevent the other's selling out.

Two clarificatory remarks are in order at this point. Though neutral consequentialism is indeed committed to these counterintuitive propositions about what it is right to do, the neutralist may respond that we find these propositions counterintuitive partly because we run together matters of right and wrong with matters of praise and blame, evaluations of acts and evaluations of agents. That the first artist does no worse wrong in violating his own integrity than he would in failing to prevent another from violating his, does not mean that *he* should he judged the same in both cases. Evaluations of acts as right or wrong is a wholly different matter from evaluating persons. For various reasons, it could be argued, lack of self-respect is a worse trait of character than is unwillingness to prevent another's loss of self-respect if it requires losing one's own respect.

Also, the neutralist insists, we must distinguish between subjective and objective rightness – between which act is right given what would actually have happened, and what act would have been right judged relatively to what the agent believed or could reasonably have believed, that is, on the assumption that those beliefs were true. The first artist's act may have been, objectively, no worse than his keeping his moral integrity intact if that would in fact have led to the other's compromising of himself. Nonetheless, if he was ignorant of this consequence his act was subjectively wrong.

For reasons that will become apparent in the next section, I am skeptical that evaluations of acts and agents should be kept separate in the way the consequentialist insists. The point is not that we cannot distinguish, at least in many cases, between what act a person should perform, regardless of motive, and how an agent is to be appraised for performing it from some particular motive, some particular set of beliefs, and so on. My point will be that one can approach the theory of right, in a general way, from a view of moral character.

Second, concern about personal integrity may lead one to think, along with Scheffler, that what consequentialism requires is simply an agent-centered prerogative that protects action for such ends. But the sort of integrity with which I am concerned is not Williams' identification of a person with his "ground projects", alienation from which is threatened by neutral consequentialism.[15] My concern is with *moral* integrity, a person's responsibility to live by principles he can reflectively accept, and, consequently, not to do what is wrong by his own lights. Here a prerogative will be insufficient.

VI

The line of thought leading to consequentialism begins, as I said, outside the moral agent with a view about the intrinsic value of states of affairs. It then works its way inside, first with a theory of right action, and then with a theory of moral character. Acts are right if they maximize the value of states of affairs. A character trait is good if inculcating it maximizes valuable states or, perhaps, if praising it does so. In this progression of external to internal, acts are the natural midpoint. They are the effect of internal causes or, less committally, the output of creatures with a certain internal constitution. But they are individuated independently of their specific internal cause or motive. And, for the consequentialist, their signal feature is that they are part of an objective external order; they partly constitute and bring about states of affairs. So acts have both an external and an internal aspect.

We may say, then, that the consequentialist approaches moral theory from the outside-in. From some basic premises about intrinsically valuable states of affairs, he builds both his theories of conduct and of character.

Now because, on this approach, both conduct and character are evaluated by their respective relation to valuable states, there is an important sense in which consequentialist appraisals of them are instrumental. Conduct is right if it brings about the best states of affairs. A trait is part of good character if it reliably produces the best states.

This may seem to be blunted by the sophisticated consequentialist's holding that the performance of an action, or the having or expressing of a character trait, may be good in itself; but that is only partly true. While a sophisticated consequentialism can hold acts and traits to be part of, and not simply means to, intrinsically good states, it will hold that a person should perform such an act, or that such a trait is a virtuous one, only if they bring about states with the most value overall. Thus a given act held to be intrinsically good will only be something one should do, or an intrinsically good trait be part of good moral character, if there is no other act or trait available that would produce even more value.

The point is really the same as the "problem of agent-centered restrictions." Even if we think of a character trait as good in itself, there will be a rationale for a person's having it only if that will bring about the most valuable states. If her having some quite contrary trait, even one held by the consequentialist to be an essential part of a state that is bad in itself, would promote greater value, say, if it would promote more people having the intrinsically good trait, then the "evil" trait will be the one the person should have, and she will be a better person for having it.

Approaching ethics from the outside-in forces one to treat moral character as derivative and instrumental. And that suggests a different approach. What I shall call the Butler/Kant view turns the line of thought leading to consequentialism on its head. It begins not with a view about the value of states of affairs but with a very general theory of moral character. It then proceeds to work toward a theory of conduct from its theory of character.

It is, I think, significant that both Butler and Kant held deontological normative positions. Kant, of course, is the paradigmatic deontologist. But Butler may seem harder to peg since, like many eighteenth century British moralists, he rarely addressed the question of what to do considered independently of motive. He did not have a theory of right properly so called. Nonetheless, in arguing that the virtues cannot simply be resolved into benevolence he anticipated what were to become stock objections to consequentialism: that "fraud," "violence," and "treachery" can be wrong, even when their overall consequences are good, and "fidelity" and "strict justice" right though their overall consequences be bad.[16]

Had they been faced with the categories of agent-centered and agent-neutral there is little doubt that both Butler and Kant would have accepted agent-centered restrictions and rejected any wholly agent-neutral theory of right. So much is familiar and uncontroversial. What is less appreciated is that these philosophers shared a fundamental approach to moral philosophy, one based on a conception of moral integrity and character, that offers hope of a rationale for agent-centered restrictions.

Very roughly put, the notion that is common to Butler and Kant is that to be subject to morality is to have a complex moral capacity, the having of which creates a fundamental responsibility to lead one's life in a way that exercises it. Exercising this capacity, moreover, is both essential to good character and constitutive of moral integrity.

The common notion, therefore, is of a sort of competence that is constitutive of character and integrity and which there is a fundamental responsibility to exercise. Thus on this view there is a link between character and right conduct that is not derivative from their respective relations to some third thing, in particular to states of affairs held to be intrinsically good. Persons ought to conduct themselves in ways necessary to maintain their moral integrity.

The requisite competence is a complex of capacities: (a) to be aware, not only of situations confronting one, but also of the sorts of motives or reasons, ("maxims," in Kant's term, "principles", in Butler's) that might move one to act in them, (b) to reflect in a certain way, and from a certain point of view, on the idea of *a person's* acting on a given reason or principle in a kind of situation (for Kant, by considering whether one could will that everyone act on the reason), (c) to take an attitude toward acting-on-that-reason-in-that-sort-of-situation on the basis of the appropriate reflection, a reflective attitude or choice that constitutes a *judgment* of so acting, and (d) to regulate one's own conduct by that judgment.[17]

For both Butler and Kant, the person of good character is one who guides his life by exercising the complex competence necessary to be subject to moral demands, a competence, more or less, for independent moral judgment. Only beings with this capacity, Butler argued, can be moral agents in the strictest sense, and by virtue of it all moral agents are "a law unto themselves."[18]

Kant, of course, held that conduct expresses good character only if it issues from the agent's own sense of what she should do. Otherwise, no matter how intrinsically "amiable" the motive of a person's act is, it will, seen from the agent's own point of view, lead her to do what she should do only "if fortunate enough to hit on something beneficial or right."[19] It will not express moral self-government.[20]

The motivation for the Butler/Kant view of moral character is not, as on the outside-in line of thought, that having it leads to intrinsically valuable states of affairs. The inside-out approach is compatible with, indeed congenial to, a profound skepticism that states can have the sort of intrinsic value they must be able to have on the outside-in approach. A theory of conduct can be justified from the outside-in only if states can have an intrinsic worth-bringing-aboutness that not only creates a *prima facie* justification for any moral agent to promote them regardless of his specific motivational and affective susceptibilities. It must also provide justification for thinking it *prima facie wrong* for him to fail to promote it.[21]

The inside-out view of character is motivated, rather, by the thought that this is what character must be if a person can be responsible for her own moral integrity simply by virtue of having the power to constitute it. Thus Butler: "[W]e are agents. Our constitution is put in our own power. We are charged with it; and therefore are accountable for any disorder or violation of it".[22]

The Butler/Kant approach is agent-centered at the outset. It begins with the idea that each person is responsible for her own moral integrity. But how is agent-centeredness at this level likely to be translated into a theory of right? There are, I think, reasons to expect agent-centeredness of at least two different kinds in a theory of right justified from the inside-out along Butler/Kant lines.

First, because it begins with the proposition that agents bear a responsibility for their own moral integrity that they do not for that of others, it will follow that persons have a duty not to compromise their own moral integrity that they do not have to do what would prevent others from compromising theirs. From the outside-in a loss of moral integrity is a loss of moral integrity. But from the inside-out it is the agent's own moral integrity that is his fundamental responsibility.

Now this duty, though fundamental on the inside-out view, is second-order. An agent violates his moral integrity by doing things he would authentically judge wrong. Ordinarily, however, we think of a theory of right as addressed to the level of the agent's first-order thoughts. True as this doubtless is, an inside-out view must hold there to be a genuine second-order duty not to do what one honestly thinks wrong using one's own best judgment, even, indeed, when one's first-order judgment is mistaken. Acting contrary to one's best judgment threatens moral integrity even if the first-order judgment is mistaken.

But is there any reason to think that approaching a theory of right in the Butler/Kant way, from the inside-out, will lead to agent-centered restrictions at the first-order level? There is, in fact, a very interesting reason for expecting that it would.

If we approach the theory of conduct from the outside-in then we think we have a rationale for evaluating acts by their relation to valuable states of affairs. What matters to us is which states of affairs would actually be brought about by the act.

If we approach the theory of conduct from the inside-out, however, our focus will rather be on the principles, considerations, or reasons that persons should be *guided by* in their deliberations about and choice of acts. Whether an act is right will depend on whether it is recommended by principles or considerations that would weigh with a person of good character.

Consequentialists are at pains to distinguish between criteria of right and wrong and considerations that should be taken account of in deliberation and choice. Their theory concerns the former and not the latter. In fact, they are often quick to point out that while the theory of right is agent-neutral, a consequentialist theory of decisionmaking may well dictate that persons take account of agent-centered considerations in deciding what to do. The best consequences may be produced only *indirectly*, that is, if persons guide their choices not by a neutral consequentialist theory of right, but by other considerations, perhaps by agent-centered ones.

A particularly good recent example of this position is advanced by Derek Parfit. After arguing against what he calls Common-Sense Morality as a theory of right because of its agent-centeredness, he then says that nonetheless "for most of us, the best *dispositions* would in the following sense roughly *correspond* to Common-Sense Morality. We should often be strongly disposed to act in the ways that this morality requires."[23]

But what is important in evaluating a consideration's status as right- or wrong-making on the inside-out view *just is* whether persons should be guided by it in making their choices, or more precisely, whether a person of good character would be guided by it. The inside-out view refuses to make the sharp distinction between criteria of right and choice-guiding considerations. Indeed, it is worth asking what the force of the consequentialist's assertion that an act was wrong *is*, over and above its simply meaning that it produced less than optimal states of affairs, when he simultaneously asserts that considerations by which the person should have been guided recommended against the act and that the person was a better person for being so guided. That is, what is the force of asserting that not only did the act have less than optimal consequences, but also that, because of that, it was the wrong thing for the agent to have done?[24]

Even consequentialists agree that the considerations a person should be guided by likely include agent-centered restrictions. The "problem" of agent-centered restrictions does not arise for them at this level. The problem concerns whether, even though it is better that agents be guided by agent-centered restrictions, they do what is right when they are so guided. It arises here because if the rationale for a view of what a person should do is to be found in the intrinsic value of states of affairs, then it seems natural to conclude that what a person should do is whatever would bring about the best states.

There are, of course, broadly consequentialist positions that deny that an act's being right depends in any simple way on the value of its consequences. Rule-consequentialists, for example, would roughly agree that since persons should be guided by agent-centered restrictions, then they act rightly when so guided. They are thus likely to endorse agent-centered restrictions. But if the rationale offered for "indirectly" consequentialist normative positions is an outside-in one, if it is argued that inculcating the relevant agent-centered rules and motives will maximize valuable states, then the "problem" reemerges. What is directly at issue in a theory of conduct is what a person should *do*, and not, directly anyway, how people should be motivated or guided in choice. So if the rationale adopted is outside-in, then a neutralist act-consequentialism seems better justified than any indirect consequentialist view.

It is open, of course, for someone who pursues the outside-in approach to define a concept of right in the way Mill did, as connected to rule-governed practices of approbation and disapprobation. If the concept is so defined, then there may well be an outside-in rationale for a rule-consequentialist account of right that will include agent-centered restrictions. But with any such definition it will still be possible to raise the further question whether a person should do what it would be right to do so defined. And if the fundamental rationale for holding a position on the latter question is outside-in, then any agent-centered response will seem problematic.

The inside-out approach does not face the problem of agent-centered restrictions in the same way. While it is similar to indirect consequentialisms in holding that what a person should do depends on what considerations and principles a person of good character would be guided by, it differs from the latter, at least when the latter is grounded in an outside-in rationale, by not basing its theory of character on a more fundamental view of objectively valuable states. Consequently the relation it asserts between principles a person of good character would be guided by and the rightness of acts is not liable to be undermined in the way indirectly consequentialisms are when their alleged support is outside-in.

The Butler/Kant approach advances a fundamental theory of character that is independent of any view of the intrinsic value of states of affairs. But if its formalist, or as I prefer to say, constitutionalist theory of character enables it to avoid self-undermining of the sort that threatens indirect consequentialisms derived from the outside-in, this very aspect seems to raise other serious problems, problems that I can no more than mention here.

Quite apart from the plausibility of its account of character and moral integrity on the one hand, and of its claim of a fundamental responsibility to maintain integrity on the other, there is a serious question whether any rationale can be mounted from these for any specific theory of right, in particular for a theory of right with specific agent-centered restrictions. The problem is that if what is fundamental is a more or less formal or procedural ideal of moral judgment, together with the proposition that no person is bound by a principle unless she could in principle approve herself of or legislate it from a certain standpoint in a way that satisfies the procedural constraints, what reason is there to think that any principles, much less any agent-centered ones, will on this basis be binding on all?

Butler and Kant, of course, thought universal principles could be so grounded, but when we consider why they did we may be less confident. Butler seems to have rested his case on a common human nature, created by a God who, by making us so that "there are certain . . . actions, which are themselves approved or disapproved by mankind, abstracted from the consideration of their tendency to the happiness or misery of the world", "may have laid us under particular obligations."[25] So, he thought, the existence of a general obligation of "fidelity," rests on fidelity's being universally approved, other things equal, and infidelity disapproved; or at least, on these judgments being universal when informed and reflectively considered in the appropriate way.

Kant's case for universal principles of duty grounded in an ideal of moral judgment, on the other hand, depends at least in part on the unpromising idea that an act is wrong if its maxim cannot consistently be conceived to hold as a universal law.[26] But if the very existence of a practice of promising (Kant's example), is vulnerable to violations in such a way that it is simply impossible for everyone to make false promises whenever it would be to their advantage to make them, so also might the existence of some thoroughly repugnant practice (such as Rawls's example of "telishment") be vulnerable to universal departures under some similar condition.[27] It might be, for example, that individual officials find telishing innocents a burden they would often like to escape, and that if they all did so when it was to their advantage then it would be impossible for anyone to telish because the practice would collapse. But this hardly seems to provide any justification for thinking it wrong not to telish.

Ignoring the "contradiction in thought" test in the Categorical Imperative, however, requires one to emphasize Kant's test of universal legislation in the *will*. The relevant question then becomes whether one could rationally will, perhaps from a standpoint that is impartial between persons (the "kingdom of ends") that everyone be guided by a given principle. But what reason is there to expect universal agreement on principles here?

Unlike Butler's, Kant's case for universal principles of right rests on no controversial theses about a common human nature that could be expected to lead to universal agreement in reflectively informed and impartial attitude. But because it lacks this common basis the question arises why there is any determinate answer to the question, What principles would it be rational to choose persons be guided by when that choice is made from a standpoint that is impartial between them?

The best hope for the Kantian project, it seems to me, is to pursue it in something like the way Rawls attempts in *A Theory of Justice*. Impartiality is modeled by a veil of ignorance and the basis for choice from this standpoint is then the agent's own interests as a rational and moral person.[28]

For this approach to provide a rationale for any principle of right, two things will have to be true. First, there must be interests that rational and moral persons have as such, relative to which a choice of principles behind a veil of ignorance can be more or less rational.[29] And second, it must be the case that relative to those interests there are principles it is rational to choose from behind a veil of ignorance. Both of these assumptions are far from trivial, but it does not seem unlikely to me that there are agent-centered principles it would be rational to choose from this standpoint.

A second problem concerns the relation of such principles, if there be any, to moral integrity. Even if a specific principle is one it would in fact be rational to choose all to act on, it may nonetheless be one that a given individual's conscientious judgment conflicts with. The Kantian can presumably rule out cases where a person simply believes something is a principle of right but has not herself genuinely embraced (legislated) it in the appropriate way. But what if she takes up the appropriate standpoint, or comes as close as can reasonably be expected, and embraces a principle that conflicts with the one it would be rational for her to choose from that point of view?

When this happens the person will apparently be under conflicting obligations on the inside-out approach. She will have a fundamental obligation to maintain moral integrity and hence not to act contrary to her own authentic moral views. On the other hand, if she does so she will contravene a principle of right grounded in a more adequate exercise of the capacity on which moral integrity depends.

This second problem should not, it seems to me, be viewed as an unwelcome consequence of the inside-out approach. For surely it is a problem that is central to the moral life and not one we should expect a philosophical account of morality to explain away. Its oddness, if not its sting, may be eased by thinking of principles of right, on the inside-out view, as primarily addressed not to the question of what a person should do when his own moral judgment on some issue is settled, but rather to the question of what his judgment on that issue should be. But if a person has a settled, and authentically gained, view on some matter, it does seem a mistake to think that the question of what he should then do is essentially unchanged.

Agent-centered restrictions seem mysterious or essentially problematic only when moral philosophy is approached from the outside-in. Whatever contribution of disvalue an act makes to the world, however bad it is, no rationale follows from that for refusing to perform it when doing so prevents more performances.

The inside-out approach is not value-based, however. It is integrity- and character-based. If moral philosophy is approached in this way, the "problem" of agent-centered restrictions dissolves in its outside-in form.

Notes

1   Two points should be kept in mind. First, I am assuming a consequential-ist/deontological distinction made with respect to the content of a theory of

right. A theory is consequentialist if, and only if, it determines whether an act is right by whether the act maximizes good consequences. Otherwise the theory is deontological. So rule-utilitarian would, for present purposes, count as a deontological theory. Consequentialism, in the present context, includes only act-consequentialist theories.

Second, deontological theories may well include principles that are not agent-centered – for example, a *prima facie* principle of general harm prevention. The point is that any such principles could also be part of a consequentialist theory if it had a suitable theory of good.

There is another way of making the consequentialist/deontological distinction, viz., with respect to a theory of right's underlying rationale. On that distinction any theory of right based on propositions about objective or impersonal value – that certain states of affairs are good or bad in a way that creates a reason for any person to promote them – is consequentialist. Deontological theories are those advanced without such a rationale. The "problem of agent-centered restrictions" is whether there exists any other rationale for a theory of right.

2   This point is made by Judith Lichtenberg in her review of Scheffler's *The Rejection of Consequentialism*, "The good, the right, and the all right", *Yale Law Journal* 92 (1983), pp. 531f. See also Michael Slote, *Common-Sense Morality and Consequentialism* (London: Routledge & Kegan Paul, 1985).

3   Samuel Scheffler, *The Rejection of Consequentialism* (Oxford: Oxford University Press, 1982), pp. 1–79. Further references to this work will be placed parenthetically in the text.

4   In addition to Scheffler, see Derek Parfit, *Reasons and Persons* (Oxford: Oxford University Press, 1984); Peter Railton, "Alienation, consequentialism, and the demands of morality", *Philosophy and Public Affairs* 13 (1984), 134–71; and Donald Regan, *Cooperative Utilitarianism* (Oxford: Oxford University Press, 1980).

5   W. D. Ross, *The Right and the Good* (Oxford University Press, 1967), p. 16.

6   G. E. Moore, *Principia Ethica* (Cambridge: Cambridge University Press, 1966), p. 147.

7   C. D. Broad, "Certain features in Moore's ethical doctrines", in *The Philosophy of G. E. Moore*, ed. P. A. Schilpp (La Salle, Ill.: Open Court, 1968), p. 46. Compare Parfit's definition that "agent-relative" principles or theories give "*different* agent *different* aims" (*Reasons and Persons*, p. 55).

8   *Principia Ethica*, p. 25.

9   *The Right and the Good*, p. 19.

10   *Ibid.*

11   *Ibid.*, p. 122.

12   Bernard Williams, "A critique of utilitarianism", in *Utilitarianism: For and Against* (Cambridge: Cambridge University Press, 1973), p. 95.

13   Thomas E. Hill, Jr., "Self-respect reconsidered", in *Respect for Persons*, Tulane Studies in Philosophy v. xxxi, ed. O. H. Green (New Orleans, Tulane University, 1982), p. 130.

14 *Ibid.*, p. 133.

15 Bernard Williams, "Persons, character, and morality", in *Moral Luck* (Cambridge: Cambridge University Press, 1981), esp. pp. 12f. See also the section titled "Integrity" in "A critique of utilitarianism".

16 Joseph Butler, *Five Sermons*, ed. S. L. Darwall (Indianapolis: Hackett, 1983), p. 66n.

17 Because this view holds there to be no external standard of moral legislation, to put the point in Kantian terms, but only procedural and formal constraints of "duly constituted" moral judgment, it is illuminating to describe it as *constitutionalist*. ("Constitution" is a central Butlerian notion.) I discuss this aspect of the view in more detail in "Self-deception, autonomy, and moral constitution", in *The Forms of Self-Deception*, ed. B. McLaughlin and A. Rorty, (University of California Press, 1988), pp. 407–30.

18 The phrase comes from Paul's *Letter to the Romans* (II:14). This passage provides the text for Butler's Sermon II and III. See *Five Sermons*, pp. 34–45 esp. p. 37.

19 Kant, *Groundwork of the Metaphysics of Morals*, trans. H. J. Paton (New York: Harper & Row, 1964), p. 66; *Preussische Akademie*, p. 398.

20 In this respect the Butler/Kant approach differs from what is often called an "ethics of virtue", such as Aristotle's, that might also be considered to be inside-out. It seems to me that "constitutionalist" projects such as Butler's and Kant's are purer cases of an inside-out approach since they do not include as essential any particular concern for states outside of the moral agent within their ideal of moral character. They thus differ in this way from a view like Hutcheson's also.

21 Whether states can be good in any purely objective or impersonal sense that provides any agent a justification to produce them, regardless of the agent's specific nature, is a completely different question than whether there can be facts of the matter about a state's being good for a person or group, or from a person or group's point of view. There might be objective values in this second sense even if there are none in the first.

22 Butler, *Five Sermons*, p. 15.

23 *Reasons and Persons*, p. 112.

24 It is, of course, open to the consequentialist to hold as did Moore in *Principia* that the only fundamental ethical notion is that of intrinsic value.

I should also point out that what I say here does not take into account the possibility that the consequentialist's account of right might be held to coincide with an account of what considerations should guide the deliberations of a perfectly impartial cognizer, like Hare's archangel, though not the deliberations of us less than perfect decisionmakers. This suggestion has promise for some cases but not for others. See Hare, *Moral Thinking* (Oxford: Oxford University Press, 1981).

25 Butler, *Five Sermons*, p. 66n.

26 Specifically, he held that the distinction between perfect and imperfect duties is to be explained by the difference between maxims that could not be

conceived to hold as a universal law and those that could not be willed so to hold. See *Groundwork, Ak.* p. 424.

27   In "Two concepts of rules", *Philosophical Review* 64 (1955), 11–12.

28   It is often complained that Rawls's original position cannot model Kant's "realm of ends" because the choice behind the veil is one of instrumental rationality relative to self-interest. But the argument would be essentially unchanged if the parties were assumed to be completely self-sacrificing trustees for the interests (as rational person) of another person. The veil makes it impossible to tailor principles to any particular individual, so by assuming a concern for the rational interests of one person the standpoint effectively expresses a concern for an arbitrary, rather than any particular, person.

   I discuss this way of modelling Kant in "Is there a Kantian interpretation of Rawlsian justice?", in *John Rawls' Theory of Social Justice*, ed. H. G. Blocker and E. Smith (Athens, Ohio: Ohio University Press, 1980), pp. 311–45.

29   The assumption that there are interests persons have as such plays a more prominent role in Rawls's writings since *A Theory of Justice*. In particular, see "Kantian constructivism in moral theory", *The Journal of Philosophy* 77 (1980), 525–7; and "Social unity and primary goods", in *Utilitarianism and Beyond*, ed. A. Sen and B. Williams (Cambridge: Cambridge University Press, 1982), pp. 164–5. Thus, from the latter: "In formulating a conception of justice for the basic structure of society, we start by viewing each person as a moral person moved by two highest-order interests, namely, the interests to realise and to exercise the two powers of moral personality. These two powers are the capacity for a sense of right and justice (the capacity to honour fair terms of cooperation), and the capacity to decide upon, to revise and rationally to pursue a conception of the good".

9

The Trolley Problem

Judith Jarvis Thomson

I

Some years ago, Philippa Foot drew attention to an extraordinarily inter-esting problem.[1] Suppose you are the driver of a trolley. The trolley rounds a bend, and there come into view ahead five track workmen, who have been repairing the track. The track goes through a bit of a valley at that point, and the sides are steep, so you must stop the trolley if you are to avoid running the five men down. You step on the brakes, but alas they don't work. Now you suddenly see a spur of track leading off to the right. You can turn the trolley onto it, and thus save the five men on the straight track ahead. Unfortunately, Mrs. Foot has arranged that there is one track workman on that spur of track. He can no more get off the track in time than the five can, so you will kill him if you turn the trolley onto him. Is it morally permissible for you to turn the trolley?

Everybody to whom I have put this hypothetical case says, Yes, it is.[2] Some people say something stronger than that it is morally *permissible* for you to turn the trolley: They say that morally speaking, you *must* turn it – that morality requires you to do so. Others do not agree that morality requires you to turn the trolley, and even feel a certain discom-fort at the idea of turning it. But everybody says that it is true, at a minimum, that you *may* turn it – that it would not be morally wrong in you to do so.

Now consider a second hypothetical case. This time you are to imagine yourself to be a surgeon, a truly great surgeon. Among other things you

Judith Jarvis Thomson, "The Trolley Problem," *The Yale Law Journal* 94 (1985): 1395–415.

do, you transplant organs, and you are such a great surgeon that the organs you transplant always take. At the moment you have five patients who need organs. Two need one lung each, two need a kidney each, and the fifth needs a heart. If they do not get those organs today, they will all die; if you find organs for them today, you can transplant the organs and they will all live. But where to find the lungs, the kidneys, and the heart? The time is almost up when a report is brought to you that a young man who has just come into your clinic for his yearly check-up has exactly the right blood-type, and is in excellent health. Lo, you have a possible donor. All you need do is cut him up and distribute *his* parts among the five who need them. You ask, but he says, "Sorry. I deeply sympathize, but no." Would it be morally permissible for you to operate anyway? Everybody to whom I have put this second hypothetical case says, No, it would not be morally permissible for you to proceed.

Here then is Mrs. Foot's problem: *Why* is it that the trolley driver may turn his trolley, though the surgeon may not remove the young man's lungs, kidneys, and heart?[3] In both cases, one will die if the agent acts, but five will live who would otherwise die – a net saving of four lives. What difference in the other facts of these cases explains the moral difference between them? I fancy that the theorists of tort and criminal law will find this problem as interesting as the moral theorist does.

II

Mrs. Foot's own solution to the problem she drew attention to is simple, straightforward, and very attractive. She would say: Look, the surgeon's choice is between operating, in which case he kills one, and not operating, in which case he lets five die; and killing is surely worse than letting die[4] – indeed, so much worse that we can even say

(I) Killing one is worse than letting five die.

So the surgeon must refrain from operating. By contrast, the trolley driver's choice is between turning the trolley, in which case he kills one, and not turning the trolley, in which case he does not *let five die*, he positively *kills* them. Now surely we can say

(II) Killing five is worse than killing one.

But then that is why the trolley driver may turn his trolley: He would be doing what is worse if he fails to turn it, since if he fails to turn it he kills five.

I do think that that is an attractive account of the matter. It seems to me that if the surgeon fails to operate, he does not kill his five patients who need parts; he merely lets them die. By contrast, if the driver fails to turn his trolley, he does not merely let the five track workmen die; he drives his trolley into them, and thereby kills them.

But there is good reason to think that this problem is not so easily solved as that.

let us begin by looking at a case that is in some ways like Mrs. Foot's story of the trolley driver. I will call her case *Trolley Driver*; let us now consider a case I will call *Bystander at the Switch*. In that case you have been strolling by the trolley track, and you can see the situation at a glance: The driver saw the five on the track ahead, he stamped on the brakes, the brakes failed, so he fainted. What to do? Well, here is the switch, which you can throw, thereby turning the trolley yourself. Of course you will kill one if you do. But I should think you may turn it all the same.[5]

Some people may feel a difference between these two cases. In the first place, the trolley driver is, after all, captain of the trolley. He is charged by the trolley company with responsibility for the safety of his passengers and anyone else who might be harmed by the trolley he drives. The bystander at the switch, on the other hand, is a private person who just happens to be there.

Second, the driver would be driving a trolley into the five if he does not turn it, and the bystander would not – the bystander will do the five no harm at all if he does not throw the switch.

I think it right to feel these differences between the cases.

Nevertheless, my own feeling is that an ordinary person, a mere bystander, may intervene in such a case. If you see something, a trolley, a boulder, an avalanche, heading towards five, and you can deflect it onto one, it really does seem that – other things being equal – it would be permissible for you to *take* charge, *take* responsibility, and deflect the thing, whoever you may be. Of course you run a moral risk if you do, for it might be that, unbeknownst to you, other things are not equal. It might be, that is, that there is some relevant difference between the five on the one hand, and the one on the other, which would make it morally preferable that the five be hit by the trolley than that the one be hit by it. That would be so if, for example, the five are not track workmen at all, but Mafia members in workmen's clothing, and they have tied the one workman to the right-hand track in the hope that you would turn the trolley onto him. I won't canvass all the many kinds of possibilities, for in fact the moral risk is the same whether you are the trolley driver, or a bystander at the switch.

Moreover, second, we might well wish to ask ourselves what exactly is the difference between what the driver would be doing if he failed to turn the trolley and what the bystander would be doing if he failed to throw the switch. As I said, the driver would be driving a trolley into the five; but what exactly would his driving the trolley into the five consist in? Why, just sitting there, doing nothing! If the driver does just sit there, doing nothing, then that will have been how come he drove his trolley into the five.

I do not mean to make much of that fact about what the driver's driving his trolley into the five would consist in, for it seems to me to be right to say that if he does not turn the trolley, he does drive his trolley into them, and does thereby kill them. (Though this does seem to me to be right, it is not easy to say exactly what makes it so.) By contrast, if the bystander does not throw the switch, he drives no trolley into anybody, and he kills nobody.

But as I said, my own feeling is that the bystander *may* intervene. Perhaps it will seem to some even less clear that morality requires him to turn the trolley than that morality requires the driver to turn the trolley; perhaps some will feel even more discomfort at the idea of the bystander's turning the trolley than at the idea of the driver's turning the trolley. All the same, I shall take it that he *may*.

If he may, there is serious trouble for Mrs. Foot's thesis (I). It is plain that if the bystander throws the switch, he causes the trolley to hit the one, and thus he kills the one. It is equally plain that if the bystander does not throw the switch, he does not cause the trolley to hit the five, he does not kill the five, he merely fails to save them – he lets them die. His choice therefore is between throwing the switch, in which case he kills one, and not throwing the switch, in which case he lets five die. If thesis (I) were true, it would follow that the bystander may not throw the switch, and that I am taking to be false.

III

I have been arguing that

(I) Killing one is worse than letting five die

is false, and a fortiori that it cannot be appealed to to explain why the surgeon may not operate in the case I shall call *Transplant*.

I think it pays to take note of something interesting which comes out when we pay close attention to

(II) Killing five is worse than killing one.

For let us ask ourselves how we would feel about *Transplant* if we made a certain addition to it. In telling you that story, I did not tell you why the surgeon's patients are in need of parts. Let us imagine that the history of their ailments is as follows. The surgeon was badly overworked last fall – some of his assistants in the clinic were out sick, and the surgeon had to take over their duties dispensing drugs. While feeling particularly tired one day, he became careless, and made the terrible mistake of dispensing chemical X to five of the day's patients. Now chemical X works differently in different people. In some it causes lung failure, in others kidney failure, in others heart failure. So these five patients who now need parts need them because of the surgeon's carelessness. Indeed, if he does not get them the parts they need, so that they die, he will have killed them. Does that make a moral difference? That is, does the fact that he will have killed the five if he does nothing make it permissible for him to cut the young man up and distribute his parts to the five who need them?

We could imagine it to have been worse. Suppose what had happened was this: The surgeon was badly overextended last fall, he had known he was named a beneficiary in his five patients' wills, and it swept over him one day to give them chemical X to kill them. Now he repents, and would save them if he could. If he does not save them, he will positively have murdered them. Does *that* fact make it permissible for him to cut the young man up and distribute his parts to the five who need them?

I should think plainly not. The surgeon must not operate on the young man. If he can find no other way of saving his five patients, he will *now* have to let them die – despite the fact that if he now lets them die, he will have killed them.

We tend to forget that some killings themselves include lettings die, and do include them where the act by which the agent kills takes time to cause death – time in which the agent can intervene but does not.

In face of these possibilities, the question arises what we should think of thesis (II), since it *looks* as if it tells us that the surgeon ought to operate, and thus that he may permissibly do so, since if he operates he kills only one instead of five.

There are two ways in which we can go here. First, we can say: (II) does tell us that the surgeon ought to operate, and that shows it is false. Second, we can say: (II) does not tell us that the surgeon ought to operate, and it is true.

For my own part, I prefer the second. If Alfred kills five and Bert kills only one, then questions of motive apart, and other things being equal, what Alfred did *is* worse than what Bert did. If the surgeon does not operate, so that he kills five, then it will later be true that he did something worse than he would have done if he had operated, killing only one – especially if his killing of the five was murder, committed out of a desire for money, and his killing of the one would have been, though misguided and wrongful, nevertheless a well-intentioned effort to save five lives. Taking this line would, of course, require saying that assessments of which acts are worse than which other acts do not by themselves settle the question what it is permissible for an agent to do.

But it might be said that we ought to by-pass (II), for perhaps what Mrs. Foot would have offered us as an explanation of why the driver may turn the trolley in *Trolley Driver* is not (II) itself, but something more complex, such as

(II′) If a person is faced with a choice between doing something *here and now* to five, by the doing of which he will kill them, and doing something else *here and now* to one, by the doing of which he will kill only the one, then (other things being equal) he ought to choose the second alternative rather than the first.

We may presumably take (II′) to tell us that the driver ought to, and hence permissibly may, turn the trolley in *Trolley Driver*, for we may presumably view the driver as confronted with a choice between here and now driving his trolley into five, and here and now driving his trolley into one. And at the same time, (II′) tells us nothing at all about what the surgeon ought to do in *Transplant*, for he is not confronted with such a choice. If the surgeon operates, he does do something by the doing of which he will kill only one; but if the surgeon does not operate, he does not do something by the doing of which he kills five; he merely fails to do something by the doing of which he would make it be the case that he has not killed five.

I have no objection to this shift in attention from (II) to (II′). But we should not overlook an interesting question that lurks here. As it might be put: *Why* should the present tense matter so much? Why should a person prefer killing one to killing five if the alternatives are wholly in front of him, but not (or anyway, not in every case) where one of them is partly behind him? I shall come back to this question briefly later.

Meanwhile, however, even if (II') can be appealed to in order to explain why the trolley driver may turn his trolley, that would leave it entirely open why the bystander at the switch may turn *his* trolley. For he does not drive a trolley into each of five if he refrains from turning the trolley; he merely lets the trolley drive into each of them.

So I suggest we set *Trolley Driver* aside for the time being. What I shall be concerned with is a first cousin of Mrs. Foot's problem, viz.: Why is it that the bystander may turn his trolley, though the surgeon may not remove the young man's lungs, kidneys, and heart? Since *I* find it particularly puzzling that the bystander may turn his trolley, I am inclined to call this The Trolley Problem. Those who find it particularly puzzling that the surgeon may not operate are cordially invited to call it The Transplant Problem instead.

IV

It should be clear, I think, that "kill" and "let die" are too blunt to be useful tools for the solving of this problem. We ought to be looking within killings and savings for the ways in which the agents would be carrying them out.

It would be no surprise, I think, if a Kantian idea occurred to us at this point. Kant said: "Act so that you treat humanity, whether in your own person or in that of another, always as an end and never as a means only." It is striking, after all, that the surgeon who proceeds in *Transplant* treats the young man he cuts up "as a means only": He literally uses the young man's body to save his five, and does so without the young man's consent. And perhaps we may say that the agent in *Bystander at the Switch* does not use his victim to save his five, or (more generally) treat his victim as a means only, and that that is why he (unlike the surgeon) may proceed.

But what exactly is it to treat a person as a means only, or to use a person? And why exactly is it wrong to do this? These questions do not have obvious answers.[6]

Suppose an agent is confronted with a choice between doing nothing, in which case five die, or engaging in a certain course of action, in which case the five live, but one dies. Then perhaps we can say: If the agent chooses to engage in the course of action, then he uses the one to save the five only if, had the one gone out of existence just before the agent started, the agent would have been unable to save the five. That is true of the surgeon in *Transplant*. He needs the young man if he is to save his five; if the young man goes wholly out of existence just before the surgeon starts to operate, then the surgeon cannot save his five. By contrast, the agent in *Bystander at the Switch* does not need the one track workman on the right-hand track if he is to save his five; if the one track workman goes wholly out of existence before the bystander starts to turn the trolley, then the bystander *can* all the same save his five. So here anyway is a striking difference between the cases.

It does seem to me right to think that solving this problem requires attending to the means by which the agent would be saving his five if he proceeded. But I am inclined to think that this is an overly simple way of taking account of the agent's means.

One reason for thinking so[7] comes out as follows. You have been thinking of the tracks in *Bystander at the Switch* as not merely diverging, but continuing to diverge, as in the following picture: pick up figure 9.1

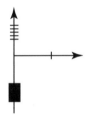

Consider now what I shall call "the loop variant" on this case, in which the tracks do not continue to diverge – they circle back, as in the following picture:

Let us now imagine that the five on the straight track are thin, but thick enough so that although all five will be killed if the trolley goes straight, the bodies of the five will stop it, and it will therefore not reach the one. On the other hand, the one on the right-hand track is fat, so fat that his body will by itself stop the trolley, and the trolley will therefore not reach the five. May the agent turn the trolley? Some people feel more discomfort at the idea of turning the trolley in the loop variant than in the original *Bystander at the Switch*. But we cannot really suppose that the presence or absence of that extra bit of track makes a major moral difference as to what an agent may do in these cases, and it really does seem right to think (despite the discomfort) that the agent may proceed.

On the other hand, we should notice that the agent here needs the one (fat) track workman on the right-hand track if he is to save his five. If the one goes wholly out of existence just before the agent starts to turn the trolley, then the agent cannot save his five[8] – just as the surgeon in *Transplant* cannot save his five if the young man goes wholly out of existence just before the surgeon starts to operate.

Indeed, I should think that there is no plausible account of what is involved in, or what is necessary for, the application of the notions "treating a person as a means only," or "using one to save five," under which the surgeon would be doing this whereas the agent in this variant of *Bystander at the Switch* would not be. If that is right, then appeals to these notions cannot do the work being required of them here.

V

Suppose the bystander at the switch proceeds: He throws the switch, thereby turning the trolley onto the right-hand track, thereby causing the one to be hit by the trolley, thereby killing him – but saving the five on the straight track. There are two facts about what he does which seem to me to explain the moral difference between what he does and what the agent in *Transplant* would be doing if *he* proceeded. In the first place, the bystander saves his five by making something that threatens them instead threaten one. Second, the bystander does not do that by means which themselves constitute an infringement of any right of the one's.

As is plain, then, my hypothesis as to the source of the moral difference between the cases makes appeal to the concept of a right. My own feeling is that solving this problem requires making appeal to that concept – or to some other concept that does the same kind of work.[9] Indeed, I think it is one of the many reasons why this problem is of such interest to moral theory that it does force us to appeal to that concept; and by the same token, that we learn something from it about that concept.

Let us begin with an idea, held by many friends of rights, which Ronald Dworkin expressed crisply in a metaphor from bridge: Rights "trump" utilities.[10] That is, if one would infringe a right in or by acting, then it is not sufficient justification for acting that one would thereby maximize utility. It seems to me that something like this must be correct.

Consideration of this idea suggests the possibility of a very simple solution to the problem. That is, it might be said (i) The reason why the surgeon may not proceed in *Transplant* is that if he proceeds, he maximizes utility, for he brings about a net saving of four lives, but in so doing he would infringe a right of the young man's.

Which right? Well, we might say: The right the young man has against the surgeon that the surgeon not kill him – thus a right in the cluster of rights that the young man has in having a right to life.

Solving this problem requires being able to explain also why the bystander may proceed in *Bystander at the Switch*. So it might be said (ii) The reason why the bystander may proceed is that if he proceeds, he maximizes utility, for he brings about a net saving of four lives, and in so doing he does *not* infringe any right of the one track workman's.

But I see no way – certainly there is no easy way – of establishing that these ideas are true.

Is it clear that the bystander would infringe no right of the one track workman's if he turned the trolley? Suppose there weren't anybody on the straight track, and the bystander turned the trolley onto the right-hand track, thereby killing the one, but not saving anybody, since nobody was at risk, and thus nobody needed saving. Wouldn't that infringe a right of the one workman's, a right in the cluster of rights that he has in having a right to life?

So should we suppose that the fact that there are five track workmen on the straight track who are in need of saving makes the one lack that right – which he would have had if that had not been a fact?

But then why doesn't the fact that the surgeon has five patients who are in need of saving make the young man also lack that right?

I think some people would say there is good (excellent, conclusive) reason for thinking that the one track workman lacks the right (given there are five on the straight track) lying in the fact that (given there are five on the straight track) it is morally permissible to turn the trolley onto him. But if your reason for thinking the one lacks the right is that it is permissible to turn the trolley onto him, then you can hardly go on to explain its being permissible to turn the trolley onto him by appeal to the fact that he lacks the right. It pays to stress this point: If you want to say, as (ii) does, that the bystander may proceed because he maximizes utility and infringes no right, then you need an independent account of what makes it be the case that he infringes no right – independent, that is, of its being the case that he may proceed.

There is *some* room for maneuver here. Any plausible theory of rights must make room for the possibility of waiving a right, and within that category, for the possibility of failing to have a right by virtue of assumption of risk; and it might be argued that that is what is involved here, i.e., that track workmen know of the risks of the job, and consent to run them when signing on for it.

But that is not really an attractive way of dealing with this difficulty. Track workmen certainly do not explicitly consent to being run down with trolleys when doing so will save five who are on some other track – certainly they are not asked to consent to this at the time of signing on for the job. And I doubt that they consciously assume the risk of it at that or any other time. And in any case, what if the six people involved had not been track workmen? What if they had been young children? What if they had been people who had been shoved out of helicopters? Wouldn't it all the same be permissible to turn the trolley?

So it is not clear what (independent) reason could be given for thinking that the bystander will infringe no right of the one's if he throws the switch.

I think, moreover, that there is *some* reason to think that the bystander will infringe a right of the one if he throws the switch, even though it is permissible for him to do so. What I have in mind issues simply from the fact that if the bystander throws the switch, then he does what will kill the one. Suppose the bystander proceeds, and that the one is now dead. The bystander's motives were, of course, excellent – he acted with a view to saving five. But the one did not volunteer his life so that the five might live; the bystander volunteered it for him. The bystander made him pay with his life for the bystander's saving of the five. This consideration seems to me to lend some weight to the idea that the bystander did do him a wrong – a wrong it was morally permissible to do him, since five were saved, but a wrong *to him* all the same.

Consider again that lingering feeling of discomfort (which, as I said, some people do feel) about what the bystander does if he turns the trolley. No doubt it is permissible to turn the trolley, but still . . . but still. . . . People who feel this discomfort also think that, although it is permissible to turn the trolley, it is not morally required to do so. My own view is that they are right to feel and think these things. We would be able to explain why this is so if we supposed that if the bystander turns the trolley, then he does do the one track workman a wrong – if we supposed, in particular, that he infringes a right of the one track workman's which is in that cluster of rights which the workman has in having a right to life.[11]

I do not for a moment take myself to have established that (ii) is false. I have wished only to draw attention to the difficulty that lies ahead of a person who thinks (ii) true, and also to suggest that there is some reason to think that the bystander would infringe a right of the one's if he proceeded, and thus some reason to think that (ii) is false. It can easily be seen that if there is some reason to think the bystander would infringe a right of the one's, then there is also some reason to think that (i) is false – since if the bystander does infringe a right of the one's if he proceeds, and may nevertheless proceed, then it cannot be the fact that the surgeon infringes a right of the young man's if *he* proceeds which makes it impermissible for *him* to do so.

Perhaps a friend of (i) and (ii) can establish that they are true. I propose that, just in case he can't, we do well to see if there isn't some other way of solving this problem than by appeal to them. In particular, I propose we grant that both the bystander and the surgeon would infringe a right of their ones, a right in the cluster of rights that the ones' have in having a right to life, and that we look for some *other* difference between the cases which could be appealed to to explain the moral difference between them.

Notice that accepting this proposal does not commit us to rejecting the idea expressed in that crisp metaphor of Dworkin's. We can still say that rights trump utilities – if we can find a further feature of what the bystander does if he turns the trolley (beyond the fact that he maximizes utility) which itself trumps the right, and thus makes it permissible to proceed.

VI

As I said, my own feeling is that the trolley problem can be solved only by appeal to the concept of a right – but not by appeal to it in as simple a way as that discussed in the preceding section. What we were attending to in the preceding section was only the fact that the agents would be killing and saving if they proceeded; what we should be attending to is the means by which they would kill and save.[12] (It is very tempting, because so much simpler, to regard a human act as a solid nugget, without internal structure, and to try to trace its moral value to the shape of its surface, as it were. The trolley problem seems to me to bring home that that will not do.)

I said earlier that there seem to me to be two crucial facts about what the bystander does if he proceeds in *Bystander at the Switch*. In the first place, he saves his five by making something that threatens them instead threaten the one. And second, he does not do that by means which themselves constitute infringements of any right of the one's.

Let us begin with the first.

If the surgeon proceeds in *Transplant*, he plainly does not save his five by making something that threatens them instead threaten one. It is organ-failure that threatens his five, and it is not *that* which he makes threaten the young man if he proceeds.

Consider another of Mrs. Foot's cases, which I shall call *Hospital*.

Suppose [Mrs. Foot says] that there are five patients in a hospital whose lives could be saved by the manufacture of a certain gas, but that this will inevitably release lethal fumes into the room of another patient whom for some reason we are unable to move.[13]

Surely it would not be permissible for us to manufacture the gas.

In *Transplant* and *Hospital*, the five at risk are at risk from their ailments, and this might be thought to make a difference. Let us by-pass it. In a variant on *Hospital* – which I shall call *Hospital'* – all six patients are convalescing. The five at risk are at risk, not from their ailments, but from the ceiling of their room, which is about to fall on them. We can prevent this by pumping on a ceiling-support-mechanism; but doing so will inevitably release lethal fumes into the room of the sixth. Here too it is plain we may not proceed.

Contrast a case in which lethal fumes are being released by the heating system in the basement of a building next door to the hospital. They are headed towards the room of five. We can deflect them towards the room of one. Would that be permissible? I should think it would be – the case seems to be in all relevant respects like *Bystander at the Switch*.

In *Bystander at the Switch*, something threatens five, and if the agent proceeds, he saves the five by making that very thing threaten the one instead of the five. That is not true of the agents in *Hospital'* or *Hospital* or *Transplant*. In *Hospital'*, for example, what threatens the five is the ceiling, and the agent does not save them by making *it* threaten the one, he saves them by doing what will make something wholly different (some lethal fumes) threaten the one.

Why is this difference morally important? Other things being equal, to kill a man is to infringe his right to life, and we are therefore morally barred from killing. It is not enough to justify killing a person that if we do so, five others will be saved: To say that if we do so, five others will be saved is merely to say that utility will be maximized if we proceed, and that is not by itself sufficient to justify proceeding. Rights trump utilities. So if that is all that can be said in defense of killing a person, then killing that person is not permissible.

But that five others will be saved is not all that can be said in defense of killing in *Bystander at the Switch*. The bystander who proceeds does not merely minimize the number of deaths which get caused: He minimizes the number of deaths which get caused by something that already threatens people, and that will cause deaths whatever the bystander does.

The bystander who proceeds does not make something be a threat to people which would otherwise not be a threat to anyone; he makes be a threat to fewer what is already a threat to more. We might speak here of a "distributive exemption," which permits arranging that something that will do harm anyway shall be better distributed than it otherwise would be – shall (in *Bystander at the Switch*) do harm to fewer rather than more. Not just any distributive intervention is permissible: It is not in general morally open to us to make one die to save five. But other things being equal, it is not morally required of us that we let a burden descend out of the blue onto five when we can make it instead descend onto one.

I do not find it clear why there should be an exemption for, and only for, making a burden which is descending onto five descend, instead, onto one. That there is seems to me very plausible, however. On the one hand, the agent who acts under this exemption makes be a threat to one something that is *already* a threat to more, and thus something that will do harm *whatever* he does; on the other hand, the exemption seems to allow those acts which intuition tells us are clearly permissible, and to rule out those acts which intuition tells us are clearly impermissible.

VII

More precisely, it is not morally required of us that we let a burden descend out of the blue onto five when we can make it instead descend onto one *if* we can make it descend onto the one by means which do not themselves constitute infringements of rights of the one.

Consider a case – which I shall call *Fat Man* – in which you are standing on a footbridge over the trolley track. You can see a trolley hurtling down the track, out of control. You turn around to see where the trolley is headed, and there are five workmen on the track where it exits from under the footbridge. What to do? Being an expert on trolleys, you know of one certain way to stop an out-of-control trolley: Drop a really heavy weight in its path. But where to find one? It just so happens that standing next to you on the footbridge is a fat man, a really fat man. He is leaning over the railing, watching the trolley; all you have to do is to give him a little shove, and over the railing he will go, onto the track in the path of the trolley. Would it be permissible for you to do this? Everybody to whom I have put this case says it would not be. But why?

Suppose the agent proceeds. He shoves the fat man, thereby toppling him off the footbridge into the path of the trolley, thereby causing him to be hit by the trolley, thereby killing him – but saving the five on the straight track. Then it is true of this agent, as it is true of the agent in *Bystander at the Switch*, that he saves his five by making something which threatens them instead threaten one.

But *this* agent does so by means which themselves constitute an infringement of a right of the one's. For shoving a person is infringing a right of his. So also is toppling a person off a footbridge.

I should stress that doing these things is infringing a person's rights even if doing them does not cause his death – even if doing them causes him no harm at all. As I shall put it, shoving a person, toppling a person off a footbridge, are *themselves* infringements of rights of his. A theory of rights ought to give an account of what makes it be the case that doing either of these things is itself an infringement of a right of his. But I think we may take it to be a datum that it is, the job which confronts the theorist of rights being, not to establish that it is, but rather to explain why it is.

Consider by contrast the agent in *Bystander at the Switch*. He too, if he proceeds, saves five by making something that threatens them instead threaten one. But the means he takes to make that be the case are these: Turn the trolley onto the right-hand track. And turning the trolley onto the right-hand track is not *itself* an infringement of a right of anybody's. The agent would do the one no wrong at all if he turned the trolley onto the right-hand track, and by some miracle the trolley did not hit him.

We might of course have imagined it not necessary to shove the fat man. We might have imagined that all you need do to get the trolley to threaten him instead of the five is to wobble the handrail, for the handrail is low, and he is leaning on it, and wobbling it will cause him to fall over and off. Wobbling the handrail would be impermissible, I should think – no less so than shoving. But then there is room for an objection to the idea that the contrast I point to will help explain the moral differences among these cases. For it might be said that if you wobble the handrail, thereby getting the trolley to threaten the one instead of the five, then the means you take to get this to be the case are just these: Wobble the handrail. But doing that is not *itself* an infringement of a right of anybody's. You would do the fat man no wrong at all if you wobbled the handrail and no harm came to him in consequence of your doing so. In this respect, then, your situation seems to be exactly like that of the agent in *Bystander at the Switch*. Just as the means he would be taking to make the trolley threaten one instead of five would not constitute an infringement of a right, so also would the means you would be taking to make the trolley threaten one instead of five not constitute an infringement of a right.

What I had in mind, however, is a rather tighter notion of "means" than shows itself in this objection. By hypothesis, wobbling the handrail will cause the fat man to topple onto the track in the path of the trolley, and thus will cause the trolley to threaten him instead of the five. But the trolley will not threaten him instead of the five unless wobbling the handrail does cause him to topple. Getting the trolley to threaten the fat man instead of the five *requires* getting him into its path. You get the trolley to threaten him instead of them by wobbling the handrail only if, and only because, by wobbling the handrail you topple him into the path of the trolley.

What I had in mind, then, is a notion of "means" which comes out as follows. Suppose you get a trolley to threaten one instead of five by wobbling a handrail. The means you take to get the trolley to threaten the one instead of the five include wobbling the handrail, *and* all those further things that you have to succeed in doing by wobbling the handrail if the trolley is to threaten the one instead of the five.

So the means by which the agent in *Fat Man* gets the trolley to threaten one instead of five include toppling the fat man off the footbridge; and doing that is itself an infringement of a right of the fat man's. By contrast, the means by which the agent in *Bystander at the Switch* gets the trolley to threaten one instead of five include no more than getting the trolley off the straight track onto the right-hand track; and doing that is not itself an infringement of a right of anybody's.

VIII

It is arguable, however, that what is relevant is not that toppling the fat man off the footbridge is itself an infringement of *a* right of the fat man's but rather that toppling him off the footbridge is itself an infringement of a particularly stringent right of his.

What I have in mind comes out in yet another variant on *Bystander at the Switch*. Here the bystander must cross (without permission) a patch of land that belongs to the one in order to get to the switch; thus in order to get the trolley to threaten the one instead of five, the bystander must infringe a right of the one's. May he proceed?

Or again, in order to get the switch thrown, the bystander must use a sharply pointed tool, and the only available sharply pointed tool is a nail-file that belongs to the one; here too the bystander must infringe a right of the one's in order to get the trolley to threaten the one instead of five. May he proceed?

For my own part, I do not find it obvious that he may. (Remember what the bystander will be doing to the one by throwing that switch.) But others tell me they think it clear the bystander may proceed in such a case. If they are right – and I guess we should agree that they are – then that must surely be because the rights which the bystander would have to infringe here are minor, trivial, non-stringent – property rights of no great importance. By contrast, the right to not be toppled off a footbridge onto a trolley track is on any view a stringent right. We shall therefore have to recognize that what is at work in these cases is a matter of degree: If the agent must infringe a stringent right of the one's in order to get something that threatens five to threaten the one (as in *Fat Man*), then he may not proceed, whereas if the agent need infringe no right of the one's (as in *Bystander at the Switch*), or only a more or less trivial right of the one's (as in these variants on *Bystander at the Switch*), in order to get something that threatens five to threaten the one, then he may proceed.

Where what is at work is a matter of degree, it should be no surprise that there are borderline cases, on which people disagree. I confess to having been greatly surprised, however, at the fact of disagreement on the following variant on *Bystander at the Switch*:

> The five on the straight track are regular track workmen. The righthand track is a dead end, unused in ten years. The Mayor, representing the City, has set out picnic tables on it, and invited the convalescents at the nearby City Hospital to have their meals there, guaranteeing them that no trolleys will ever, for any reason, be turned onto that track. The one on the right-hand track is a convalescent having his lunch there; it would never have occurred to him to do so if the Mayor had not issued his invitation and guarantee. The Mayor was out for a walk; he now stands by the switch.[14]

For the Mayor to get the trolley to threaten the one instead of the five, he must turn the trolley onto the right-hand track; but the one has a right against the Mayor that he not turn the trolley onto the right-hand track – a right generated by an official promise, which was then relied on by the one. (Contrast the original *Bystander at the Switch*, in which the one had no such right.) My own feeling is that it is plain the Mayor may not proceed. To my great surprise, I find that some people think he may. I conclude they think the right less stringent than I do.

In any case, that distributive exemption that I spoke of earlier is very conservative. It permits intervention into the world to get an object that already threatens death to those many to instead threaten death to these few, but only by acts that are not themselves gross impingements on the few. That is, the intervenor must not use means that infringe stringent rights of the few in order to get his distributive intention carried out.

It could of course be argued that the fact that the bystander of the original *Bystander at the Switch* makes threaten the one what already threatens the five, and does so by means that do not themselves constitute infringements of any right of the one's (not even a trivial right of the one's), shows that the bystander in that case infringes no right of the one's at all. That is, it could be argued that we have here that independent ground for saying that the bystander does not infringe the one's right to life which I said would be needed by a friend of (ii).[15] But I see nothing to be gained by taking this line, for I see nothing to be gained by supposing it never permissible to infringe a right; and something is lost by taking this line, namely the possibility of viewing the bystander as doing the one a wrong if he proceeds – albeit a wrong it is permissible to do him.

IX

What counts as *"an* object which threatens death"? What marks one threat off from another? I have no doubt that ingenious people can construct cases in which we shall be unclear whether to say that if the agent proceeds, he makes threaten the one the very same thing as already threatens the five.

Moreover, which are the interventions in which the agent gets a thing that threatens five to instead threaten one by means that themselves constitute infringements of stringent rights of the one's? I have no doubt that ingenious people can construct cases in which we shall all be unclear whether to say that the agent's means do constitute infringements of stringent rights – and cases also in which we shall be unclear whether to say the agent's means constitute infringements of any rights at all.

But it is surely a mistake to look for precision in the concepts brought to bear to solve this problem: There isn't any to be had. It would be enough if cases in which it seems to us unclear whether to say "same threat," or unclear whether to say "non-right-infringing-means," also seemed to us to be cases in which it is unclear whether the agent may or may not proceed; and if also coming to see a case as one to which these expressions do (or do not) apply involves coming to see the case as one in which the agent may (or may not) proceed.

X

If these ideas are correct, then we have a handle on anyway some of the troublesome cases in which people make threats. Suppose a villain says to us "I will cause a ceiling to fall on five unless you send lethal fumes into the room of one." Most of us think it would not be permissible for us to accede to this threat. Why? We may think of the villain as part of the world around the people involved, a part which is going to drop a burden on the five if we do not act. On this way of thinking of him, nothing *yet* threatens the five (certainly no ceiling as yet threatens them) and a fortiori we cannot save the five by making what (already) threatens them instead threaten the one. Alternatively, we may think of the villain as himself a threat to the five. But sending the fumes in is not making *him* be a threat to the one instead of to the five. The hypothesis I proposed, then, yields what it should: We may not accede.

That is because the hypothesis I proposed says nothing at all about the source of the threat to the five. Whether the threat to the five is, or is caused by, a human being or anything else, it is not permissible to do what will kill one to save the five except by making what threatens the five itself threaten the one.

By contrast, it seems to me very plausible to think that if a villain has started a trolley towards five, we may deflect the trolley towards one – other things being equal, of course. If a trolley is headed towards five, and we can deflect it towards one, we *may*, no matter who or what caused it to head towards the five.

I think that these considerations help us in dealing with a question I drew attention to earlier. Suppose a villain says to us "I will cause a ceiling to fall on five unless you send lethal fumes into the room of one." If we refuse, so that he does what he threatens to do, then he surely does something very much worse than we would be doing if we acceded to his threat and sent the fumes in. If we accede, we do something misguided and wrongful, but not nearly as bad as what he does if we refuse.

It should be stressed: The fact that he will do something worse if we do not send the fumes in does not entail that we ought to send them in, or even that it is permissible for us to do so.

How after all could that entail that we may send the fumes in? The fact that we would be saving five lives by sending the fumes in does not itself make it permissible for us to do so. (Rights trump utilities.) How could adding that the taker of those five lives would be doing what is worse than we would tip the balance? If we may not infringe a right of the one in order to save the five lives, it cannot possibly be thought that we may infringe the right of that one in order, not merely to save the five lives, but to make the villain's moral record better than it otherwise would be.

For my own part, I think that considerations of motives apart, and other things being equal, it does no harm to say that

(II) Killing five is worse than killing one

is, after all, true. *Of course* we shall then have to say that assessments of which acts are worse than which do not by themselves settle the question of what is permissible for a person to do. For we shall have to say that, despite the truth of (II), it is not the case that we are required to kill one in order that another person shall not kill five, or even that it is everywhere permissible for us to do this.

What is of interest is that what holds inter-personally also holds intra-personally. I said earlier that we might imagine the surgeon of *Transplant* to have caused the ailments of his five patients. Let us imagine the worst: He gave them chemical X precisely in order to cause their deaths, in order to inherit from them. Now he repents. But the fact that he would be saving five lives by operating on the one does not itself make it permissible for him to operate on the one. (Rights trump utilities.) And if he may not infringe a right of the one in order to save the five lives, it cannot possibly be thought that he may infringe the right of that one in order, not merely to save the five lives, but to make his own moral record better than it otherwise would be.

Another way to put the point is this: Assessments of which acts are worse than which have to be directly relevant to the agent's circumstances if they are to have a bearing on what he may do. If A threatens to kill five unless B kills one, then although killing five is worse than killing one, these are not the alternatives open to B. The alternatives open to B are: Kill one, thereby forestalling the deaths of five (and making A's moral record better than it otherwise would be), or let it be the case that A kills five. And the supposition that it would be worse for B to choose to kill the one is entirely compatible with the supposition that killing five is worse than killing one. Again, the alternatives open to the surgeon are: Operate on the one, thereby saving five (and making the surgeon's own moral record better than it otherwise would be), or let it be the case that he himself will have killed the five. And the supposition that it would be worse for the surgeon to choose to operate is entirely compatible with the supposition that killing five is worse than killing one.

On the other hand, suppose a second surgeon is faced with a choice between here and now giving chemical X to five, thereby killing them, and operating on, and thereby killing, only one. (It taxes the imagination to invent such a second surgeon, but let that pass. And compare *Trolley Driver*.) Then, other things being equal, it does seem he may choose to operate on the one. Some people would say something stronger, namely that he is required to make this choice. Perhaps they would say that

> (II′) If a person is faced with a choice between doing something *here and now* to five, by the doing of which he will kill them, and doing something else *here and now* to one, by the doing of which he will kill only the one, then (other things being equal) he ought to choose the second alternative rather than the first

is a quite general moral truth. Whether or not the second surgeon is morally required to make this choice (and thus whether or not (II′) is a general moral truth), it does seem to be the case that he may. But this did seem puzzling. As I put it: Why should the present tense matter so much?

It is plausible to think that the present tense matters because the question for the agent at the time of acting is about the present, viz., "What may I here and now do?," and because that question is the same as the question "Which of the alternatives here and now open to me may I choose?" The alternatives now open to the second surgeon are: kill five or kill one. If killing five is worse than killing one, then perhaps he ought to, but at any rate he may, kill the one.

Notes

1   See Philippa Foot, "The Problem of Abortion and the Doctrine of Double Effect," in *Virtues and Vices* (Oxford: Basil Blackwell, 1978), pp. 19–32.
2   I think it possible (though by no means certain) that John Taurek would say No, it is not permissible to (all simply) turn the trolley; what you ought to do is flip a coin. See John Taurek, "Should the Numbers Count?" *Philosophy & Public Affairs* 6 (1977): 293–316. (But he is there concerned with a different kind of case, namely that in which what is in question is not whether we may do what harms one to avoid harming five, but whether we may or ought to

choose to save five in preference to saving one.) For criticism of Taurek's article, see Derek Parfit, "Innumerate Ethics," *Philosophy & Public Affairs* 7 (1978): 285–301.

3   I doubt that anyone would say, with any hope of getting agreement from others, that the surgeon ought to flip a coin. So even if you think that the trolley driver ought to flip a coin, there would remain, for you, an analogue of Mrs. Foot's problem, namely: Why ought the trolley driver flip a coin, whereas the surgeon may not?

4   Mrs. Foot speaks more generally of causing injury and failing to provide aid; and her reason for thinking that the former is worse than the latter is that the negative duty to refrain from causing injury is stricter than the positive duty to provide aid. See Foot, "The Problem of Abortion," pp. 27–9.

5   A similar case (intended to make a point similar to the one that I shall be making) is discussed in Nancy Davis, "The Priority of Avoiding Harm," in Bonnie Steinbock, ed., *Killing and Letting Die* (Englewood Cliffs, NJ: Prentice-Hall, 1980), pp. 172, 194–5.

6   For a sensitive discussion of some of the difficulties, see Nancy Davis, "Using Persons and Common Sense," *Ethics* 94 (1984): 387–406. Among other things, she argues (I think rightly) that the Kantian idea is not to be identified with the common sense concept of "using a person" (p. 402).

7   For a second reason to think so, see note 13 below.

8   It is also true that if the five go wholly out of existence just before the agent starts to turn the trolley, then the one will die whatever the agent does. Should we say, then, that the agent uses one to save five if he acts, *and* uses five to save one if he does not act? No: What follows *and* is false. If the agent does not act, he uses nobody. (I doubt that it can even be said that if he does not act, he lets them *be used*. For what is the active for which this is passive? Who or what would be using them if he does not act?)

9   I strongly suspect that giving an account of what makes it wrong to *use* a person, see text accompanying notes 6–8 above, would also require appeal to the concept of a right.

10   Ronald Dworkin, *Taking Rights Seriously* (Cambridge, MA: Harvard University Press, 1977), p. ix.

11   Many of the examples discussed by Bernard Williams and Ruth Marcus plainly call out for this kind of treatment. See Bernard Williams, "Ethical Consistency," in *Problems of the Self* (Cambridge: Cambridge University Press, 1973), pp. 166–86; Ruth Barcan Marcus, "Moral Dilemmas and Consistency," *Journal of Philosophy* 77 (1980): 121–36.

12   It may be worth stressing that what I suggest calls for attention is not (as some construals of "double effect" would have it) whether the agent's killing of the one is his means to something, and not (as other construals of "double effect" would have it) whether the death of the one is the agent's means to something, but rather what are the means by which the agent both kills and saves. For a discussion of "the doctrine of double effect," see Foot, "The Problem of Abortion."

13   Ibid., p. 29. As Mrs. Foot says, we do not *use* the one if we proceed in *Hospi-tal*. Yet the impermissibility of proceeding in *Hospital* seems to have a common source with the impermissibility of operating in *Transplant*, in which the surgeon *would* be using the one whose parts he takes for the five who need them. This is my second reason for thinking that an appeal to the fact that the surgeon would be using his victim is an over-simple way of taking account of the means he would be employing for the saving of his five. See note 7 above.

14   Notice that in this case too the agent does not *use* the one if he proceeds. (This case, along with a number of other cases I have been discussing, comes from Judith Jarvis Thomson, "Killing, Letting Die, and the Trolley Problem," *The Monist* 59 (1976): 204–17. Mrs. Thomson seems to me to have been blunder-ing around in the dark in that paper, but the student of this problem may possibly find some of the cases she discusses useful.)

15   See text accompanying notes 9–11 above.

10

Harming Some to Save Others

Frances Myrna Kamm

Some moral philosophers with nonconsequentialist leanings have puzzled over how to reconcile their apparently conflicting intuitions that it is morally permissible to redirect fatal threats away from a greater number of people to a lesser number of people, but that it is not morally permissible to kill one person in order to transplant his organs into a greater number of people merely because this alone will save their lives.[1]

In this article I wish to present, as succinctly as possible, criticisms of some answers that others have given to this question and then present what I believe to be a new answer, an answer with broad implications. I will sacrifice detail in order to provide the broad outlines of positions. In addition, I should say at the outset that my aim is to find a principle which accounts for what I take to be "common-sense" moral intuitions, putting to one side for the time being the question of whether these intuitions are ultimately correct. (Of course how we account for these intuitions may play a part in deciding whether they are correct.) Such a principle, essentially, tells us when people have a right not to be killed and when they lack such a right. The question then arises, whether we show greatest concern for the right if we violate it in order to minimize violations of it? I shall argue that we do not show greatest concern for *rights* by violating them to minimize violations, and that the explanation of this is what I call *victim-* rather than *agent-* focused. However, this still leaves the question why we should be concerned with rights when ignoring them could minimize *lives* lost?

Frances Myrna Kamm, "Harming Some to Save Others," *Philosophical Studies* 57 (1989): 227–60.

I. *Other Proposals*: It is commonly assumed by nonconsequentialists that it is impermissible for us to chop up an innocent person simply because we could transplant organs only from him and so could save the lives of five other innocent people (Transplant Case). It would be impermissible for us to do this even if *we* were responsible for endangering the lives of the five and so would otherwise be the killers of five rather than of just the (different) one.[2] Yet it is also commonly assumed by nonconsequentialists that it is permissible for us to turn a fatal trolley away from killing five toward killing one, even if we have not set the trolley in motion toward the five and are just bystanders watching it (Trolley Case).[3] What is the difference between the cases?

A. Let us first consider proposals others have made. James Montmarquet[4] suggests that we may kill the one – call him Joe – in the Trolley Case (although not in the Transplant Case) because (1) Joe is already threatened with death by the trolley, since someone is already threatened by any threat that can be redirected to him, (2) we do not create a new threat; he dies of one that already exists, and (3) we maximize lives saved.

All these claims seem incorrect. First, it is simply not true that someone to whom a threat can be redirected is already under a threat if the threat is headed in a totally different direction. Secondly, it would be impermissible to turn a trolley headed to one toward five (who are already threatened according to (1)) even if this maximized lives saved by defusing a bomb threatening another twenty people. Third, it would be permissible to redirect a trolley away from the five even if we *did* create a new threat that killed Joe. We might, for example, imagine a case in which we redirect a trolley in such a way that it stopped far away from Joe, but its movement started a rockslide, a threat that did not previously exist, which killed Joe (Rockslide Case).

Perhaps some might object that the rockslide, because it is an effect of the trolley's stopping, is a part of the trolley threat itself. Two other cases might then be considered. First imagine a case in which I must press a switch to turn the trolley headed toward the five onto a track where no one sits. This switch also controls another trolley which has been inactive till now. When the switch is pressed it not only turns the first trolley away from the five but also turns the second trolley toward one person on another track (Two-trolley Case). In this case the switch action, not the first trolley, produces the new threat; yet, I believe, it is still permissible to redirect the first trolley.

Second, suppose it is not possible for us to redirect the trolley headed toward the five, but it *is* possible to move the five out of the way of the trolley, because they are seated on one end of a Lazy Susan-type device which we can turn. However, seated on the other side of the Lazy Susan is Joe, and we foresee that, when we move the five out of the way of the trolley, he will be moved into an electric pole which will kill him (Lazy-Susan Case). I believe it is as permissible to move the Lazy Susan as it would be to redirect the trolley if we could, even though a new threat kills Joe. (This case also serves as an answer to those who think we can turn the trolley only because we are doing something to the threat itself; here we do something to the Lazy Susan rather than to the threat.)

B. Judith Thomson[5] has suggested that we may kill a few in order to save a greater number of people, provided that we do not save the greater number *by* infringing significant rights of the few, *and* provided that the few die of the same threat that faced the greater number. Therefore, we may not kill in the Transplant Case because we would have to save the greater number *by* violating a significant right of the few (i.e., we save the many by chopping one man up). Likewise, we may not throw someone off a bridge so that his body will fall in the way of the trolley and stop it in its path (Bridge Case). This is because we would stop the trolley *by* violating the right of the person not to be toppled in front of trains. But killing in the Trolley Case is permissible because we bring about the better state by redirecting a trolley, and this in itself does not violate Joe's significant rights – Joe dies *as a result* of the redirection of the trolley, which redirection saves the five, but we do not save the five *by* harming Joe – and, secondly, because Joe dies of the same threat that would have killed the five. Thomson further suggests that if it would have been permissible to redirect the trolley if Joe had not been present, this indicates that we act permissibly in doing the same thing even if he is present.

I have already argued (in discussing Montmarquet's proposal) by constructing the Rockslide, Two-trolleys, and Lazy-Susan cases that whether the few and the many would die from the *same* threat seems not to be decisive, and so that part of Thomson's proposal is wrong. Let us, therefore, consider the question of the infringement of Joe's rights by itself. Several questions can be raised for this proposal, I believe. Suppose the trolley is a very valuable antique that *belongs to Joe* (Owned-trolley Case). Ordinarily it would be a significant violation of Joe's rights to do something to *his* trolley, but, presumably, if it is a threat to five, it *is* permissible to redirect it even toward Joe, and this even if he and it will be destroyed in the process. Here we save the five *by* turning Joe's trolley and so *by* infringing on a significant right of his. How does this gibe with Thomson's theory?

Thomson herself introduces another case and asks why, by her criterion of permissibility, it is not permissible to wiggle a publicly owned bridge (this in itself violates no right of Joe's), in order to topple Joe off it, so that he will fall in the path of the trolley and thus stop it from heading toward the five (Wiggle-the-Bridge Case). Thomson suggests that this is not permissible because we *require* Joe's being in front of the trolley (a serious infringement of his rights) in order to stop the trolley, and this amounts to stopping the trolley *by* violating his rights. However, in another case which we can construct (Prevented-Return Case) in which harm to Joe is similarly *required* in order to save the five, I believe that our action *is* permissible; here we turn the trolley away from the five toward Joe, and we *require* that it actually grind itself into Joe because otherwise it would roll back and hit the five anyway.[6]

How does the Wiggle-the-Bridge Case differ from the Prevented-Return Case, since in both we cause, require (and therefore intend) that the victim be hit by the trolley? (Furthermore, suppose that wiggling the bridge *by itself* would stop the trolley, but we foresaw that the wiggling would also topple Joe off the bridge into the trolley's path. In this case we do not require Joe's being hit in order to stop the trolley; yet I believe it is still *im*permissible to wiggle the bridge. (This case (Wiggle II) has the same structure as the Grenade Case to be discussed next.)

Now suppose that the only way to stop the trolley is to throw a grenade which will stop it, but we foresee that pieces of the grenade will also hit and kill Joe, an innocent bystander, whose death will play no causal role in saving the five (Grenade Case). Even though the grenade does not belong to Joe and it would be permissible to throw it if he were not present, – referring back to Thomson's test – it is impermissible, I believe, to use it if it will kill Joe in the manner described. (It might be suggested that we may turn the trolley toward Joe but not throw the grenade because in the Grenade Case Joe would die of a different threat from the threat that faced the five. But then how does the Grenade Case differ from the Lazy-Susan and Two-trolley cases, of which this is also true? Notice also that it cannot be said in the Grenade Case that we save the five by doing something to Joe because we require his death as a means to their being saved. His death has no causal role to play in saving them; it is only a foreseen consequence of the grenade.) If we do not save the five either by laying hands on Joe or anything of his, or by requiring that he be harmed, *by* infringement of what rights of Joe's would we save the five in the Grenade Case?

Let us go back to the Lazy-Susan Case. It seems correct to say of this case that while we prevent the five from being killed *by* moving them, *in so doing* we also move Joe, which is an infringement of his rights. Is this close enough to saving them "by" doing something to Joe, so that Thomson's theory should condemn the turning, when, in fact, it is permissible? It might be said that, in itself, moving Joe is only a *minor* not significant infringement of his rights. But if we know that a minor infringement of someone's rights will lead to his death, wouldn't this *ordinarily* stand in the way of our committing the minor infringement? Why does it not do so here? Furthermore, Joe might be under the Lazy Susan, so that we know that if we moved it, thereby saving the five from the trolley, we would, *in doing this*, crush him (Lazy-Susan Case II). Crushing him is itself a significant infringement. Yet I believe it may well be permissible to do even this.

Despite the questions I have raised about Thomson's proposal, I believe its underlying idea is sound and I will return to it below.

C. Bruce Russell has offered another proposal[7] In some respects similar to Thomson's, and comparison of the two may prove useful at this point. As I understand it, Russell has suggested that we may not save lives by *illegitimate plans*. An illegitimate plan is a plan that involves means for saving those lives which either require deaths as causally necessary or involve deaths that are merely side effects of the means we use. Russell's idea of an illegitimate plan for saving people is broader than Thomson's proposal, at least insofar as he disallows some merely foreseen, not causally required, deaths. She restricts herself to the impermissibility of significant direct intrusions on someone or something of his and the impermissibility of causing some events because we require some eventual serious infringement of someone's rights as a means to stopping a threat to others.

Employing his criterion, Russell could argue that it is permissible to kill neither in the Transplant Case nor in the Grenade Case. But how then will it be permissible to kill in the Trolley Case, if our plan is to redirect a trolley, foreseeing Joe's death as an absolutely certain side effect? Furthermore, Russell also believes that there is no intrinsic moral difference between killing and letting die. Therefore, if actively *causing* a death that is not intended, but merely foreseen to be a side effect of the means used to save the five is not permissible, it would follow that just passing by a dying person on the way to saving the five should also be impermissible. But this makes it impossible ever to save some rather than others in situations where we cannot save everyone; there will always be an illegitimate plan. For if we do not rush off to save five, leaving one to die, but instead save the one, we shall be letting the five die as a foreseen side effect instead.[8]

II. *A New Proposal*: Let me now present a new proposal for dealing with these cases, describing it first as briefly as possible and then elaborating on it. The explanation I propose to account for the various permissible and impermissible killings we have so far considered (and others as well) is based on what I will call the *Principle of (Im)Permissible Harm* (PI/PH):

> It is permissible to cause harm to some in the course of achieving the greater good of saving a greater number of others from comparable harm, if events which produce the greater good are not more intimately causally related to the production of harm than they are to the production of the greater good (or put another way, if events which produce the greater good are at least as intimately causally related to the production of the greater good as they are to the production of the lesser harm).[9]

If an event is more intimately causally related to the harm than to the good, then we will perceive this as having achieved the good "by" harming others, and this may produce moral problems.[10] Therefore, the PI/PH tells us exactly what this "by" relation which may create moral problems amounts to. (The PI/PH is being presented as both a sufficient condition for permissibility, and as a requirement which if not met will result in prima facie impermissibility. However, we may be able to justify acts which do not abide by PI/PH's restrictions by pointing to overriding considerations.)[11] The PI/PH allows us to introduce new threats as we remove old ones – a homeostasis of threats – so long as the events which produce the greater good are no more intimately causally related to the lesser harm that the new threat produces than they are to the greater good. For example, an event which removes a direct threat to the greater number may cause a comparable direct threat to the lesser number, but may not itself be the direct threat. Let us now consider how this PI/PH applies to the cases we have so far introduced and, in the process, try to make clearer what is meant by "degrees of intimacy in causal relations."

First, the original Trolley Case: When we turn the trolley, the five's being saved (the greater good) is an effect causally quite immediately related to the trolley's turning. In a sense the five's being saved "fills the space" of the trolley's being moved; it is the flipside of the trolley's being removed. However, it is of some significance for later discussions to note that it would be wrong to identify the five's being saved as *an aspect of* the turning of the trolley itself in the way that the trolley's rattling as it goes down the tracks is an aspect of the trolley's turning. What of the causal relation between the trolley's turning and Joe's death? The trolley we turn directly causes Joe's death, though again its causing the death is not merely an aspect of the turning (as it would be if Joe were attached to the bottom of the trolley and turning it fatally dragged him).

DIAGRAM 1

5 Saved
↗
Turn Trolley → 1 dead

In the Trolley Case, therefore, the turning trolley, our means to the greater good, has at least as intimate a causal relation to the greater good (five saved) as to the lesser harm (one dead). (This need not mean that *temporally* Joe's death occurs at the same time as or after the five are saved, though this is true in this case; one causal relation may be more intimate than another even though its components are temporally more separated, as we shall see below.) The conclusion is that the redirection is permissible.[12]

In the first Lazy-Susan Case, the greater good seems to be an aspect of the turning of the Lazy Susan, and turning the Lazy Susan eventually pushes Joe into the pole.

DIAGRAM 2

Lazy Susan I

(Save 5) Lazy Susan Turned → 1 Dead

In this case the good seems even more intimately related to our turning of the Lazy Susan than it was when we turned the trolley, since it is an aspect of our turning it. After all, the five are seated on the Lazy Susan and are moved to safety. It may even be inappropriate to speak of a causal relation between an event and an aspect of it, but only because the intimacy has gone beyond causation. In Lazy Susan II, where Joe's being killed is an aspect of the turning of the Lazy Susan itself (since he is crushed in the turning), the relation of the Lazy Susan's turning to the lesser harm is also so intimate that it may not even be appropriate to say the turning caused the crushing, since crushing is an aspect of the very event of the turning.

DIAGRAM 3

Lazy Susan II

(5 saved) Lazy Susan Turned (1 dead)

Still, that turning has no more intimate a causal relation to the lesser harm than it has to the greater good, and therefore the turning is permissible.

Suppose our turning the *trolley* left the five unmoved but free of the threat, and crushed Joe because he was attached to the bottom of the moving trolley (Trolley II)?

DIAGRAM 4

5 Saved
↗
Turn Trolley (1 dead)

What has been said so far suggests that we should feel reluctant to turn the trolley in this case, in a way in which we do not feel reluctant to turn the Lazy Susan in Lazy Susan II. This is because the turning trolley is a means, with the greater good as its effect (albeit an intimate effect), but the lesser harm is thought of as an aspect of the turning. I believe, in fact, that our intuitive responses to these two cases confirm this analysis, and we think that turning the trolley is impermissible. We think of the turning Lazy Susan in Lazy Susan II as having both the good and bad as its aspects, and we think of the relation "aspect of" as more intimate than the relation "effect of."

Turning the trolley in the Rockslide Case is permissible because the turning trolley is causally *more* intimately related to the greater good than to the lesser harm. In this case, the trolley is not even the direct cause of death, it is only the indirect cause since it causes the rockslide which is the direct cause of death.

DIAGRAM 5

5 saved
↗
Trolley Turned → Rockslide → 1 Dead

The PI/PH also permits us to do something to produce a greater good when the greater good itself will produce a lesser harm. In such a case, the greater good *causes* the lesser harm, so there is no need to worry about a cause of the greater good being more intimately related to the harm than to the good. When the lesser harm is a side effect of the greater good, the greater good does not occur *by* way of the lesser harm to others, according to the analysis of "by" provided by the PI/PH. In these cases what we do, – or any other event that helps to cause the greater good – is more directly related to the greater good than to the harm, since the greater good either is the direct cause or the indirect cause of the lesser harm. This would be the case, for example, if we saved the lives of five patients (GG) whose normal breathing then caused a shift in air patterns which led fatal germs, hitherto safely closeted, to approach and kill Joe (Germ Case).

DIAGRAM 6

Cause → GG → 1 Dead

What about cases in which it would be impermissible to act? It was said that, if a grenade that we set off to stop the trolley would itself kill one person, it would be *im*permissible to use it. According to the PI/PH this is because the grenade itself directly kills the bystanders but the grenade only indirectly produces the greater good; for it directly turns the trolley and the (very intimate) effect of this movement – not of the grenade going off itself – is that the five are saved.

DIAGRAM 7

5 Saved
↗
Trolley Turned
↗
Grenade → 1 Dead

(This case can help highlight the distinction between "causal intimacy" and temporal priority, for it is quite possible that the grenade delivers the fatal blow to the bystander *after* the five are saved, but this is irrelevant for the PI/PH.)

Most importantly, if we thought the grenade directly saved the five (for example, if its going off under them lifted them into the air and away from the trolley), as well as directly killed Joe (Grenade II), it would be permissible to set off the grenade, according to the PI/PH. It seems that stopping a threat from reaching people does not (or does not seem to us to) involve as intimate a relation to the good of their being saved as moving them to safety.

DIAGRAM 8

5 Saved

↗

Grenade → 1 Dead

The contrast between the original Grenade Case, in which the grenade has an indirect relation to the greater good but a direct relation to the lesser harm, and Grenade Case II in which it has a direct relation to both greater good and lesser harm, also has important bearing on a case presented by P. Foot.[13] She argued that our duty not to harm is stronger than our duty to do good. In particular, she argued that we may not use a gas in performing surgery to save five if we foresee that this gas will seep next door and kill one innocent bystander. The PI/PH endorses this conclusion *if* the gas indirectly contributes to the greater good but directly kills. This is so, for example, if the gas runs a machine which helps save the five patients, but kills the bystander because it is poisonous for him to inhale. However, if the gas is poisonous to one person who inhales it but livesaving to five who inhale it, then the PI/PH says that it is permissible to spray the gas into the air, since its relation to greater good and lesser harm is causally equally intimate. (Of course, another objection to Foot's general claim that not harming takes precedence over aiding is provided by the case discussed above in which the greater good itself causes harm, e.g., if the successful surgery on the five causes them to breathe normally and this, in turn, changes air currents so that germs safely closeted up to now move so as to kill one person in an adjoining room.)

According to the PI/PH it would be permissible to set off the grenade if it only indirectly caused the greater good but also *indirectly* killed Joe. For example, if the gas is used to melt a tumor (remove a threat) in five people and also moves germs which kill one, the relation to greater good is as indirect as the relation to lesser harm. Likewise, if the grenade that moved the trolley, also caused some rocks to fall which killed Joe (Rockslide II Case), the PI/PH would permit use of the grenade. The grenade would get rid of one threat, and introduce another, but not itself be a new direct threat.

DIAGRAM 9

5 Saved
↗
Trolley Moved
↗
Grenade → Rockslide → 1 Dead

Indeed the Two-trolley Case has this same structure, only with our pressing of the switch, instead of the grenade going off, in the role of indirect cause of greater good and lesser harm.

DIAGRAM 10

5 Saved
↗
Trolley Moved
↗
Press Switch → Trolley Moved → 1 Dead

That is, our pressing of the switch moves one trolley and so indirectly saves the five and also starts another trolley which directly kills Joe (homeostasis of threats). By contrast, if I pressed a switch to set off a grenade when the exploding grenade *itself* moved the trolley *and* itself also killed Joe, then the grenade that only indirectly saved the five would directly kill the one. (Compare Diagram 10 with 11 below.)

DIAGRAM 11

5 Saved
↗
Trolley Moved
↗
Press Switch → Grenade → 1 Dead

In the original Grenade Case (Diagram 7), pressing a switch to start the grenade – something we do – is indirectly related both to the death of Joe and to the saving of the five, but it is more intimately related to the former (i.e., less indirectly related to it) than to the latter. The threat (grenade going off) that our act produces which itself plays a causal role in saving the five, is not as intimately related to the greater good as it is to the lesser harm.

In the Bridge Case, where we throw a bystander off a bridge to stop the trolley in its tracks, throwing him off the bridge is causally more intimately related to harm to him than it is to the greater good.

DIAGRAM 12

5 Saved
↗
Trolley Stopped
↗
Trolley Crushes 1
↗
Topple before Trolley

This is necessarily so where the harm to the bystander is a means to the greater good, not just a foreseen side effect; since the good is achieved as an effect of the harm to him, what plays a causal role in achieving the good *must* be more intimately related to the lesser harm, since it *is* (in part) the lesser harm. In the Wiggle-the-Bridge Case, where we require the bystander to fall in the path of the trolley, the same is true, even though the act we perform (wiggling the bridge) indirectly causes the lesser harm. Suppose we wiggle the bridge and this alone is enough to stop the trolley, but we also foresee that it will topple the bystander to his death. If we understand this to be a case in which wiggling indirectly causes the five to be saved by stopping the trolley, but directly infringes a significant right by *toppling* the bystander (the infringement occurring even if he doesn't die), we will think it impermissible to wiggle, according to the PI/PH.

DIAGRAM 13

5 Saved
↗
Stop Trolley
↗
Wiggle → Topple → 1 Dead

To return to cases where significant infringement of rights is intended as a means to the greater good, it might be argued that it is *not* true that in all such cases an event that helps bring about the greater good is causally more intimately related to the lesser harm (because, for example, it *is* the lesser harm, or first causes the lesser harm) than to the greater good. This could be true if we accept a possible equivocation on "greater good." When either a greater good itself (Diagram 14) or something that directly brings about a greater good (such as turning the trolley) (Diagram 15) begins a chain of events which causes the lesser harm, then, according to the PI/PH, it is permissible to act with the intention that the lesser harm occur as a way of *maintaining the greater good* already achieved. (This is what happens when we turn the trolley in the Prevented-Return Case.) Notice that this is different from the less controversial intention that a *foreseen* harmful side effect of a greater good which is itself sufficient to justify the existence of the harm, be used to achieve a totally different good. In this case we would proceed to produce the first good even if the harmful side effect had no further good effect. This is not so in the Prevented-Return Case, since if the harmful side effect did not keep the trolley away, we would not turn the trolley at all, for six people would then die.

DIAGRAM 14

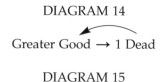

Greater Good → 1 Dead

DIAGRAM 15

Greater Good ←
↗   ⬂
Trolley Turned → 1 Dead

The key to understanding this case, I believe, is (1) to see the five's being free of *one threat* (i.e., free of the trolley originally coming at them) as an intrinsically good state of affairs, which is a greater good in comparison to its bad side effect (the one's being hit), and (2) to understand that though this greater good alone would not justify turning the trolley (if the *second threat* of the trolley's coming back at the five occurred), the good of their being free of this one threat *is* a *component* (not a mere means) to the final greater good of the five's being saved from all threats. So long as what produces the causally useful lesser harm is either the first greater good itself, or a means to this greater good which is at least as intimately related to the greater good as to the lesser harm, the fact that the lesser harm is causally necessary to the maintenance of the greater good is not a reason against acting.[14]

The Prevented-Return Case is problematic because there remains a temptation to say we have achieved the greater good *by* harm, because we think of the *true* greater good as the *continued freedom* of the five from the threat, not their being free of one threat that comes from turning the trolley initially. Then the greater good (or a cause more intimately related to the greater good) will *not* seem to be the cause of the harm. If this is an irresistible conclusion, we should accept that it is permissible for a certain type of component of greater good (i.e., one that is in itself something which if not wiped out would be a greater good than the harm it causes) or the means to it to cause lesser harm.[15]

Suppose we are permitted by the PI/PH to turn the trolley in the Prevented-Return Case, although we would not do so unless we believed the trolley would stick to the bystander. It is very important to understand that this does not mean that we may cause the trolley to stick to the bystander when it would otherwise not reach him at all, by an act (or aspect of an act) *not needed* to turn the trolley temporarily away from the five. For example, we may not give the trolley an extra-hard push (Extra-Push Case), so that it hits and sticks to the bystander when it would not otherwise have done so. (This of course means that, if the extra push were needed, we should not bother to turn the trolley at all when sticking to the bystander is needed to prevent return.) This is because the cause of the trolley's hitting the bystander (i.e., the extra push) is not causally more intimately related to the greater good than to the lesser harm (where the greater good is taken to be the five's being free of the trolley initially). This is because it is not causally necessary to give the extra push for purposes of getting the trolley temporarily away from the five to begin with; what causes the lesser harm is more than what we must do to get the trolley away initially.[16]

III. *Understanding and Comparing the PI/PH:* Having considered its application to cases, let us return to a more general discussion of the PI/PH and the "by" relation. For purposes of the following discussion, I will assume that case results support the following components of the PI/PH, which summarize ideas of necessary and sufficient conditions for the permissibility of causing the deaths of nonthreatening innocents in particular cases:

(1) It is acceptable that greater good have lesser harm as one of its aspects or as its direct or indirect effect.[17]
(2) It is permissible that a mere means to a greater good have
    (a) lesser harm as an indirect effect, if it has greater good as a direct effect or as an indirect effect achieved by a causal route independent of the lesser harm, or
    (b) lesser harm as a direct effect, if it has greater good as a direct effect.

> (c)   lesser harm as its aspect, if it has greater good as its aspect also (as in Lazy Susan II).

In (2) (a), "achieved by a causal route independent of the lesser harm" is intended to exclude as permissible the using of a means that indirectly produces greater good by indirectly causing harm, when that harm is what causes the greater good. (In such a case, the factor that helps cause the greater good is causally more intimately related to the lesser harm than to the greater good.) So (2) (a) achieves the same result as requiring that the greater good have no more indirect a causal relation than the lesser harm has to what causes them both, since a good achieved via a harm *will* be more *in*directly related to what causes both it and the lesser harm than the lesser harm is. The greater good and lesser harm should branch off from a common point, though they need not be equidistant from the point, given that it is acceptable that the greater good be *more* intimately related to the cause they both share than the lesser harm is. The PI/PH, therefore, (only) comes close to involving a *principle of symmetry of good and harm.*[18]

To repeat, an event that is causally involved in producing a greater good is permissible if it has no more (it may have less) intimate a causal connection to the lesser harm than it has to the greater good (where it is understood that something that is an aspect of an event is more intimately connected to it than something that is a direct effect, and something that is a direct effect is more intimately connected to it than something that is an indirect effect).

As noted above, (p. 166) I believe that what underlies the PI/PH is a version of Thomson's proposal, that we will avoid moral problems if we do not bring about a greater good *by* infringing someone's rights in a significant way. The important point is that the "by" relation we should avoid is given specific meaning by the PI/PH. That is, the "by" relation we should avoid is understood as present when our act or another event causally involved in producing the greater good has a *more* intimate causal relation to the significant right-infringing harm than it has to the greater good – for example, when our means directly causes harm but indirectly brings about greater good. Furthermore, I take this to mean that the point of the PI/PH is to recommend that we save the greater number in a way that preserves morally appropriate relations between victims and beneficiaries who are moral equals. Saving some *by* harming others, as explicated in the PI/PH, is not sanctioned as an *appropriate* relation by the PI/PH.[19] (Though this does not mean it cannot sometimes be justified nevertheless; the PI/PH could be overridden.)

The PI/PH has been discussed in the context of our acts. I suspect that we may use its standards even in making judgments, analogous to moral judgments, about natural events. For example, suppose nature were organized along purely consequentialist lines so that when five people became ill their being ill always caused another person to die, making his organs available which would then be used to save the five. I suggest that we would think that such a course of nature offended our conception of appropriate relations between people. This is a case in which a bad state of affairs (the illness of five) causes a lesser harm (the death of one) which then causes the greater good (preventing the death of five). An event causally involved in producing the greater good has a causally more intimate relation to the lesser harm than to the greater good.

Since there is no agent here who acts to save five by using one person, the primary immorality is not an inappropriate relation between an agent and his victim, or a sullying of an agent by his being more intimately causally related to harm than to good; the primary immorality is the potential for an inappropriate relation established between victim and beneficiaries. When there is an agent and he acts contrary to the PI/PH, the PI/PH focusses on the fact that he may (barring special other justifications) establish an inappropriate relation between his victim and those who are saved.

Thus the PI/PH seems to contrast with theories, such as that proposed by Thomas Nagel,[20] which locate what is wrong with harming non-threatening innocents to help others in the special relation established between agent and victim that involves intending a victim's death. This is wrong, in part because intending a death is not crucial to violating the PI/PH. Furthermore, in cases where five people would be killed in violation of the PI/PH to save others unless we kill one in violation of the PI/PH, Nagel, I believe, would see no reason for an agent not to minimize violation of the PI/PH *except* that from the agent's point of view he would have to be the one to do the minimizing, thereby establishing a special (intending-a-death) relation to one victim, namely *his*. (He would only foresee the deaths of the others.) I would propose, by contrast, that the PI/PH itself provides a sufficient explanation of why and when we may not kill the one to minimize violations of the PI/PH. If we did think it permissible to kill him, we would sanction as permissible some relations between victims and beneficiaries that are simply ruled out by the PI/PH. Contrary to Nagel, therefore, deontological constraints are not a function of an agent's subjective point of view, wherein things that he intends loom larger than things others intend. They are, rather, part of an objective and complete understanding of victims as persons protected by the PI/PH. (We shall return to the question of why we should not minimize violations of the PI/PH below.)

The PI/PH also contrasts in several respects with the Doctrine of Double Effect (DDE) which says that we may not intentionally harm the innocent as an end in itself or as a means to a greater good, but may do a neutral or good act as a means to a greater good even though we foresee that an innocent will be harmed as a side effect. The PI/PH suggests the DDE may be too restrictive; for when a death is caused in accord with the PI/PH it is sometimes permissible to *intend* the death, i.e. it is permissible to take an action that leads to a death, which we would not take unless we expected it to lead to the death. This is exemplified by the Prevented-Return Case discussed above. The PI/PH suggests that it is not one's state of mind – intending a harm – that is significant, but whether we make any movements or cause other events that are not more intimately causally related to greater good (or a component which if not wiped out would be greater good) than to lesser harm. (In Extra-Push Case we would make such movements.)

The PI/PH also suggests that the DDE may allow too much in permitting lesser foreseen (but not intended) harm in the course of achieving a greater good. This is because the DDE fails to differentiate, for example, a foreseen lesser harm that is the side effect of the greater good itself (permitted according to the PI/PH) from the direct effect of a means when the means has no direct good effects (as when the grenade kills Joe but only indirectly saves the five in the original Grenade Case, not permitted by the PI/PH).[21]

The PI/PH, however, coincides with the DDE when it rules out bringing about harm as a means to greater good; for according to the PI/PH, we would be using a means that has a causally more intimate relation to the harm than to the greater good (as in the Bridge Case). I am not sure, however, that the PI/PH provides a complete substitute for an explanation of the moral significance of harm as an intended means. For a merely foreseen death that is the direct effect of an act whose indirect effect is a greater good also involves an act's being more intimately related to the lesser harm than to the greater good. While the PI/PH does not sanction producing this harm, I do not believe it implies (nor do we find) that it is *as* morally bad as harm that is an intended means.

We might, however, get a clue to a complete explanation of the moral difference between intending and merely foreseeing harm, even when both are *impermissible*, from our discussion of the Prevented-Return Case. There we concluded that it was *permissible* to intend that the bystander be killed because what we did to remove the trolley was not more intimately related to the lesser harm than to the greater good. A necessary, but not sufficient, reason for this occurring is that all the acts or aspects of our acts which bring about the harm are done to get the trolley away from the five initially. If there had been, for example, a separate act undertaken to bring about harm, its relation to the harm would have been causally more intimate than its relation to the greater good (as in the Extra-Push Case).

But there can be cases in which it is *not* permissible to bring about the foreseen harm, because there is a more intimate causal relation to harm than to greater good, and yet there is still no separate act undertaken to bring about the harm. When the harm is a side effect, the event which brings it about, even if it is in an inappropriately close causal relation to the harm, is brought about for the sake of its causal relation to other events, each of which is also brought about for the sake of other events which do not in themselves involve harm. In the case of every event which has harm as a mere side effect, there is always a line of justification leading *directly* from the event in a direction away from the harm. There is no act or aspect of an act done solely for its ability to bring about the harm. So even if the event is too distantly related to the greater good to make the event permissible, it is as directly related to (and justified by its causing) some other non-harm event as it is to the harm, and the same is true of this other event, in a chain all justified by its leading to the greater good. (See Diagram 17, where "E" stands for "event".) (Of course, in speaking of a line of justification, we are employing the idea of intending the neutral or greater good event, rather than the too-intimately related harmful side effect.)

The event which produces intended harm in the case where intending harm is impermissible, however, is not justified by any causal relation to a greater good occurring causally prior to the harmful event. It is done for the sake of bringing about the harm.

DIAGRAM 17*

Foreseen Harm   *Intended Harm*

Greater Good
↑
E → harm SE
↑
E → harm SE   Act → harm → E → E → Greater Good
↑   or
E → harm SE   Act → harm → Greater Good
↑   or
Act → harm SE   Act → E → harm → Greater Good

---

* Numbering of diagrams incorrect in original.

All this, of course, does not mean that I would not *seek* to bring about the harm when it is a mere side effect, as I seek to bring it about when it is intended. If there is an unavoidable causal link between the harmful side effect and the innocent means that I intend to the greater good, I know that if the harm does not occur, then neither does my intended means. So I keep my eye out to see that the harm does occur.[22] But I am still not prompted to do anything separate I would not do anyway in bringing about the non-harmful means to the greater good. There is nothing separate I do (or omit doing) for the sake of producing the harm, so there is at least some motivated *direct* causal relation to non-harmful events in everything I do. Likewise, I would not do what I am doing if the bad side effect did not occur, because given the unavoidable causal links, if it doesn't occur that would mean my neutral means and/or good end would also not occur. But my actions are not *explained* by every event which is such that had it not occurred, I would not have acted.

Imagine, however, a case in which the five are not only threatened by the trolley, but by a runaway tractor as well. Turning the trolley will result in it hitting and dragging Joe under the tractor, which stops it (Double Threat Case). Since it is only if Joe is crushed in this way that the tractor stops, we should be intending Joe's death if we turn the trolley. In this case, I believe, it is impermissible to turn the trolley, though we make no extra movements we wouldn't make to turn the trolley away. This is because we are here more intimately causally related to the lesser harm than to the greater good, i.e., turning the trolley initially leaves us with a state of affairs in which the five still have the tractor headed to them, and this is not a state of affairs which if not undone is a greater good than the lesser harm. Yet it would be worse to act here than in other cases in which we are also causally more intimately related to lesser harm than to greater good, because we intend Joe's death, and yet not because this is associated with making extra movements. Why?

The answer, I believe, is that in the Prevented-Return Case we create the second threat (returning trolley) and the way of stopping it by removing the first (initial trolley) threat. Therefore, when we turn the trolley in the Prevented-Return Case we do not do so *in order* to stop the second threat, though we intend it be stopped. (In Extra-Push Case we say we turn the trolley *in order* to stop the second threat we will create, only because we make extra movements for that aim.) But in Double Threat Case we do turn the trolley *in order* to stop the second threat (as well as the first) though we do nothing extra, because the second threat already exists. Intention must take this form to make some violations of the PI/PH worse than others.

IV. *Limitations and Variations*: First, so far as limitations are concerned, the PI/PH speaks of "innocents," but it should be restricted to non-threatening innocents. That is, it does not apply to what are known as (morally) innocent threats, e.g., individuals who, through no fault of their own, will pose a threat to others. It also does not apply as a constraint on pre-emptive attacks against those who have a culpable intention to do harm, but have not yet done it. Against such persons, I believe, we may permissibly use means that have a more direct causal relation to harm than to good, indeed the same means that we may permissibly use against guilty aggressors. The PI/PH is also limited by what I shall call the *Principle of Secondary Permissibility*: If something we are permitted by the PI/PH to do to someone is something we physically can do (even if it is not something we would do) and if this act would cause the victim more harm than something which we physically could do but which is otherwise prohibited by the PI/PH, then we may substitute the less harmful act for the more harmful one. That is, we may do secondarily, as a substitute for what we may and could do, something that we would not be permitted to do if it were our only option, when doing this is in the best interests of the person who will be harmed.

A second limitation is the difficulty of giving precise characterizations of "causally more intimately related to," and the associated concepts of "indirect cause of," "direct cause of," and "aspect of." As troublesome as this difficulty may be, I believe that these concepts must nonetheless be used for a correct understanding of common-sense morality. This discussion has aimed at setting the course in the right direction, rather than at providing a precise characterization of these concepts. (A related problem is whether the requirement that there be no more intimate relation to harm than to greater good holds no matter how indirect the relation to harm is.)

A third problem concerns the view that moving the trolley is a means to the greater good, rather than the greater good itself. (Support for the view that removing a threat is itself a greater good comes from the fact that removing a barrier to a harm should be treated like a harm by the PI/PH. For example, if the grenade which turns the trolley only blows away a shield to falling rocks and so indirectly causes rocks to kill Joe, it is still impermissible, I believe, to use the grenade.) If turning the trolley is itself the greater good, how can the PI/PH exlain why it is not permissible to use the grenade in the Grenade Case? Two other principles do.

PI/PH(2) – a principle I originally favored offers the following alternative account: (a) Lesser evil is allowed to be an aspect or effect of greater good itself (the trolley being turned away from the five is a greater good);

lesser evil is not allowed to be even the indirect effect of mere means to greater good. (In support of this view, it might be argued that it is only a confusion between greater indirectness of harmful effects and their decreased probability that leads us to think setting a grenade in Rockslide II is permissible.[23])

PI/PH(3) repeats (a), but (b) allows that lesser harm be an indirect effect of a means which directly produces a greater good, e.g., the grenade which moves the trolley may cause death by a rockslide. This alternative principle, in essence, requires that one have a *more* intimate relation to the greater good than to the lesser evil.

Certain cases raise questions about accepting either of these alternatives to the PI/PH. For example, if in Grenade II it is permissible to set off a grenade that both lifts the five up and directly kills Joe, PI/PH(3) will be satisfied only if lifting the five somehow puts us in a more intimate relation to the greater good than does moving the trolley from the five. But this begins to reintroduce the views underlying the PI/PH. (The same sort of issue arises if we may turn the Lazy Susan crushing Joe underneath, but may not turn the trolley when Joe will be crushed underneath, because it is only in the first case that good is an aspect of what we do.)

Returning to the distinctions between direct, indirect, and aspect of, used in the PI/PH, the fourth problem also concerns the possibility that the PI/PH allows too much. In particular, there may be resistance (from within common-sense morality itself) to the idea that an agent may permissibly use means that *directly* cause harm (even if they directly cause greater good as well) and may also permissibly cause harm as an aspect of an act whose other aspect is a greater good. (There may also be objections to one of these permissions but not to the other.) Therefore, some might think it impermissible to release a gas the inhaling of which saves many and kills few, and some might think it impermissible to turn a Lazy Susan with the five on it away from the trolley when Joe, attached to its bottom, is crushed in the process. As noted above, the PI/PH is essentially concerned with preventing the agent from violating appropriate relations between moral equals, some of whom will be victims and others beneficiaries in the choice of who will live and who will die. This concern is part of a wider concern about how the qualities of being a person limit what it is permissible to do to victims. The PI/PH is thus what I would call "victim-focused," concerned that victims be treated appropriately relative to beneficiaries, and simply in their own right. By contrast, the objections to turning in Lazy Susan II, and releasing a gas which directly saves and harms, I believe, are founded more directly on concern for the agent. These concerns are what I would call "agent-focused."

One way to express the agent-focused concern is to say agents must not *do* harm (e.g., crush people) though they may sometimes *bring about harm* (i.e., bring about that people are crushed).[24] (This way of talking may not capture what is wrong with setting off a gas, which, when inhaled, kills some and saves others; that depends on how we analyze "do." However it does capture what happens when we turn the Lazy Susan with Joe attached under it, as that is an act of crushing.)

There is another point of view which takes issue with the PI/PH. It too is agent-focused, but it would not find crushing Joe by turning the Lazy Susan objectionable, although it would condemn releasing the gas which directly harms *and* benefits. This point of view does not emphasize doing versus bringing about, but emphasizes rather the agent's having a sufficient hands-on *buffer* between himself and the harm he does. Greater good (moving the five) would provide such a buffer for a harmful aspect of the act – you can't get your hands dirty when you are wearing "greater-good gloves." But a mere in itself neutral act (setting off a gas) would not be a sufficient buffer between the agent and the gas's direct harmful effect.

It might be suggested that the PI/PH, amplified to include such additional agent-focused concerns, would more accurately describe common-sense intuitions about what may and may not be done. I am not at all sure that this is so. At the very least, if the PI/PH plays some role, this shows that these types of agent-focused accounts of non-consequentialism require a victim-focused component if they are to be complete. On the other hand, if the PI/PH alone is sufficient to ground true moral prohibitions, the agent-focused limitations described above will be dealing with something less than the full-blooded moral. I suspect that this is the correct conclusion. It remains true, however, that we may care more about *our* violating the PI/PH with any given victim, than about the PI/PH being violated by someone else even with the *same* victim. (Where the same person would be harmed anyway, his interests are not affected differently whether I or someone else harm him.) If this is what is meant by a focus on the agent in morality – the content of the wrong being given totally by the PI/PH, but any given agent being worried about his doing the wrong to a person who would be wronged by someone else anyway – then I agree that the agent-focus concern may be a component, though not the major one, of nonconsequentialist thought.[25]

V. *Minimizing Rights Violations?* Cases in which the victim will be different depending on who does the killing can, I believe, be handled by a victim-focused approach alone. It is worth expanding on this point, and hence reopening the discussion of minimizing violations of the PI/PH. Let us think of the PI/PH as excluding certain types of acts because it characterizes certain rights individuals have. One way in which the issue of victim versus agent focus in morality comes up is in the attempt to understand how any principles (such as the PI/PH) that tell us what we should not do to individuals, can restrict our minimizing violations of *those very principles themselves*, i.e., can exclude minimizing as a justification for not abiding by the PI/PH. That is, suppose the PI/PH is true, and in the Bridge Case we may not throw Joe off a bridge to stop a trolley. Nevertheless, someone else who does not appreciate the truth of the PI/PH is about to throw two different people (Jim and Susan) off another bridge in order to stop the trolley, thus violating the PI/PH rights against interference of those two people. Suppose that our toppling Joe will save the other two people from being toppled by causing a rail to pop up on their bridge. Even assuming that this still does violate Joe's PI/PH-given rights, we would thereby minimize the number of such rights violated. Why is it not permissible, indeed obligatory, for us to do this – i.e., engage in what has been referred to as a utilitarianism of rights – as an expression of respect and concern for rights?[26]

I suggest, in answer to this question, that a moral system – where a moral system is our attempt to represent moral truth – that permits minimization of the violations of a certain right by transgression of that very right essentially eliminates that right from the system, hence it would be futile as a way of showing respect for rights; it would be a "futilitarianism" of rights. This is so, at least, if the right is what I shall call a *specified* right, and rights with at least some sort of specification, we shall see, are the serious rights. Permission to minimize violations, therefore, destroys a component of the moral system itself and alters its essential structure, in the effort to minimize violations in the realm of practice.

Let us consider this point in some detail. By a "specified right" I mean a right that implicitly or explicitly tells us to what extent the individual is protected from transgressions against him, a right that does not leave this matter of extent entirely vague. Suppose the right not to be killed in violation of the PI/PH were absolute, so that we had a right not to be toppled from the bridge no matter how many other people could be saved from being toppled by our being toppled. To say that it is permissible to violate one person's absolute right not to be toppled in order to prevent the violation of other people's absolute right not to be toppled, eliminates from the structure of the moral system by which we live the representation of the absolute right that people have (assuming that in moral reality they do have the right). This is because, if that permissibility were accepted, it would no longer be true that the moral system includes the claim that it is absolutely wrong to kill in violation of the PI/PH. Under such an interpretation, if we minimized violations, fewer people might in fact die of violations of this right, but people would no longer really be held to have the right. This also means that our concept of the person would be changed; we would no longer think that a person did not exist for the purpose of improving the fates of others.

Suppose the right not to be killed in transgression of the PI/PH is not absolute. For example, suppose (just for the sake of argument) that it specifically forbids killing one person as a means to saving up to five others, but permits such a killing when more could be saved. Given a situation in which five people will be killed in violation of their nonabsolute PI/PH right unless we kill one, the decision to minimize the violation of the PI/PH by killing the one would be morally confused. This is because the PI/PH *specifically* excludes this as a correct course, and so to follow it would involve eliminating this version of the PI/PH from the moral system. Then if this PI/PH correctly describes the rights people in fact have, our moral system would not accurately represent reality and we would have an incorrect concept of the person. (This system is arranged hierarchically: avoiding the wrong of violating a specific directive not to minimize wrongs takes precedence, and violating the directive cannot be considered just one more wrong on the same level, and to be weighed against the many wrongs that will occur without minimization.)

Once we understand how minimization of rights violations makes no sense as an expression of concern for a right, we can also see how it would make more sense – even if it were ultimately wrong – to transgress a right for the sake of utility, or some other item that is not part of the very same conceptual network as the right, than to minimize rights violations.[27]

What if the right is not "specified"? That is, what if we recognize a PI/PH in our moral system, but without any explicit specifications of how many lives can be lost due to respect for it. Suppose that, on a given occasion, we decide that in order to save a thousand people from having their PI/PH rights violated, we will transgress the PI/PH rights of one person. One understanding of this decision is that we have then specified the strength of the right, removed the vagueness that existed before. Since there was no specification to begin with, however, we cannot, strictly speaking, eliminate the right from the system by granting permission to minimize violations of it for any given number of violations, at least not before the specification.[28]

I have maintained that concern for a specified right should not involve acting against its clear demands and eliminating it from a moral system (intended to represent what is morally true). However, we must then face the crucial question: Why specify one way rather than another? For a moral realist, at least, the answer is that if people really do have a high degree of inviolability (i.e., the PI/PH should not be violated even to save many people from violation of their PI/PH rights), then we should so specify.

It is important to see that it is the *permission* to kill, not any killing, that eliminates the right not to be killed from the moral system. If the PI/PH is violated many times over, this does not involve our *endorsing* any such violation; though many people may die, we do not say that it was correct that any of them died, which is what an endorsement would involve. Accordingly, the constraining effect of the PI/PH derives not from its resulting in fewer rights violated or from its moral consequences (it does not make rights come to exist as part of moral reality), but from its illumination of truth, leading to our understanding of, and acting in accord with, moral reality. For if rights would exist whether we recognized them or not and if violations of rights could be minimized if we did not abide by the PI/PH, it is only representation of truth in us and in events that is at stake. Indeed, our worth – our being the sort of creatures wrongs to whom we are most tempted to minimize – arises in part through our recognition of moral truth.

This point is connected to the question of whether, if we do not minimize rights violations by violating comparable rights, we tolerate a worse world than we could otherwise have. For example, it may seem that a world in which someone kills one person to prevent others from being killed in a way that violates the PI/PH is better than a world in which he does not kill and more rights are violated. But, I believe, the temptation to say this exists only when we also think that the person who kills is doing the wrong thing. If we were to think that he did the right thing, we would be endorsing the permissibility of the act, changing our moral system and altering our concept of the person, and this might very well make the world a worse place from our point of view.

The world would become worse for us because we would have to live believing in a less sublime and elevated conception of ourselves. We might save more people, but they would, in a sense, be less worth saving in our eyes. This is because individuals whose rights stand as a barrier to action are more potent individuals than they would be otherwise. This benefit of a more sublime and elevated self-conception accrues even to the five (or more) who will die because our system represents this truth about

persons: They die as individuals who ought not to have been killed in violation of the PI/PH even to save five (or more) other lives. If we understand these cases we have been discussing as cases in which the single
person who will be protected by the PI/PH might have been one among
the five who will die, then – because if we killed the one to save the five
and each person has a five times greater chance of being among the five
than of being the one who is sacrificed, each has a greater likelihood of
survival if we minimize violations – both the one who survives and those
who die will be exchanging the opportunity to increase the probability of
physical survival for the dignity of retaining a more elevated conception
of themselves which, they believe, represents the truth.[29]

To return to our jumping-off point, this analysis of why we may not
kill one in order to prevent greater violations of rights is victim-focused:
People have certain properties that give them rights which constrain our
actions. It is not agent-focused; it is not that one agent should avoid being
a killer, even though he would not in the first place wrong (by violating
the constraining right of) the person he kills. It is true that an agent may
not kill the first potential victim *he* meets, – his potential victim is important to him – but this is not because something about the agent constrains
the agent. It is rather that the agent will necessarily be present whenever
he meets the constraining force of the PI/PH-given rights of the potential
victim. It would certainly be wrong to say that an agent should not kill
the one person to save five others from being killed because the agent
should avoid *his* being a killer. This is because it might be that the agent
was himself responsible for the plight of the five others, so that if he
doesn't kill the one now he will be the killer of the five, and yet it would
still be wrong of him to kill the one. For example, suppose he had planted
a bomb to kill the five and now would like to defuse it, but this is only
possible if he throws one other person onto the bomb. (To explain the
impermissibility of killing even in this case – what we could refer to as
deontology of the (present) moment – an agent-centered approach would
have to develop a time-slice approach to agents. That is, it would have to
claim that the present time slice of an agent is not permitted to do certain
acts in order to prevent consequences of past acts done by his past self.[30])

An account has been offered of why minimizing rights violations is not
the way to show greatest concern either for rights or the concept of the
person which they express. However, there is another, more straightforward, reason that could be offered for minimizing rights violations by
violating the rights of one person. It might be argued that minimization,
rather than being the way to show maximal respect and concern for rights,
is simply a policy which ignores rights in order to maximize lives saved.

Further, when the person sacrificed seemed to be at risk of being one among the larger number, and the policy is adopted at a time when he did not know he would, in fact, not be among the larger number, then this policy also maximizes each person's own chance of survival. The question then becomes, why should we not bargain away rights, and agree to a policy to achieve these alternate goals in all sorts of cases? The answer to this question is part of a theory of permissible and impermissible bargains and is a subject for another time.[31]

Notes

1   For example, Philippa Foot in "The Problem of Abortion and the Doctrine of Double Effect," reprinted in Steinbock, ed., *Killing and Letting Die* (N.J.: Prentice-Hall 1979), and Judith Thomson in "The Trolley Problem," *Yale Law Journal*, Spring 1986. I have argued (in a longer version of this article) that a nonconsequentialist should think that it is sometimes permissible to kill one person in order to transplant his organs into others. These are very special cases, however, and I omit them here.

2   I discuss this latter point in more detail in an unpublished paper "Constraints and You," a short version of which was presented at the Pacific APA in 1984. Judith Thomson also discusses such a case in "The Trolley Problem."

3   This implies, contrary to what Foot suggested, that we may turn the trolley even when it is not a choice between our *killing* five and our *killing* one, but a choice between our *letting* five *die* and our *killing* one. Foot originated the Trolley case in which we have set the trolley in motion, Thomson originated the case in which we are bystanders.

4   In "Doing Good: The Right and the Wrong Way," in *The Journal of Philosophy*, August 1982.

5   In "The Trolley Problem."

6   Thomson would agree this is permissible since she endorses the permissibility of turning the trolley in a case similar to this one: The trolley is directed away from the five onto a track which, however, loops back toward them. The only reason it does not kill the five anyway, is that it slams into Joe who is seated on that track and whose weight stops it from going all the way around.

7   In "The Relative Strictness of Positive and Negative Duties," reprinted in B. Steinbock, *Killing and Letting Die* (N.Y.: Prentice-Hall, 1979).

8   Suppose now that Russell tells us that if, no matter what we do, saving some will involve a plan that involves the death of others, it will be permissible to *then* save the greater number. The problem with this is that he would then have no way to distinguish morally between our chopping up one to save five and our spending our time and resources on saving the five at the

expense of letting one die. It might be suggested that a reason why we might permissibly do the latter, but not the former, is that, if we spent our resources on the one rather than the five, we would save him by a plan that costs five lives, but, if we merely do not chop up one person, we do *not* have a plan to save his life that costs five lives – after all he was not under any threat (but ours potentially) from which he needed saving. So there is a moral difference after all. But this difference would disappear if the single person who is not chopped up *is* in need of the organs of the five and will get them if they die. Then Russell's analysis, revised as I have suggested, will again imply that it is indifferent whether we chop the one up to save the five, or use our resources to save the five and let the one die. (Notice that if Russell, in order to deal with these problems, emphasized intending a death rather than merely foreseeing it, but did not reintroduce the moral distinction between killing and letting die, he would not be able to account for its being wrong to kill in the Grenade Case where we only foresee the death of the one.)

9   I here omit any attempt to formulate the analogue condition of permissibility for omissions (e.g., if the trolley is headed toward the one, why is it permissible to not redirect toward the five?).

10 The harm to others will at least be prior to the greater good in order of causation, mimicking the causal structure that would exist if it were actually a cause of the good.

11 I owe the emphasis on the fact that the PI/PH may be overridden to Keith Lehrer.

12 The redirection of a trolley already on its way to the five has the same structure, for moral purposes, as the direction of a trolley which is at a crosspoint and must be directed to either the one or five. In both cases the turning to the one has the direct effect of saving the five. This similarity in *moral* structure may account for Montmarquet's view that the one is already under a threat even when the trolley is headed to the five, since he is as much (or as little) under a threat (relative to the five) as the one is (relative to the five) when we must decide what to do with a trolley which is at a crosspoint.

13 In "The Problem of Abortion and the Doctrine of Double Effect."

14 The explanation here is complicated by the need to show that because of the difference in numbers of people involved (5 vs. 1), fairness does *not* require (as I believe it sometimes does) that we *not* take advantage of the intrinsically valueless period of temporary removal of the threat to the five (which is all that would exist but for the trolley sticking to the one) in order to produce the sustained greater good. In addition, it should be emphasized that there is a distinction between (1) *components* of the greater good which are not greater goods than the bad side effects (for example, saving one of the five) causing the lesser harm which is to be used as a means to producing the total greater good (not permitted), and (2) the initial removal of the trolley threat to the five eventually causing the five to be saved for a significantly long period of time, which is the case we are discussing (permitted). The PI/PH analysis

should also account for Thomson's Loop Case described in Endnote 6. But how can we say that the greater good of the five being free of a threat (even temporarily) occurs when we turn a trolley along another track that also leads to the five, as it does in her case? I suggest that we do, in fact, conceive of the initial redirection of the trolley in Thomson's case as reducing one threat to the five, since we eliminate a trolley from being a threat from one direction, a component in eliminating its being a threat from two directions.

15 Our results here apply to a case which is a variant of a type well known in discussion of the Doctrine of Double Effect: We foresee that if we bomb a crucial munitions plant during a just war, children next door will die. The plant would be rebuilt immediately by their parents, were it not that they are consumed by grief over the deaths of their children. It is here permissible to bomb the plant, even though we would not bomb unless the children were killed, and even though it would be impermissible to terror bomb the children per se.

16 This case should also be distinguished from one in which our doing what we must do to turn the trolley from the five *will* kill the one person, but we must do something *not* causally necessary for turning the trolley in order to get it to stick to the *already dead* bystander. In this case, doing the separate act which gets the trolley to stick is permissible. This is because the separate act or separate component does not increase the damage to the one person, whose death is the result of the parts of our act necessary for merely turning the trolley away from the five. [This is true even though if this separate act or component were not permissible, it would not be permitted to turn the trolley away from the five (because it would be a waste of six lives), and then the bystander would not be harmed at all.]

17 In the morality of character, an analogous thesis is present in the view that someone is allowed the (lesser) vices of his (greater) virtues, even if he may not cultivate lesser vices in order to achieve greater virtues.

18 In an earlier attempt at answering these questions I emphasized the (supposed) symmetry between good and harm in another, much more straightforward way.

19 An alternative explanation for the PI/PH that might be suggested is that it ensures that a lesser harm will not be in vain, by requiring that the harm be the effect or aspect of a greater good that already exists. (This would deal with a common objection to consequentialism, namely that we cannot be sure that a greater good will result from the lesser harm which is our means.) However this would only explain part of what the PI/PH endorses, i.e. clause (1). It does not even explain the permissibility of turning the trolley in the Prevented-Return Case, since it is only the expectation that the five will *continue* to be unthreatened that justifies our turning the trolley, and we are not absolutely ensured that the trolley will not return. [Any time we depend on a causal connection (in the real world) certainty is eliminated. It is also possible that the greater good will not result as a direct or indirect effect

of a means though the lesser harm does result, since causality can fail in producing the good and not in producing the harm.]

20 As described in his *The View From Nowhere* (N.Y.: Oxford University Press 1986).

21 It might be argued – I once argued in this way and I believe Warren Quinn does – that what is crucial for (prima facie) wrongdoing is not whether we intend death or other significant harm, but rather whether we intend any intrusion on a person – or any event that is, in fact identical with such an intrusion – that will lead to foreseen significant harm. However, not only does such a view run afoul of the PI/PH, but it represents a radically watered down version of the original DDE. If an intentional intrusion which would be quite permissible on its own (e.g., tapping someone lightly for the sake of a great good), is only wrong when we foresee that it will lead to a great harm (e.g., tapping someone lightly will cause the person to bleed to death), then the objection to the act is no longer that it involves intending harm. The objection to it seems rather to exhibit a concern with making something that belongs to someone (his body) play a part in a chain of events that is against his interests. As such it has much more in common with the concern that we not do things that are harmful to people "by" doing something to them, than with the DDE. If we intrude in an intrinsically minor way with what belongs to someone, as a means to a greater good, we achieve our end by intruding on him, even if we do not bring about the greater good *by* the larger harm that befalls the person – as the PI/PH explains "by." However, the Owned-trolley Case shows that it is not always wrong to do harm to someone by doing something to what is his, when his item is a threat. But if Joe owned the Lazy Susan (a non-threat) on which he and the five sit (Owned-Lazy-Susan Case), it is impermissible, I believe, to turn what is his when this has the consequence of causing his death. This is a case in which we violate the "not-by" condition though we are not more intimately related to the lesser evil than the greater good.

22 It is wrong, therefore, to try to distinguish intending from foreseeing harm by associating only the former with following the harm wherever it goes, seeking to increase it if it diminishes.

23 This point was made by both Warren Quinn and David Wasserman.

24 This mode of expression is used by Thomas Nagel in "War and Massacre," in *Mortal Questions* (Cambridge University Press, 1979). However, he seems to believe that what we *do* is given by what we *intend*. This does not seem to be true when we turn the Lazy Susan in Lazy Susan II, for we do not intend to crush Joe yet what we do is crush him.

25 I believe that an agent's reluctance to kill such a victim who would die anyway only exists when the same person would be the victim of another agent's violation of the PI/PH, not when a natural event (proceeding according to an ordinary, not a consequentialist, schema in nature) does the victim in.

26   Samuel Scheffler discusses this issue in *The Rejection of Consequentialism* (Oxford: Oxford University Press, 1982). The idea of a utilitarianism of rights was, I believe, first discussed by Robert Nozick in *Anarchy, State and Utopia* (N.Y.: Basic Books, 1975). My discussion here is based on an unpublished paper, "Prerogatives and Restrictions," a short version of which was presented at the American Philosophical Association Meeting, Pacific Division, 1985. (It also contains other criticisms of Scheffler.)

27   Notice the contrast between this position and the right-as-goals position for which Amartya Sen argues in "Rights and Agency," *Philosophy and Public Affairs*, Vol. 11, no. 1, Winter 1982. He believes we may violate a right to minimize rights violations, but not to maximize utility.

28   However, note the following objection to this argument: Consider first an unspecified right not to be used in violation of the PI/PH. Suppose we decide to kill someone as a means to save one thousand people from being killed as a means to save yet others. It may be said that the right of the one not to be so used still exists and is recognized in our moral system even in the breach; without thinking that we act impermissibly, we may think that there is a negative residue produced by our acting for which we would owe compensation to the victim. The claim is that there would be no such negative residue unless he still had a right not to be so used. The claim would be that deciding that it is permissible to kill the person in this case does not conflict with the claim that he has a right not to be used to save one thousand people, though we may infringe the right. But, then, why in the case of a *specified* right not to be used to save one thousand people who will otherwise themselves be used, may it not also be said that granting permission to kill the one to save the one thousand does *not* involve a denial of the right not to be killed to save the one thousand? Here too can we not use the language of permissibly infringing a right and owing compensation for infringing a right we recognize as still in force? Certainly these infringeable rights will be weaker than non-infringeable ones and so involve a different concept of the person, but the right will still be represented in our moral system in some form. In fact, this system will have a concept of the person as more inviolable than one which claimed that he had no right not to be sacrificed when preventing one thousand rights violations was at stake. I believe that the crucial question about this proposal so far as the present topic is concerned is whether it is permissible to infringe the right only for some reason other than concern for rights violations, e.g. utility, or whether concern for one thousand rights violations qua rights violations can prompt the infringement as well. It is consistent with the argument presented in the text that utility be a reason, but not that concern for the right per se be such a reason for transgressing a specified right while retaining it in the moral system.

29   That one is a more elevated type of being if the PI/PH is true of one need not mean that complete pacifism, i.e. the refusal ever to kill someone, represents a true and even more elevated conception of the person, since, for example,

killing an aggressor because he must bear responsibility for his actions may represent the more elevated conception of the person.

30 This case presents a problem for the view Sen develops. That is, Sen adds to his system of rights as goals (described above) an agent-relative perspective from which an agent's killing one person produces a worse state of affairs from that agent's perspective than five people being killed by another agent produces. In this way Sen (thinks that he) generates a prohibition on killing the one to save five that is (supposedly) co-extensional with that generated by a victim-focused account. But would an agent not find it worse to be the killer of five than the killer of one? A constraint on killing the one is still generated only if being a person who does an act of killing now is worse from the agent's perspective than having been a person who did an act in the past that will make him a killer. I first argued that deontology is not to be identified with agent-focused constraints or the agent giving himself more weight in minimizing wrongs in "Constraints and You," a short version of which was presented at the American Philosophical Association, Pacific Division, meetings in March 1984.

31 Further discussion of these issues is present in my *Morality, Mortality*, vol. 2 (New York: Oxford University Press, 1996); "Non-consequentialism, the Person as an End-in-Itself, and the Significance of Status," *Philosophy and Public Affairs* 21 (1992): 358–89; "Inviolability," Midwest Studies in Philosophy 20 (1995): 167–75.

11

Actions, Intentions, and Consequences: The Doctrine of Double Effect

Warren S. Quinn

Situations in which good can be secured for some people only if others suffer harm are of great significance to moral theory.[1] Consequentialists typically hold that the right thing to do in such cases is to maximize overall welfare. But nonconsequentialists think that many other factors matter. Some, for example, think that in situations of conflict it is often more acceptable to let a certain harm befall someone than actively to bring the harm about. I believe that this view, which I call the Doctrine of Doing and Allowing, is correct, and I defend it elsewhere.[2] But there is a different and even better known anticonsequentialist principle in the Doctrine of Double Effect (for short, the DDE).[3] According to one of the common readings of this principle, the pursuit of a good tends to be less acceptable where a resulting harm is intended as a means than where it is merely foreseen.[4] It is this controversial idea that I wish to examine here.

There are two major problems with the DDE. First, there is a difficulty in formulating it so that it succeeds in discriminating between cases that, intuitively speaking, should be distinguished. In particular, I will need to find a formulation that escapes the disturbing objection that under a strict enough interpretation the doctrine fails to rule against many or most of the choices commonly taken to illustrate its negative force. Second, there is a question of rationale. What, apart from its agreeing with our particular intuitions, can be said in favor of the doctrine? Indeed, why should we accept the intuitions that support it? In answer, I shall suggest a rationale with clear Kantian echoes.

Warren S. Quinn, "Actions, Intentions, and Consequences: The Doctrine of Double Effect," *Philosophy and Public Affairs* 18 (1989): 334–51.

I

Like the Doctrine of Doing and Allowing, the DDE discriminates between two kinds of morally problematic agency. It discriminates against agency in which there is some kind of intending of an objectionable outcome as conducive to the agent's end, and it discriminates in favor of agency that involves only foreseeing, but not that kind of intending, of an objectionable outcome. That is, it favors and disfavors these forms of agency in allowing that, *ceteris paribus*, the pursuit of a great enough good might justify one but not the other. The doctrine is meant to capture certain kinds of fairly common moral intuitions about pairs of cases which have the *same* consequential profile – in which agents bring about the same good result at the same cost in lives lost and harm suffered – but in which the character of the intention differs in the indicated way.

One such pair of contrasting cases is drawn from modern warfare: In the Case of the Strategic Bomber (SB), a pilot bombs an enemy factory in order to destroy its productive capacity. But in doing this he foresees that he will kill innocent civilians who live nearby. Many of us see this kind of military action as much easier to justify than that in the Case of the Terror Bomber (TB), who deliberately kills innocent civilians in order to demoralize the enemy. Another pair of cases involves medicine: In both there is a shortage of resources for the investigation and proper treatment of a new, life-threatening disease. In the first scenario doctors decide to cope by selectively treating only those who can be cured most easily, leaving the more stubborn cases untreated. Call this the Direction of Resources Case (DR). In the contrasting and intuitively more problematic example, doctors decide on a crash experimental program in which they deliberately leave the stubborn cases untreated in order to learn more about the nature of the disease. By this strategy they reasonably expect to do as much long-term medical good as they would in DR. Call this the Guinea Pig Case (GP). In neither case do the nontreated know about or consent to the decision against treating them.

Another pair of medical examples is found in most discussions of double effect. In the Craniotomy Case (CC) a woman will die unless the head of the fetus she is trying to deliver is crushed. But the fetus may be safely removed if the mother is allowed to die. In the Hysterectomy Case (HC), a pregnant mother's uterus is cancerous and must be removed if she is to be saved. This will, given the limits of available medical technology, kill the fetus. But if no operation is performed the mother will eventually die after giving birth to a healthy infant. Many people see less of a moral difference between these two cases than between the other pairs. This might be for a variety of reasons extraneous to the doctrine: because the fetus is not yet a person and therefore not yet within the moral framework, because the craniotomy is seen as a way of defending the mother against the fetus, because the fetus's position within the mother's body gives her special rights over it, and so on. But the relative weakness of the intuitive contrast here might also signal something important about the doctrine's central distinction. I shall say more about this later. But for the present it will be useful to include this pair of cases under the DDE, if only because it naturally illustrates the objection mentioned earlier.

According to that objection, the doctor in CC does not intend, at least not strictly speaking, that the fetus actually die.[5] On the contrary, we would expect the doctor to be glad if, by some miracle, it survived unharmed. It is not death itself, or even harm itself, that is strictly intended, but rather an immediately physical effect on the fetus that will allow its removal.[6] That effect will of course be fatal to the fetus, but it is not intended *as* fatal. The intentions in CC are therefore really no different from those in HC.

It might seem that this kind of point cannot be made about the bombing and nontreatment cases. In GP the doctors seem to need the disease to continue so that they can observe its effects. And in TB the pilot seems to need the deaths of the civilians to lower enemy morale. But Jonathan Bennett suggests a way of extending the objection to the bombing case.[7] The terror bomber does not, he argues, need the civilians actually to be dead. He only needs them to be as good as dead and to seem dead until the war ends. If by some miracle they "came back to life" after the war was over, he would not object. And something similar might be said about the doctors in GP. While they need the disease to continue its course, they do not need the victims actually to be harmed by it. If by some miracle the victims developed special ways of withstanding the disease so that they remained comfortable and well-functioning despite its progress, the doctors would be glad.[8]

This line of objection clearly threatens to deprive the doctrine of most of its natural applications. One reply is to say that it surely matters how *close* the connection is between that which is, strictly speaking, intended and the resulting foreseen harm. If the connection is close enough, then the doctrine should treat the harm as if it were strictly intended.[9] And, the reply might go on, the connection is close enough in the cases I have used to illustrate the doctrine's negative force. But what does this idea of closeness amount to? H. L. A. Hart suggests a possible answer by way of the example of someone violently striking a glass just in order to hear the sound of the initial impact. In such a case the further outcome, the shattering of the glass, is "so immediately and invariably" connected with the intended impact that the connection seems conceptual rather than contingent.[10] The death of the fetus in CC is, arguably, connected with the intended impact on its skull in just this immediate and invariable way. And the deaths, or at lease some harms, in TB and GP seem just as closely connected with what is strictly intended in those cases.

But what of the contrasting cases? Since hysterectomies are rarely performed on pregnant women, they rarely result in the death of a fetus. So we might say that what is strictly intended in HC (that the uterus be removed) is not, in the relevant sense, closely connected with the fetus's death. And we might hope to find something similar to say in SB and DR. But in taking this way of preserving the contrasts, we would be making everything depend on which strictly intended outcomes of the various choices we fasten upon.

This leads to a new problem. For certain things that the doctor in CC strictly intends for the fetus lack an invariable fatal upshot. Indeed, if craniotomies are ever performed on fetuses that are already dead, then a craniotomy is already such a thing. Even more obviously, the doctor in HC might strictly intend something that is invariably fatal to a fetus. Suppose, for example, that hysterectomies performed on patients who are in the early months of pregnancy are distinguished by the use of a special anesthetic that is safer for the patient and, in itself, harmless to the fetus. This peculiarity could hardly make the operation in HC more difficult to justify, but it would imply that the strictly intended medical means were immediately and invariably connected with the death of a fetus.[11] Perhaps similar things can be said about the other cases. A strategic bomber might have as his mission the bombing of automotive factories. This would not make him a terror bomber, for he would still not aim at civilian casualties. But, for obvious reasons, no automobile factories have ever existed completely apart from civilian populations. So the kind of thing the bomber strictly intends immediately and invariably results in some innocent deaths.

Two problems have emerged: First, since more than one thing may be strictly intended in a given choice, the pronouncements of the doctrine may depend on how the choice happens to be described. This relativity is embarrassing. We would like the doctrine to speak with one voice in any given case. Second, if we try to get around this problem by saying that the doctrine discriminates against a choice in which anything that is strictly intended is also closely connected with death or harm, the doctrine will make uninviting moral distinctions. As we have seen, it will speak against HC if hysterectomies performed on pregnant patients have some distinguishing surgical feature. Otherwise it will speak in favor. And it will speak against the strategic bomber's attack on an urban factory if he was looking specifically for an automotive plant but not, perhaps, if he was looking for a strategically important productive facility.[12] Another approach clearly seems called for.

Instead of looking for a way to identify intrinsically bad effects that are "close enough" to what is intended, we might look instead for a way to identify choices that are intended under some intrinsically negative description. We might then find a way to show that the actions in TB and CC, but not in SB or HC, are intentional *as killings* and that the inaction in GP, but not in DR, is intentional *as a letting die*. Elizabeth Anscombe gives us one such criterion.[13] If we ask a man why he is pushing a mower, he will perhaps say "to cut the grass"; if we ask why he is cutting the grass, he may say "to get things spruced up around here," and so on. The "to . . ." answers, or answers that can be understood in terms of them, give further intentions with which the agent acts. If, his choice being described in a certain way, he accepts the "why" question and replies with a "to . . ." answer, then his choice is intentional under that description. But if he rejects the question in a certain familiar way, his choice is unintentional. If asked why he is cutting the grass he replies, for example, "I don't care about that, I'm just out to annoy the neighbors" or "Can't be helped – it goes with this terrific form of exercise," his cutting the grass is not, as such, intentional.

This seems to give the desired result when applied to our cases. If we ask the doctor in CC why he is killing the fetus, he will naturally say "to save the mother." If we ask the pilot in TB why he is killing the civilians, he will say "to help with the war." And if we ask the doctors in GP why they withhold treatment, they will say "to observe the progress of the disease." And it might be thought that if we ask similar questions in the other cases, the "why" question will be rejected in a way that shows the choices to be unintentional. Thus, if asked why he is killing the fetus, the doctor in HC will avoid a "to . . ." answer, saying instead something like "It can't be helped if I am to save the mother."

Actually, this seems not quite right. If the doctors in DR were asked why they weren't treating the group in question, they might naturally reply "*to* save our resources for more easily treated cases." And this, by Anscombe's criterion, would seem to make the nontreatment intentional.

But waiving this difficulty, there is another worry. What if the agents in the problematic cases (TB, GP, and CC) become philosophically sophisticated? Perhaps they will then come to reject the "why" questions in the manner of their counterparts. The terror bomber, for example, might respond by saying, "The actual deaths can't be helped if I am to create the realistic appearance of death and destruction." By giving such answers, he and the others will be opting for a more demanding criterion of the intentional. All aspects of an action or inaction that do not in the strictest sense contribute to an agent's goal will be trimmed away as unintentional. By this criterion, the action in CC is intentional as a crushing and that in TB is intentional as an apparent killing. But neither is intentional as a killing. And in GP the inaction is intentional as a way of facilitating medical research, but not as a letting die.

Now it would be very natural to object that the ordinary, more relaxed criterion of the intentional is the right one, and that the stricter criterion is specious. But how is this to be made out? We might try to introduce a form of essentialism here, claiming that the surgery in CC and the bombing in TB are essentially killings or harmings, while the surgery in HC and the bombing in SB are not. But surely the ground of this essentialism would be the prior conviction that the killings in CC and TB are intentional while those in HC and SB are not. The issue about intentionality seems to be the basic one. And what would we say about the inaction in GP – that it was essentially a failure to prevent harm? But then this would also seem true of the inaction in DR.

On the one side we have Anscombe's criterion of the intentional, which pretty well maps our ordinary ways of speaking, while on the other we have a criterion that is structurally similar but stricter. The problem here about intention is reminiscent of a problem about causality that arises in connection with the Doctrine of Doing and Allowing. Certain defenses of that doctrine (which discriminates against active harming and in favor of allowing harm) appeal to a familiar conception of causality according to which active harming *causes* harm while inactively allowing harm does not. But opponents counter that according to other, philosophically superior conceptions of causality, inaction can be every bit as much a cause of harm. Now I have argued that if DDA is sound theory, it ought to have force on any plausible conception of causality.[14] And I feel much the same here. If the DDE is sound, its force ought to be capturable on any plausible theory of the intentional, even one that would revise ordinary ways of speaking. So, for purposes of argument, I shall grant opponents of the doctrine the greatest latitude in paring back intentional actions to their indisputably intentional cores.

II

We must therefore find a different reply to the difficulty with which we started. And I think I see a way. For we have been neglecting one striking respect in which members of our contrasting pairs differ. Take TB and SB. In the former case, but not the latter, the bomber undeniably intends in the strictest sense that the civilians be involved in a certain explosion, which he produces, precisely because their involvement in it serves his goal. He may not, if Bennett is right, intend their deaths. But his purpose requires at least this – that they be violently impacted by the explosion of his bombs. That this undeniably intended effect can be specified in a way that does not strictly entail their deaths is, on the view I am proposing, beside the point. What matters is that the effect serves the agent's end precisely because it is an effect *on civilians*. The case with SB is quite different. The bomber in that case intends an explosion, but not in order that any civilians be affected by it. Of course he is well aware that his bombs will kill many of them, and perhaps he cannot honestly say that this effect will be "unintentional" in any standard sense, or that he "does not mean to" kill them. But he can honestly deny that their involvement in the explosion is anything to his purpose.

The same contrast is found in the medical cases. The doctor in CC strictly intends to produce an effect on the fetus so that the mother can be saved by that effect. But the doctor in HC has, as we have seen, no such intention. Even if he cannot deny that, in some ordinary sense, he "intends" the fetus's death, he can rightly insist that the effects on the fetus of his surgery are nothing toward his medical purpose. Similarly, the doctors in GP intend, as something toward their further goal, that the disease in the untreated patients work its course. And this could be true even if, wishing to investigate only the effects of the disease within cells, they had no interest in the pain and loss of function it also causes. But in DR nothing that happens to the untreated patients serves the doctors' further goal.[15]

The important way in which the cases differ should not be obscured by the following complication. We have seen that a doctor in HC might intend to use the special anesthetic "safest for a *pregnant* patient." Would it follow from this allusion to the fetus that the doctor does, after all, strictly intend something for it? No. The medical relevance of the patient's pregnancy does not mean that any of the surgical effects on the fetus are medically useful. Something similar holds in SB. Suppose the bomber wants, for moral reasons, to target factories in the least populated district of a certain city. If so, the formulation of his strictly intended means contains an indirect reference to the civilians whom he may kill. But this hardly turns him into a terror bomber. The impact of his bombs on those civilians is still nothing to his military purpose.

This clear distinction between the intentional structures of the contrasting cases is the key to a new and better formulation of the doctrine. To put things in the most general way, we should say that it distinguishes between agency in which harm comes to some victims, at least in part, from the agent's deliberately involving them in something in order to further his purpose precisely by way of their being so involved (agency in which they figure as *intentional objects*)[16] and harmful agency in which either nothing is in that way intended for the victims or what is so intended does not contribute to their harm.[17] Let us call the first kind of agency in the production of harm *direct* and the second kind *indirect*. According to this version of the doctrine, we need, *ceteris paribus*, a stronger case to justify harmful direct agency than to justify equally harmful indirect agency.[18] Put this way, the doctrine solves the original problem of showing a genuine difference in the intentional structures of our contrasting cases, even under a strict interpretation of what is intended. And it makes no appeal to the problematic notion of "closeness." For direct agency requires neither that harm itself be useful nor that what is useful be causally connected in some especially close way with the harm it helps bring about.[19] There is another, related advantage. With this version of the doctrine, we can sidestep all potentially controversial questions about whether the agents in our various cases kill or harm intentionally. It is enough that we can identify the things they uncontroversially intend as contributing to their goal.

Our further bit of line-drawing remains. We have not yet defined the difference between the more pronounced moral asymmetry of DR and GP, or SB and TB, and the apparently weaker asymmetry of HC and CC. This difference may partly depend on whether the agent, in his strategy, sees the victim as an advantage or as a difficulty. In CC the doctor wants the fetus removed from the birth canal. Its presence there is the problem. In GP and TB, on the other hand, the availability of potential victims presents an opportunity. By bringing it about that certain things are true of them, the agents positively further their goals. Perhaps it would not be surprising if we regarded fatal or harmful exploitation as more difficult to justify than fatal or harmful elimination. If so, we might say that the doctrine strongly discriminates against direct agency that benefits from the presence of the victim (direct *opportunistic* agency) and more weakly discriminates against direct agency that aims to remove an obstacle or difficulty that the victim presents (direct *eliminative* agency).

III

The DDE, of course, has only prima facie moral force. Special rights may allow us to harm someone's interests by way of direct (and even direct opportunistic) agency. Various rights of competition and the right to punish seem to be examples. Certain other cases may prompt qualifications or special interpretations of the doctrine. Suppose that the doctor in HC needs to alter, harmlessly, the position of the fetus before the womb can be safely removed. Whether the overall surgical procedure would still count as indirect harming seems a matter of interpretation. If we saw the manipulation of the fetus as a partial cause of its later removal, we would presumably count the harming as direct. If we saw the manipulation as a precondition, but not a partial cause, of the removal, we would count the harming as indirect.

Another problematic kind of case involves innocent hostages or other persons who physically get in the way of our otherwise legitimate targets or projects. Does our shooting through or running over them involve a direct intention to affect them? I think not. It is to our purpose, in the kind of case I am imagining, that a bullet or car move through a certain space, but it is not to our purpose that it in fact move through or over someone occupying that space. The victims in such cases are of no use to us and do not constitute empirical obstacles (since they will not deflect the missile or vehicle in question). If we act despite their presence, we act exactly as we would if they were not there. If, on the other hand, we needed to aim at someone in order to hit a target, that person would clearly figure as an intentional object. Another tricky case is one in which we could, and would if we had to, accomplish our end by harmful indirect agency; but it is better, perhaps safer for those to be benefited, to pursue the end by harmful agency that is direct. It seems clear why we might wish to make this kind of case an exception.

Before we turn to the defense of the doctrine, we should briefly consider the way in which it interacts with the distinction, mentioned in connection with the Doctrine of Doing and Allowing, between what is actively brought about and what is merely allowed to happen. I have claimed that DDE, with the exceptions noted, discriminates against harmful direct agency. But, as we have seen, people may figure as intentional objects not only of a choice to act but also of a choice not to act. DDE therefore cuts across the distinction between harming and allowing harm. Sometimes, as in TB and CC, it discriminates against direct agency in which harm is done. And sometimes, as in GP, it discriminates against direct agency in which harm is allowed.

In all of these cases we seem to find an original negative or positive right that, while opposed by other rights, seems to be strengthened by the fact that harm will come via direct agency.[20] Civilians in wartime have negative rights not to be killed. But if their government is waging an unjust war, these rights may conflict with strong rights of self-defense. A sufficiently developed fetus *in utero* might also have some negative right not to be killed. But this right may not prevail, either because the fetus is not yet fully one of us or because its mother has strong rights over her body. In TB and CC, the directness of the threatening agency apparently serves to strengthen these negative rights, perhaps giving them a power to stand against moral forces to which they would otherwise give way. Something similar happens in GP. The untreated people have, presumably, some positive right to medical aid. This right might not be binding if doctors could cure more people by directing aid elsewhere. But it stands against any attempt to maximize medical benefit *by* deliberately letting the people deteriorate. Again, the directness of the intention strengthens the force of the opposing right or claim.

It is interesting to consider whether DDE might also come into play where no independent negative or positive right is present. Suppose, in an act of pure supererogation, I am about to aid you but am checked by the realization that your difficulty can be turned either to my advantage or to that of someone I care more for. Does my change of mind, for that reason, violate any of your rights? I am inclined to think not. It might be bad of me to be checked by such a reason, but its appearance cannot create an obligation where none existed before. Rights not to be caught up, to one's disadvantage, in the direct agency of others seem to exist only where some positive or negative right already applies. Their effect always seems to be that of strengthening some other right.

The effect of the doctrine is therefore to *raise* rather than to lower moral barriers. So we should not expect a proponent of DDE to be more tolerant of harmful indirect agency than those who reject the doctrine but share the rest of his moral outlook. We should rather expect him to be *less* tolerant of harmful direct agency. This point is important. For casual critics of the doctrine sometimes seem to suppose that its defenders must be ready to allow killings or harmings simply on the ground that the agency is indirect. But nothing could be further from the truth. The doctrine in no way lessens the constraining force of any independent moral right or duty.

IV

We must now turn to the question of rationale. At first glance, harmful direct agency might seem harder to justify because it requires that the agent welcome something bad for the victim. The terror bomber, for example, must welcome the news that the innocent civilians are blown up, even if he is not glad that they won't be miraculously resurrected after the war. The trouble is that it also seems the strategic bomber must, in some sense, welcome the same news, since if the civilians had been unharmed the factory would not in fact have been destroyed.[21] Of course the news is good for different reasons. It is good news for the terror bomber because it announces the very thing that he intended, while it is good news for the strategic bomber because it announces the thing that he foresaw would be evidence of what he intended. But this difference does little more than register what we already knew – that the terror bomber strictly intended the deaths while the strategic bomber merely foresaw them as necessary costs. So it is hard to see how it could be used to explain the moral difference between direct and indirect agency.

Nor is it the case that harms of direct agency need be worse than those of indirect agency. If someone threatened by a terror bomber and someone equally threatened by a strategic bomber both needed rescuing, the former would not seem to have the stronger claim to help. Indeed, there would seem to be no reason to rescue either in preference to someone threatened by purely natural causes.[22] And if we sometimes think that the first rescue must have priority, it seems to be only because we are tempted to regard the violation of a special right against harmful direct agency as a distinctive and additional kind of moral evil. But then it would be circular simply to appeal to the evil in order to explain the existence or force of the right.

Perhaps the following rationale is more promising. Someone who unwillingly suffers because of what we intend for him as a way of getting our larger goal seems to fall under our power and control in a distinctive way. And there may be something morally problematic in this special relation – something over and above what is morally objectionable in the simpler relation of bringing about or not preventing harm. If this is right, then harmful direct agency must have two things against it, while equally harmful indirect agency need have only one. This additional negative element can be seen most clearly in the contrast between the doctors' attitudes in GP and DR. In the former, but not the latter, they show a shocking failure of respect for the persons who are harmed; they treat their victims as they would treat laboratory animals. DDE might therefore seem to rest on special duties of respect for persons, duties over and above any duty not to harm or to prevent harm.

While this is surely on the right track, we must proceed with caution. For there is also a kind of disrespect in typical cases of wrongful indirect agency. A strategic bomber who ought to have refrained from destroying a rather unimportant target because of likely civilian casualties has failed to treat his victims with the consideration that they and their interests deserve. So we must look for a kind of disrespect that is peculiar to wrongful direct agency – a kind different from that shown in wrongly giving a victim's interests too little weight.

What seems specifically amiss in relations of direct harmful agency is the particular way in which victims enter into an agent's strategic thinking. An indirect agent may be certain that his pursuit of a goal will leave victims in its wake. But this is not because their involvement in what he does or does not do will be useful to his end. The agent of direct harm, on the other hand, has something in mind for his victims – he proposes to involve them in some circumstance that will be useful to him precisely because it involves them. He sees them as material to be strategically shaped or framed by his agency.

Someone who harms by direct agency must therefore take up a distinctive attitude toward his victims. He must treat them as if they were then and there *for* his purposes. But indirect harming is different. Those who simply stand unwillingly to be harmed by a strategy – those who will be incidentally rather than usefully affected – are not viewed strategically at all and therefore not treated as for the agent's purposes rather than their own. They may, it is true, be treated as beings whose harm or death does not much matter – at least not as much as the achievement of the agent's goals. And that presumption is morally questionable. But in a counterpart case of direct agency there is the *additional* presumption that the victim may be cast in some role that serves the agent's goal.

The civilians in TB serve the bomber's goal by becoming casualties, and the infected people in GP serve the doctors' goal by becoming guinea pigs. If things were different, the victims might become these things only voluntarily. Suppose, for example, the civilians had effective bomb shelters and the sick people medicines of their own. Then the bomber or doctors could succeed only with the cooperation of the victims. The service exacted would then be voluntary. But in cases of indirect agency the victims make *no* contribution. If the civilians in SB had shelters and if the sick people in DR had medicines, the bomber and the doctors would see no point in their refusing to use them.

The DDE rests on the strong moral presumption that those who can be usefully involved in the promotion of a goal only at the cost of something protected by their independent moral rights (such as their life, their bodily integrity, or their freedom) ought, prima facie, to serve the goal only voluntarily.[23] The chief exceptions to this strong presumption are cases in which people have or would have strong moral obligations to give themselves to the service of a goal even at such personal costs – especially cases in which it would be indecent of them to refuse. But surely there is not, or may not be, any such obligation in the cases we have been considering; noncombatants (even those on the wrong side) are not morally obligated to serve the right side by accepting the role of demoralizing civilian casualties, victims of dangerous diseases are not typically obligated to become guinea pigs for the sake of others, and I suppose it is at least open to question whether the fetus in CC, if it could grasp its predicament, would have to accept, for the sake of its mother, the sacrifice of its life.

In these cases, but not in their indirect counterparts, the victims are made to play a role in the service of the agent's goal that is not (or may not be) morally required of them. And this aspect of direct agency adds its own negative moral force – a force over and above that provided by the fact of harming or failing to prevent harm.[24] This additional force seems intuitively clearest in direct opportunistic agency, such as TB and GP, where unwilling victims are not only harmed but, in some sense, used. And this must be why the doctrine seems most plausible when it discriminates against opportunistic direct agency. It must also help explain why some of the most perverse forms of opportunistic agency, like torture, can seem absolutely unjustifiable.

It is less plausible, on the other hand, to think of the victims of direct eliminative agency as used. This may be why the doctrine seems to discriminate against eliminative agency less forcefully. And it may therefore help explain why some people feel that the direct agency of CC is not much harder to justify than the indirect agency of HC. But something of the questionable character of direct opportunistic agency also seems present in direct eliminative agency. Someone who gets in your way presents a strategic problem – a causal obstacle whose removal will be a service to your goals. And this is quite unlike what we find in harmful indirect agency, where victims can be obstacles only in a moral sense.

In discriminating to some extent against both forms of direct agency, the doctrine reflects a Kantian ideal of human community and interaction.[25] Each person is to be treated, so far as possible, as existing only for purposes that he can share. This ideal is given one natural expression in the language of rights. People have a strong prima facie right not to be sacrificed in strategic roles over which they have no say. They have a right not to be pressed, in apparent violation of their prior rights, into the service of other people's purposes. Sometimes these additional rights may be justifiably infringed, especially when the prior right is not terribly important and the harm is limited, but in all cases they add their own burden to the opposing moral argument.

The Doctrine of Double Effect thus gives each person some veto power over a certain kind of attempt to make the world a better place at his expense. This would be absurd if the entire point of morality were to maximize overall happiness or welfare. But that is not its entire point. An equally urgent basic task is to define the forms of respect that we owe to one another, and the resulting limits that we may not presume to exceed. The doctrine embodies our sense that certain forms of forced strategic subordination are especially inappropriate among free and equal agents.

Notes

1   Harm is meant in a very broad sense that includes the loss of life, rightful property, privacy, and so on. In my examples, the relevant harm will usually be the loss of life.

2   Warren S. Quinn, "Actions, Intentions, and Consequences: The Doctrine of Doing and Allowing," *Philosophical Review*, July 1989, pp. 287–312.

3   The doctrine, which is usually traced to Thomas Aquinas, *Summa Theologiae*, II-II, Q. 64, art. 7, is typically put as a set of necessary conditions on morally permissible agency in which a morally questionable bad upshot is foreseen: (a) the intended final end must be good, (b) the intended means to it must be morally acceptable, (c) the foreseen bad upshot must *not* itself be willed (that is, must not be, in some sense, intended), and (d) the good end must be proportionate to the bad upshot (that is, must be important enough to justify the bad upshot). The principle that follows in the text, which I henceforth treat as if it were itself the doctrine, is really what I find most important and plausible in its first three conditions. I ignore the fourth condition both because it is probably best understood in a way that makes it noncontroversial and because I am concerned here not so much with how choices with a "second effect" can be justified as with whether, *ceteris paribus*, the structure of intention makes a justificatory difference. That seems to me the fundamental question.

4 The principle is sometimes put in terms of the difference between a harmful *result* that is "directly" intended and one that is "indirectly" (or "obliquely") intended. But it also might be put in terms of the difference between a directly and an indirectly intended *act* of harming. In either variant, the point of calling the merely foreseen result or action "indirectly *intended*" is to mark a species of linguistic impropriety in an agent's asserting, with a completely straight face, that a clearly foreseen harm or harming is quite *un*intended. If I have no desire to wake you but simply do not care that my fiddling will have that effect, I cannot say that your waking or my waking you is purely unintentional. Whether there is any natural sense in which they are intentional is a debated point. In the final analysis, I shall sidestep this controversy, concerning myself with a species of intention that an agent clearly does not have toward a merely foreseen result of his agency – namely, the intention that the result occur, or that he bring it about, as a means of achieving his purpose.

5 See Herbert L. A. Hart, "Intention and Punishment," in *Punishment and Responsibility* (Oxford: Clarendon Press, 1968), p. 123. Hart finds the intentions in CC and HC to be parallel. But he does not argue, and does not seem to think, that a similar point can be made about most other cases that the doctrine might seem to distinguish. Nancy Davis finds more general problems along these lines in "The Doctrine of Double Effect: Problems of Interpretation," *Pacific Philosophical Quarterly* 65 (1984): 107–23.

6 If the miracle happened, and after its removal the fetus were quickly restored to its previous healthy condition, we would say that the craniotomy had done no real harm. In the actual case, the harm done to the fetus by the craniotomy consists in the *combination* of the desired immediate effect on it (which permits its removal) and the further natural effects that flow from that first effect. Since these further effects are not strictly intended, the objection holds that the harm itself is not strictly intended. See Jonathan Bennett, *Morality and Consequences*, The Tanner Lectures on Human Values II (Salt Lake City: University of Utah Press, 1981), pp. 110–11.

7 Ibid., p. 111.

8 Perhaps then it would not really be, at least in these people, a disease. But then it might be said that the doctors don't really need it to be a disease in *them*. It would be good enough if, due to their special powers of compensation, it is for them a harmless condition very much like a disease in others.

9 Philippa Foot perhaps suggests this kind of reply in "The Problem of Abortion and the Doctrine of the Double Effect," in *Virtues and Vices and Other Essays* (Berkeley and Los Angeles: University of California Press, 1978), pp. 21–2.

10 Hart, "Intention and Punishment," p. 120.

11 Of course this special operation could, however inappropriately, be performed on patients who were not pregnant. And this might lead someone to speculate that the doctrine speaks against a strictly intended and invariably

harmful kind of action or omission only if the harm is an empirically necessary consequence. But this cannot be right. Suppose there is some good that will arise immediately upon your being injected with a certain fatal poison. The good does not require that you actually die. But that is what will happen, since the very real and naturally abundant antidote that could save you has not been, and in fact never will be, discovered. In such a case, the doctrine should certainly speak against my poisoning you. But the directly and invariably connected harm would not follow of empirical necessity.

12 If the latter intention sometimes gets fulfilled, for example, by bombing electric power facilities built into remote and isolated dams.

13 G. E. M. Anscombe, *Intention*, 2nd ed. (Oxford: Blackwell, 1963), sec. 25, pp. 41–5.

14 See Quinn, "Actions, Intentions, and Consequences: The Doctrine of Doing and Allowing," pp. 293–4.

15 Not even, I would argue, the fact of their not receiving the treatment. What really furthers the goal is the treatment received by the other, more tractable cases. The nontreatment of the first group contributes, at most, in an odd and secondary sense. This point applies, I think, to a wide range of intentional expressions. Suppose we decide to combat a disease by spending our limited resources on education rather than on inoculation. Education, and not non-inoculation, will then be our *means* of combat; and the *way* we fight the disease will be by educating, not by not inoculating.

16 I might instead have said "agency in which harm comes to victims ... from the agent's deliberately producing some *effect on them* in order to further his purpose precisely by way of their being so affected." But there is a certain kind of ingenious case, attributed to David Lewis, that such a formulation might seem to miss. Suppose that another terror bomber wishes to demoralize enemy leaders by bombing a major center of population, and suppose he knows that these leaders will be convinced that the city is destroyed by seeing, from afar, the explosion of his bombs over it. The explosion occurs an instant before the fatal effects below. So in this case the bomber does not, strictly speaking, intend to blow up the civilians, or produce any *physical* effects on them, as a means to his end. Yet the case seems, morally speaking, to be like TB rather than SB. But notice that while such a strategy does not aim at *physically* affecting its victims, it does strictly aim at exploding bombs in their vicinity. Whether or not this change in their situation could be counted as an effect on them, as I think it could, the bomber strictly intends to involve them in something (to make his bombs explode over them) in order to further his purpose precisely by way of their being involved.

17 This way of drawing the distinction excludes a pair of cases sometimes used to illustrate double effect: in one we give powerful analgesics to lessen the terrible pain of a dying patient, where we foresee that he will die as a side effect. In the other we relieve his suffering by intentionally killing him with the same or other drugs. In both cases we are to suppose that life is no longer

a good and that we act with his explicit or correctly presumed consent. So we cannot see ourselves as infringing, justifiably or unjustifiably, any of his moral rights. For this reason I see these cases as really quite different from the others, in which there is conflict between the moral claims of different people. Indeed, I think that the doctrine is misapplied in nonconflict cases. I see, for example, no difference between amputating someone's leg to save him and proceeding with some life-saving treatment that, as a side effect, results in the loss of the limb. And by parity of reasoning it seems to me that if stopping pain is urgent enough from the patient's perspective to make death acceptable as a side effect, it ought to make death acceptable as a means.

18 A terminological point: Something counts as "harmful direct agency" only insofar as harm comes to the very people who are deliberately affected by the agency. Insofar as harm comes to others, the agency also counts as "indirectly harmful". A single act or omission can thus be both directly and indirectly harmful.

19 Nor, of course, does it require that the agent have *particular* victims in mind. It is enough, as in the case of a terrorist's car bomb, that he intends something for someone or other.

20 Positive rights are rights to aid while negative rights are rights to noninterference. While borrowed originally from the law, these terms are here used in a moral sense.

21 See Bennett, *Morality and Consequences*, pp. 102–3.

22 Samuel Scheffler makes a similar point in *The Rejection of Consequentialism* (Oxford: Clarendon Press, 1982), p. 109.

23 I am deliberately not considering cases where the sacrifice is financial. What to think in such cases partly depends on the sorts of moral rights people really have to keep money or property that is legally or conventionally theirs when others have more pressing material needs. It is quite consistent with everything I say here to deny that the doctrine speaks against liberal schemes of redistributing wealth.

24 Although it is, as we have seen, a kind of negative moral force that is activated only when other rights are present.

25 But there is a way in which the rationale I have provided is not Kantian. For it draws a sharp moral line between adversely affecting someone in the pursuit of an end that he does not share (not treating him as an end in itself) and adversely affecting someone because his being so affected is strategically important to achieving an end that he does not share (very roughly, treating him as a means). Neither the terror nor the strategic bomber treats his victims as ends in themselves, but only the former treats them as something like means. And I have argued that this difference is significant – that morality erects an extra barrier against the strategic posture of harmful direct agency. Kant might disagree, focused as he is on the alleged status of people as ends in themselves. But I have difficulty attaching any sense to that idea except via intuitions that certain forms of treatment are unacceptably disrespectful of

rational beings. And the intuition that it is more disrespectful, all other things being equal, to treat someone as if he existed for purposes he does not share than simply not to be constrained by his purposes, seems to me plausible enough to be worth incorporating in a proper idea of what it means for persons to be ends in themselves. On this conception, one aspect of being an end in itself would be to have, *ceteris paribus*, a stronger right against directly harmful agency than against indirectly harmful agency.

The Right to Lie: Kant on Dealing with Evil

Christine M. Korsgaard

One of the great difficulties with Kant's moral philosophy is that it seems to imply that our moral obligations leave us powerless in the face of evil. Kant's theory sets a high ideal of conduct and tells us to live up to that ideal regardless of what other persons are doing. The results may be very bad. But Kant says that the law "remains in full force, because it commands categorically" (G, 438–39/57).[1] The most well-known example of this "rigorism," as it is sometimes called, concerns Kant's views on our duty to tell the truth.

In two passages in his ethical writings, Kant seems to endorse the following pair of claims about this duty: first, one must never under any circumstances or for any purpose tell a lie; second, if one does tell a lie one is responsible for all the consequences that ensue, even if they were completely unforeseeable.

One of the two passages appears in the *Metaphysical Principles of Virtue*. There Kant classifies lying as a violation of a perfect duty to oneself. In one of the casuistical questions, a servant, under instructions, tells a visitor the lie that his master is not at home. His master, meanwhile, sneaks off and commits a crime, which would have been prevented by the watchman sent to arrest him. Kant says:

> Upon whom . . . does the blame fall? To be sure, also upon the servant, who here violated a duty to himself by lying, the consequence of which will now be imputed to him by his own conscience. (*MMV*, 431/93)

Christine M. Korsgaard, "The Right to Lie: Kant on Dealing with Evil," *Philosophy and Public Affairs* 15 (1986): 325–49.

The other passage is the infamous one about the murderer at the door from the essay, "On A Supposed Right to Lie From Altruistic Motives." Here Kant's claims are more extreme, for he says that the liar may be held legally as well as ethically responsible for the consequences, and the series of coincidences he imagines is even more fantastic:

> After you have honestly answered the murderer's question as to whether his intended victim is at home, it may be that he has slipped out so that he does not come in the way of the murderer, and thus that the murder may not be committed. But if you had lied and said he was not at home when he had really gone out without your knowing it, and if the murderer had then met him as he went away and murdered him, you might justly be accused as the cause of his death. For if you had told the truth as far as you knew it, perhaps the murderer might have been apprehended by the neighbors while he searched the house and thus the deed might have been prevented. (*SRL*, 427/348)

Kant's readers differ about whether Kant's moral philosophy commits him to the claims he makes in these passages. Unsympathetic readers are inclined to take them as evidence of the horrifying conclusions to which Kant was led by his notion that the necessity in duty is rational necessity – as if Kant were clinging to a logical point in the teeth of moral decency. Such readers take these conclusions as a defeat for Kant's ethics, or for ethical rationalism generally; or they take Kant to have confused principles which are merely general in their application and *prima facie* in their truth with absolute and universal laws. Sympathetic readers are likely to argue that Kant here mistook the implications of his own theory, and to try to show that, by careful construction and accurate testing of the maxim on which this liar acts, Kant's conclusions can be blocked by his own procedures.

Sympathetic and unsympathetic readers alike have focused their attention on the implications of the first formulation of the categorical imperative, the Formula of Universal Law. The *Foundations of the Metaphysics of Morals* contains two other sets of terms in which the categorical imperative is formulated: the treatment of humanity as an end in itself, and autonomy, or legislative membership in a Kingdom of Ends. My treatment of the issue falls into three parts. First, I want to argue that Kant's defenders are right in thinking that, when the case is treated under the Formula of Universal Law, this particular lie can be shown to be permissible. Second, I want to argue that when the case is treated from the perspective provided by the Formulas of Humanity and the Kingdom of Ends, it becomes clear why Kant *is* committed to the view that lying is wrong in every case. But from this perspective we see that Kant's rigorism about lying is not the result of a misplaced love of consistency or legalistic thinking. Instead, it comes from an attractive ideal of human relations which is the basis of his ethical system. If Kant is wrong in his conclusion about lying to the murderer at the door, it is for the interesting and important reason that morality itself sometimes allows or even requires us to do something that from an ideal perspective is wrong. The case does not impugn Kant's ethics as an *ideal* system. Instead, it shows that we need special principles for dealing with evil. My third aim is to discuss the structure that an ethical system must have in order to accommodate such special principles.

Universal Law

The Formula of Universal Law tells us never to act on a maxim that we could not at the same time will to be a universal law. A maxim which cannot even be conceived as a universal law without contradiction is in violation of a strict and perfect duty, one which assigns us a particular action or omission. A maxim which cannot be willed as universal law without contradicting the will is in violation of a broad and imperfect duty, one which assigns us an end, but does not tell us what or how much we should do toward it. Maxims of lying are violations of perfect duty, and so are supposed to be the kind that cannot be conceived without contradiction when universalized.

The sense in which the universalization of an immoral maxim is supposed to "contradict" itself is a matter of controversy. On my reading, which I will not defend here, the contradiction in question is a "practical" one: the universalized maxim contradicts itself when the efficacy of the action as a method of achieving its purpose would be undermined by its universal practice.[2] So, to use Kant's example, the point against false promising as a method of getting ready cash is that if everyone attempted to use false promising as a method of getting ready cash, false promising would no longer *work* as a method of getting ready cash, since, as Kant says, "no one would believe what was promised to him but would only laugh at any such assertion as vain pretense" (*G*, 422/40).

Thus the test question will be: could this action be the universal method of achieving this purpose? Now when we consider lying in general, it looks as if it could not be the universal method of doing anything. For lies are usually efficacious in achieving their purposes because they deceive, but if they were universally practiced they would not deceive. We believe what is said to us in a given context because most of the time people in that context say what they really think or intend. In contexts in which people usually say false things – for example, when telling stories that are jokes – we are not deceived. If a story that is a joke and is false counts as a lie, we can say that a lie in this case in not wrong, because the universal practice of lying in the context of jokes does not interfere with the *purpose* of jokes, which is to amuse and does not depend on deception. But in most cases lying falls squarely into the category of the sort of action Kant considers wrong: actions whose efficacy depends upon the fact that most people do not engage in them, and which therefore can only be performed by someone who makes an exception of himself (*G*, 424/42).

When we try to apply this test to the case of the murderer at the door, however, we run into a difficulty. The difficulty derives from the fact that there is probably already deception in the case. If murderers standardly came to the door and said: "I wish to murder your friend – is he here in your house?" then perhaps the universal practice of lying in order to keep a murderer from his victim would not work. If everyone lied in these circumstances the murderer would be aware of that fact and would not be deceived by your answer. But the murderer is not likely to do this, or, in any event, this is not how I shall imagine the case. A murderer who expects to conduct his business by asking questions must suppose that you do not know who he is and what he has in mind.[3] If these are the circumstances, and we try to ascertain whether there could be a universal practice of lying in these circumstances, the answer appears to be yes. The lie will be efficacious even if universally practiced. But the reason it will be efficacious is rather odd: it is because the murderer supposes you do not know what circumstances you are in – that is, that you do not know you are addressing a murderer – and so does not conclude from the fact that people in those circumstances always lie that *you* will lie.

The same point can be made readily using Kant's publicity criterion (*PP*, 381–3/129–31). Can we announce in advance our intention of lying to murderers without, as Kant says, vitiating our own purposes by publishing our maxims? (*PP*, 383/131). Again the answer is yes. It does not matter if you say publicly that you will lie in such a situation, for the murderer supposes that you do not know you are in that situation.[4]

These reflections might lead us to believe, then, that Kant was wrong in thinking that it is never all right to lie. It is permissible to lie to deceivers in order to counteract the intended results of their deceptions, for the maxim of lying to a deceiver is universalizable. The deceiver has, so to speak, placed himself in a morally unprotected position by his own deception. He has created a situation which universalization cannot reach.

Humanity

When we apply the Formula of Humanity, however, the argument against lying that results applies to any lie whatever. The formula runs:

> Act so that you treat humanity, whether in your own person or in that of another, always as an end and never as a means only. (*G*, 429/47)

In order to use this formula for casuistical purposes, we need to specify what counts as treating humanity as an end. "Humanity" is used by Kant specifically to refer to the capacity to determine ends through rational choice (*G*, 437/56; *MMV*, 392/50). Imperfect duties arise from the obligation to make the exercise, preservation, and development of this capacity itself an end. The perfect duties – that is, the duties of justice, and, in the realm of ethics, the duties of respect – arise from the obligation to make each human being's capacity for autonomous choice the condition of the value of every other end.

In his treatment of the lying promise case under the Formula of Humanity, Kant makes the following comments:

> For he whom I want to use for my own purposes by means of such a promise cannot possibly assent to my mode of acting against him and cannot contain the end of this action in himself. . . . he who transgresses the rights of men intends to make use of the persons of others merely as means, without considering that as rational beings, they must always be esteemed at the same time as ends, i.e., only as beings who must be able to contain in themselves the end of the very same action. (*G*, 429–30/48)

In these passages, Kant uses two expressions that are the key to understanding the derivation of perfect duties to others from the Formula of Humanity. One is that the other person "cannot possibly assent to my mode of acting toward him" and the second is that the other person cannot "contain the end of this action in himself." These phrases provide us with a test for perfect duties to others: an action is contrary to perfect duty if it is not possible for the other to assent to it or to hold its end.

It is important to see that these phrases do not mean simply that the other person *does not* or *would not* assent to the transaction or that she does not happen to have the same end I do, but strictly that she *cannot* do so: that something makes it impossible. If what we cannot assent to means merely what we are likely to be annoyed by, the test will be subjective and the claim that the person does not assent to being used as a means will sometimes be false. The object you steal from me may be the gift I intended for you, and we may both have been motivated by the desire that you should have it. And I may care about you too much or too little to be annoyed by the theft. For all that, this must be a clear case of your using me as a mere means.[5]

So it must not be merely that your victim will not like the way you propose to act, that this is psychologically unlikely, but that something makes it impossible for her to assent to it. Similarly, it must be argued that something makes it impossible for her to hold the end of the very same action. Kant never spells out why it is impossible, but it is not difficult to see what he has in mind.

People cannot *assent* to a way of acting when they are given no chance to do so. The most obvious instance of this is when coercion is used. But it is also true of deception: the victim of the false promise cannot assent to it because he doesn't know it is what he is being offered. But even when the victim of such conduct does happen to know what is going on, there is a sense in which he cannot assent to it. Suppose, for example, that you come to me and ask to borrow some money, falsely promising to pay it back next week, and suppose that by some chance I know perfectly well that your promise is a lie. Suppose also that I have the same end you do, in the sense that I want you to have the money, so that I turn the money over to you anyway. Now here I have the same end that you do, and I tolerate your attempts to deceive me to the extent that they do not prevent my giving you the money. Even in this case I cannot really assent to the transaction *you* propose. We can imagine the case in a number of different ways. If I call your bluff openly and say "never mind that nonsense, just take this money" then what I am doing is not accepting a false promise, but giving you a handout, and scorning your promise. The nature of the transaction is changed: now it is not a promise but a handout. If I don't call you on it, but keep my own counsel, it is still the same. I am not accepting a false promise. In this case what I am doing is *pretending* to accept your false promise. But there is all the difference in the world between actually doing something and pretending to do it. In neither of these cases can I be described as accepting a false promise, for in both cases I fix it so that it is something else that is happening. My knowledge of what is going on makes it *impossible* for me to accept the deceitful promise in the ordinary way.

The question whether another can assent to your way of acting can serve as a criterion for judging whether you are treating her as a mere means. We will say that knowledge of what is going on and some power over the proceedings are the conditions of possible assent; without these,

the concept of assent does not apply. This gives us another way to formulate the test for treating someone as a mere means: suppose it is the
case that if the other person knows what you are trying to do and has the
power to stop you, then what you are trying to do cannot be what is really
happening. If this is the case, the action is one that by its very nature is
impossible for the other to assent to. You cannot wrest from me what I
freely give to you; and if I have the power to stop you from wresting something from me and do not use it, I am in a sense freely giving it to
you. This is of course not intended as a legal point: the point is that any
action which depends for its nature and efficacy on the other's ignorance
or powerlessness fails this test. Lying clearly falls into this category of
action: it only deceives when the other does not know that it is a lie.[6]

A similar analysis can be given of the possibility of holding the end
of the very same action. In cases of violation of perfect duty, lying
included, the other person is unable to hold the end of the very same
action because the way that you act prevents her from *choosing* whether
to contribute to the realization of that end or not. Again, this is obviously
true when someone is forced to contribute to an end, but it is also true in
cases of deception. If you give a lying promise to get some money, the
other person is invited to think that the end she is contributing to is your
temporary possession of the money: in fact, it is your permanent possession of it. It doesn't matter whether that would be all right with her if she
knew about it. What matters is that she never gets a chance to choose the
end, not knowing that it is to be the consequence of her action.[7]

According to the Formula of Humanity, coercion and deception are the
most fundamental forms of wrongdoing to others – the roots of all evil.
Coercion and deception violate the conditions of possible assent, and all
actions which depend for their nature and efficacy on their coercive or
deceptive character are ones that others cannot assent to. Coercion and
deception also make it impossible for others to choose to contribute to our
ends. This in turn makes it impossible, according to Kant's value theory,
for the ends of such actions to be good. For on Kant's view "what we call
good must be, in the judgment of every reasonable man, an object of the
faculty of desire" (C2, 60/62–3). If your end is one that others cannot
choose – not because of what they want, but because they are not in a
position to choose – it cannot, as the end of that action, be good. This
means that in any cooperative project – whenever you need the decisions
and actions of others in order to bring about your end – everyone who is
to contribute must be in a position to *choose* to contribute to the end.

The sense in which a good end is an object for everyone is that a good
end is in effect one that everyone, in principle, and especially everyone

who contributes to it, gets to cast a vote on. This voting, or legislation, is the prerogative of rational beings; and the ideal of a world in which this prerogative is realized is the Kingdom of Ends.

The Kingdom of Ends

The Kingdom of Ends is represented by the kingdom of nature; we determine moral laws by considering their viability as natural laws. On Kant's view, the will is a kind of causality (*G*, 446/64). A person, an end in itself, is a free cause, which is to say a first cause. By contrast, a thing, a means, is a merely mediate cause, a link in the chain. A first cause is, obviously, the initiator of a causal chain, hence a real determiner of what will happen. The idea of deciding for yourself whether you will contribute to a given end can be represented as a decision whether to initiate that causal chain which constitutes your contribution. Any action which prevents or diverts you from making this initiating decision is one that treats you as a mediate rather than a first cause; hence as a mere means, a thing, a tool. Coercion and deception both do this. And deception treats you as a mediate cause in a specific way: it treats your reason as a mediate cause. The false promiser thinks: if I tell her I will pay her back next week, then she will choose to give me the money. Your reason is worked, like a machine: the deceiver tries to determine what levers to pull to get the desired results from you. Physical coercion treats someone's person as a tool; lying treats someone's *reason* as a tool. This is why Kant finds it so horrifying; it is a direct violation of autonomy.

We may say that a tool has two essential characteristics: it is there to be used, and it does not control itself – its nature is to be directed by something else. To treat someone as a mere means is to treat her as if these things were true of her. Kant's treatment of our duties to others in the *Metaphysical Principles of Virtue* is sensitive to *both* characteristics. We are not only forbidden to use another as a mere means to our private purposes. We are also forbidden to take attitudes toward her which involve regarding her as not in control of herself, which is to say, as not using her reason.

This latter is the basis of the duties of respect. Respect is violated by the vices of calumny and mockery (*MMV*, 466–8/131–3): we owe to others not only a practical generosity toward their plans and projects – a duty of aid – but also a generosity of attitude toward their thoughts and motives. To treat another with respect is to treat him as if he were using his reason and as far as possible as if he were using it well. Even in a case where someone evidently *is* wrong or mistaken, we ought to suppose he must have what he takes to be good reasons for what he believes or what he does. This is not because, as a matter of fact, he probably does have good reasons. Rather, this attitude is something that we *owe* to him, something that is his right. And he cannot forfeit it. Kant is explicit about this:

> Hereupon is founded a duty to respect man even in the logical use of his reason: not to censure someone's errors under the name of absurdity, inept judgment, and the like, but rather to suppose that in such an inept judgment there must be something true, and to seek it out. . . . Thus it is also with the reproach of vice, which must never burst out in complete contempt or deny the wrongdoer all moral worth, because on that hypothesis he could never be improved either – and this latter is incompatible with the idea of man, who as such (as a moral being) can never lose all predisposition to good. (*MMV*, 463–4/128–9)

To treat others as ends in themselves is always to address and deal with them as rational beings. Every rational being gets to reason out, for herself, what she is to think, choose, or do. So if you need someone's contribution to your end, you must put the facts before her and ask for her contribution. If you think she is doing something wrong, you may try to convince her by argument but you may not resort to tricks or force. The Kingdom of Ends is a democratic ideal, and poor judgment does not disqualify anyone for citizenship. In the *Critique of Pure Reason*, Kant says:

> Reason depends on this freedom for its very existence. For reason has no dictatorial authority; its verdict is always simply the agreement of free citizens, of whom each one must be permitted to express, without let or hindrance, his objections or even his veto.[8]

This means that there cannot be a good reason for taking a decision out of someone else's hands. It is a rational being's prerogative, as a first cause, to have a share in determining the destiny of things.

This shows us in another way why lying is for Kant a paradigm case of treating someone as a mere means. Any attempt to control the actions and reactions of another by any means except an appeal to reason treats her as a mere means, because it attempts to reduce her to a mediate cause. This includes much more than the utterance of falsehoods. In the *Lectures on Ethics*, Kant says "whatever militates against frankness lowers the dignity of man" (*LE*, 231).[9] It is an everyday temptation, even (or perhaps especially) in our dealings with those close to us, to withhold something, or to tidy up an anecdote, or to embellish a story, or even just to place a certain emphasis, in order to be sure of getting the reaction we want.[10] Kant holds the Socratic view that any sort of persuasion that is aimed at distracting its listener's attention from either the reasons that she ought to use or the reasons the speaker thinks she will use is wrong.[11]

In light of this account it is possible to explain why Kant says what he does about the liar's responsibility. In a Kantian theory our responsibility has definite boundaries: each person as a first cause exerts some influence on what happens, and it is your part that is up to you. If you make a straightforward appeal to the reason of another person, your responsibility ends there and the other's responsibility begins. But the liar tries to take the consequences out of the hands of others; he, and not they, will determine what form their contribution to destiny will take. By refusing to share with others the determination of events, the liar takes the world into his own hands, and makes the events his own. The results, good or bad, are imputable to him, at least in his own conscience. It does not follow from *this*, of course, that this is a risk one will never want to take.

Humanity and Universal Law

If the foregoing casuistical analyses are correct, then applying the Formula of Universal Law and the Formula of Humanity lead to different answers in the case of lying to the murderer at the door. The former seems to say that this lie is permissible, but the latter says that coercion and deception are the most fundamental forms of wrongdoing. In a Kingdom of Ends coercive and deceptive methods can never be used.

This result impugns Kant's belief that the formulas are equivalent. But it is not necessary to conclude that the formulas flatly say different things, and are unrelated except for a wide range of coincidence in their results. For one thing, lying to the murderer at the door was not shown to be permissible in a straightforward manner: the maxim did not so much pass as evade universalization. For another, the two formulas can be shown to be expressions of the same basic theory of justification. Suppose that your maxim is in violation of the Formula of Universal Law. You are making an exception of yourself, doing something that everyone in your circumstances could not do. What this means is that you are treating the reason *you* have for the action as if it were stronger, had more justifying force, than anyone else's exactly similar reason. You are then acting as if the fact that it was in particular *your* reason, and not just the reason of a human being, gave it special weight and force. This is an obvious violation of the idea that it is your humanity – your power of rational choice – which is the condition of all value and which therefore gives your needs and desires the justifying force of *reasons*. Thus, any violation of the Formula of Universal Law is also a violation of the Formula of Humanity. This argument, of course, only goes in one direction: it does not show that the two formulas are equivalent. The Formula of Humanity is stricter than the Formula of Universal Law – but both are expressions of the same basic theory of value: that your rational nature is the source of justifying power of your reasons, and so of the goodness of your ends.

And although the Formula of Humanity gives us reason to think that all lies are wrong, we can still give an account in the terms it provides of what vindicates lying to a liar. The liar tries to use your reason as a means – your honesty as a tool. You do not have to passively submit to being used as a means. In the *Lectures on Ethics*, this is the line that Kant takes. He says:

> If we were to be at all times punctiliously truthful we might often become victims of the wickedness of others who were ready to abuse our truthfulness. If all men were well-intentioned it would not only be a duty not to lie, but no one would do so because there would be no point in it. But as men are malicious, it cannot be denied that to be punctiliously truthful is often dangerous . . . if I cannot save myself by maintaining silence, then my lie is a weapon of defence. (*LE*, 228)

The common thought that lying to a liar is a form of self-defense, that you can resist lies with lies as you can resist force with force, is according to this analysis correct.[12] This should not be surprising, for we have seen that deception and coercion are parallel. Lying and the use of force are attempts to undercut the two conditions of possible assent to actions and of autonomous choice of ends, namely, knowledge and power. So, although the Formula of Universal Law and the Formula of Humanity give us different results, this does not show that they simply express different moral outlooks. The relation between them is more complex than that.

Two Casuistical Problems

Before I discuss this relation, however, I must take up two casuistical problems arising from the view I have presented so far. First, I have argued that we *may* lie to the murderer at the door. But most people think something stronger: that we ought to lie to the murderer – that we will have done something wrong if we do not. Second, I have argued that it is permissible to lie to a deceiver in order to counter the deception. But what if someone lies to you for a good end, and, as it happens, you know about it? The fact that the murderer's *end* is evil has played no direct role in the arguments I have given so far. We have a right to resist liars and those who try to use force because of their methods, not because of their purposes. In one respect this is a virtue of my argument. It does not license us to lie to or use violence against persons *just* because we think their purposes are bad. But it looks as if it may license us to lie to liars whose purposes are good. Here is a case: suppose someone comes to your door and pretends to be taking a survey of some sort.[13] In fact, this person is a philanthropist who wants to give his money to people who meet certain criteria, and this is his way of discovering appropriate objects for his beneficence. As it happens, you know what is up. By lying, you could get some money, although you do not in fact meet his criteria. The argument that I derived from the Formula of Universal Law about lying to the murderer applies here. Universalizing the lie to the philanthropist will not destroy its efficacy. Even if it is a universal law that everyone will lie in these circumstances, the philanthropist thinks you do not know you are in these circumstances. By my argument, it is permissible to lie in this case. The philanthropist, like the murderer, has placed himself in a morally unprotected position by his own deception.

Start with the first casuistical problem. There are two reasons to lie to the murderer at the door. First, we have a duty of mutual aid. This is an imperfect duty of virtue, since the law does not say exactly what or how much we must do along these lines. This duty gives us *a* reason to tell the lie. Whether it makes the lie imperative depends on how one understands the duty of mutual aid, on how one understands the "wideness" of imperfect duties.[14] It may be that on such an urgent occasion, the lie is imperative. Notice that if the lie were impermissible, this duty would have no force. Imperfect duties are always secondary to perfect ones. But if the lie is permissible, this duty will provide a reason, whether or not an imperative one, to tell the lie.

The second reason is one of self-respect. The murderer wants to make you a tool of evil; he regards your integrity as a useful sort of predictability. He is trying to use you, and your good will, as a means to an evil end. You owe it to humanity in your own person not to allow your honesty to be used as a resource for evil. I think this would be a perfect duty of virtue; Kant does not say this specifically, but in his discussion of servility (the avoidance of which is a perfect duty of virtue) he says "Do not suffer your rights to be trampled underfoot by others with impunity" (*MMV*, 436/99).

Both of these reasons spring from duties of virtue. A person with a good character will tell the lie. Not to tell it is morally bad. But there is no duty of justice to tell the lie. If we do not tell it, we cannot be punished, or, say, treated as an accessory to the murder. Kant would insist that even if the lie ought to be told this does not mean that the punctiliously truthful person who does not tell it is somehow implicated in the murder. It is the murderer, not the truthful person, who commits this crime. Telling the truth cannot be part of the crime. On Kant's view, persons are not supposed to be responsible for managing each other's conduct. If the lie were a duty of justice, we would be responsible for that.

These reflections will help us to think about the second casuistical problem, the lie to the philanthropist. I think it does follow from the line of argument I have taken that the lie cannot be shown to be impermissible. Although the philanthropist can hardly be called evil, he is doing something tricky and underhanded, which on Kant's view is wrong. He should not use this method of getting the information he wants. This is especially true if the reason he does not use a more straightforward method is that he assumes that if he does, people will lie to him. We are not supposed to base our actions on the assumption that other people will behave badly. Assuming this does not occur in an institutional context, and you have not sworn that your remarks were true, the philanthropist will have no recourse to justice if you lie to him.[15] But the reasons that favor telling the lie that exist in the first case do not exist here. According to Kant, you do not have a duty to promote your own happiness. Nor would anyone perform such an action out of self-respect. This is, in a very trivial way, a case of dealing with evil. But you can best deal with it by telling the philanthropist that you know what he is up to, perhaps even that you find it sneaky. This is *because* the ideal that makes his action a bad one is an ideal of straightforwardness in human relations. This would also be the best way to deal with the murderer, if it *were* a way to deal with a murderer. But of course it is not.

Ideal and Nonideal Theory

I now turn to the question of what structure an ethical theory must have in order to accommodate this way of thinking. In *A Theory of Justice*, John Rawls proposes a division of moral philosophy into ideal and nonideal theory.[16] In that work, the task of ideal theory is to determine "what a perfectly just society would be like," while nonideal theory deals with punishment, war, opposition to unjust regimes, and compensatory justice (Sec. 2, pp. 8–9). Since I wish to use this feature of Rawls's theory for a model, I am going to sketch his strategy for what I will call a double-level theory.

Rawls identifies two conceptions of justice, which he calls the general conception and the special conception (Secs. 11, 26, 39, 46). The general conception tells us that all goods distributed by society, including liberty and opportunity, are to be distributed equally unless an unequal distribution is to the advantage of everyone, and especially those who fall on the low side of the inequality (Sec. 13). Injustice, according to the general conception, occurs whenever there are inequalities that are not to the benefit of everyone (Sec. 11, p. 62). The special conception in its most developed form removes liberty and opportunity from the scope of this principle and says they must be distributed equally, forbidding tradeoffs of these goods for economic gains. It also introduces a number of priority rules, for example, the priority of liberty over all other considerations, and the priority of equal opportunity over economic considerations (Secs. 11, 46, 82).

Ideal theory is worked out under certain assumptions. One is strict compliance: it is assumed that everyone will act justly. The other, a little harder to specify, is that historical, economic, and natural conditions are such that realization of the ideal is feasible. Our conduct toward those who do not comply, or in circumstances which make the immediate realization of a just state of affairs impossible, is governed by the principles of nonideal theory. Certain ongoing natural conditions which may always prevent the full realization of the ideal state of affairs also belong to nonideal theory: the problems of dealing with the seriously ill or mentally disturbed, for instance, belong in this category. For purposes of constructing ideal theory, we assume that everyone is "rational and able to manage their own affairs" (Sec. 39, p. 248). We also assume in ideal theory that there are no massive historic injustices, such as the oppression of blacks and women, to be corrected. The point is to work out our ideal view of justice on the assumption that people, nature, and history will behave themselves so that the ideal can be realized, and then to determine – in light of that ideal – what is to be done in actual circumstances when they do not. The special conception is not applied without regard to circumstances. Special principles will be used in nonideal conditions.

Nonideal conditions exist when, or to the extent that, the special conception of justice cannot be realized effectively. In these circumstances our conduct is to be determined in the following way: the special conception becomes a goal, rather than an ideal to live up to; we are to work toward the conditions in which it is feasible. For instance, suppose there is a case like this: widespread poverty or ignorance due to the level of economic development is such that the legal establishment of equal liberties makes no real difference to the lot of the disadvantaged members of society. It is an empty formality. On the other hand, some inequality, temporarily instituted, would actually tend to foster conditions in which equal liberty could become a reality for everyone. In these circumstances, Rawls's double-level theory allows for the temporary inequality (Secs. 11, 39). The priority rules give us guidance as to which features of the special conception are most urgent. These are the ones that we should be striving to achieve as soon as possible. For example, if formal equal opportunity for blacks and women is ineffective, affirmative action measures may be in order. If some people claim that this causes inefficiency at first, it is neither here nor there, since equality of opportunity has priority over efficiency. The special conception may also tell us which of our nonideal options is least bad, closest to ideal conduct. For instance, civil disobedience is better than resorting to violence not only because violence is bad in itself, but because of the way in which civil disobedience expresses the democratic principles of the just society it aspires to bring about (Sec. 59). Finally, the general conception of justice commands categorically. In sufficiently bad circumstances none of the characteristic features of the special conception may be realizable. But there is no excuse *ever* for violation of the general conception. If inequalities are not benefiting those on the lower end of them in some way, they are simply oppression. The general conception, then, represents the point at which justice becomes uncompromising.[17]

A double-level theory can be contrasted to two types of single-level theory, both of which in a sense fail to distinguish the way we should behave in ideal and nonideal conditions, but which are at opposite extremes. A consequentialist theory such as utilitarianism does not really distinguish ideal from nonideal conditions. Of course, the utilitarian can see the difference between a state of affairs in which everyone can be made reasonably happy and a state of affairs in which the utilitarian choice must be for the "lesser of evils," but it is still really a matter of degree. In principle we do not know what counts as a state in which everyone is "as happy as possible" absolutely. Instead, the utilitarian wants to make everyone as happy as possible relative to the circumstances, and pursues this goal regardless of how friendly the circumstances are to human happiness. The difference is not between ideal and nonideal states of affairs but simply between better and worse states of affairs.

Kant's theory as he understood it represents the other extreme of single-level theory. The standard of conduct he sets for us is designed for an ideal state of affairs: we are always to act as if we were living in a Kingdom of Ends, regardless of possible disastrous results. Kant is by no means dismissive toward the distressing problems caused by the evil conduct of other human beings and the unfriendliness of nature to human ideals, but his solution to these problems is different. He finds in them grounds for a morally motivated religious faith in God.[18] Our rational motive for belief in a moral author of the world derives from our rational need for grounds for hope that these problems will be resolved. Such an author would have designed the laws of nature so that, in ways that are not apparent to us, our moral actions and efforts do tend to further the realization of an actual Kingdom of Ends. With faith in God, we can trust that a Kingdom of Ends will be the consequence of our actions as well as the ideal that guides them.

In his *Critique of Utilitarianism*, Bernard Williams spells out some of the unfortunate consequences of what I am calling single-level theories.[19] According to Williams, the consequentialist's commitment to doing whatever is necessary to secure the best outcome may lead to violations of what we would ordinarily think of as integrity. There is no kind of action that is so mean or so savage that it can *never* lead to a better outcome than the alternatives. A commitment to always securing the best outcome never allows you to say "bad consequences or not, this is not the sort of thing I do; I am not that sort of person." And no matter how mean or how savage the act required to secure the best outcome is, the utilitarian thinks that you will be irrational to regret that you did it, for you will have done what is in the straightforward sense the right thing.[20] A Kantian approach, by defining a determinate *ideal* of conduct to live up to rather than setting a *goal* of action to strive for, solves the problem about integrity, but with a high price. The advantage of the Kantian approach is the definite sphere of responsibility. Your share of the responsibility for the way the world is is well-defined and limited, and if you act as you ought, bad outcomes are not your responsibility. The trouble is that in cases such as that of the murderer at the door it seems grotesque simply to say that I have done my part by telling the truth and the bad results are not my responsibility.

The point of a double-level theory is to give us both a definite and well-defined sphere of responsibility for everyday life and some guidance, at least, about when we may or must take the responsibility of violating ideal standards. The common-sense approach to this problem uses an intuitive quantitative measure: we depart from our ordinary rules and standards of conduct when the consequences of following them would be "very bad." This is unhelpful for two reasons. First; it leaves us on our own about determining *how* bad. Second, the attempt to justify it leads down a familiar consequentialist slippery slope: if very bad consequences justify a departure from ordinary norms, why do not slightly bad consequences justify such a departure? A double-level theory substitutes something better than this rough quantitative measure. In Rawls's theory, for example, a departure from equal liberty cannot be justified by the fact that the consequences of liberty are "very bad" in terms of mere efficiency. This does not mean that an endless amount of inefficiency will be tolerated, because presumably at some point the inefficiency may interfere with the effectiveness of liberty. One might put the point this way: the measure of "very bad" is not entirely intuitive but rather, bad enough to interfere with the reality of liberty. Of course this is not an algorithmic criterion and cannot be applied without judgment, but it is not as inexact as a wholly intuitive quantitative measure, and, importantly, does not lead to a consequentialist slippery slope.

Another advantage of a double-level theory is the explanation it offers of the other phenomenon Williams is concerned about: that of regret for doing a certain kind of action even if in the circumstances it was the "right" thing. A double-level theory offers an account of at least some of the occasions for this kind of regret. We will regret having to depart from the ideal standard of conduct, for we identify with this standard and think of our autonomy in terms of it. Regret for an action we would not do under ideal circumstances seems appropriate even if we have done what is clearly the right thing.[21]

Kantian Nonideal Theory

Rawls's special conception of justice is a stricter version of the egalitarian idea embodied in his general conception. In the same way, it can be argued that the Formula of Universal Law and the Formula of Humanity are expressions of the same idea – that humanity is the source of value, and of the justifying force of reason. But the Formula of Humanity is stricter, and gives implausible answers when we are dealing with the misconduct of others and the recalcitrance of nature. This comparison gives rise to the idea of using the two formulas and the relation between them to construct a Kantian double-level theory of individual morality, with the advantages of that sort of account. The Formulas of Humanity and the Kingdom of Ends will provide the ideal which governs our daily conduct. When dealing with evil circumstances we may depart from this ideal. In such cases, we can say that the Formula of Humanity is inapplicable because it is not designed for use when dealing with evil. But it can still guide our conduct. It defines the goal toward which we are working, and if we can generate priority rules we will know which features of it are most important. It gives us guidance about which of the measures we may take is the least objectionable.

Lying to deceivers is not the only case in which the Formula of Humanity seems to set a more ideal standard than the Formula of Universal Law. The arguments made about lying can all be made about the use of coercion to deal with evildoers. Another very difficult case in which the two formulas give different results, as I think, is suicide. Kant gives an argument against suicide under the Formula of Universal Law, but that argument does not work.[22] Yet under the Formula of Humanity we can give a clear and compelling argument against suicide: nothing is of any value unless the human person is so, and it is a great crime, as well as a kind of incoherence, to act in a way that denies and eradicates the source of all value. Thus it might be possible to say that suicide is wrong from an ideal point of view, though justifiable in circumstances of very great natural or moral evil.

There is also another, rather different sense of "rigorism" in which the Formula of Humanity seems to be more rigorous than that of Universal Law. It concerns the question whether Kant's theory allows for the category of merely permissible ends and actions, or whether we must always be doing something that is morally worthy: that is, whether we should *always* pursue the obligatory ends of our own perfection and the happiness of others, when no other duty is in the case.

The Formula of Universal Law clearly allows for the category of the permissible. Indeed, the first contradiction test is a test for permissibility. But in the *Metaphysical Principles of Virtue*, there are passages which have sometimes been taken to imply that Kant holds the view that our conduct should always be informed by morally worthy ends (*MMV*, 390/48). The textual evidence is not decisive. But the tendency in Kant's thought is certainly there. For complete moral worth is only realized when our actions are not merely in accordance with duty but from duty, or, to say the same thing a different way, perfect autonomy is only realized when our actions and ends are completely determined by reason, and this seems to be the case only when our ends are chosen as instantiations of the obligatory ends.

Using the Formula of Humanity it is possible to argue for the more "rigorous" interpretation. First, the obligatory ends can be derived more straightforwardly from Humanity than from Universal Law. Kant does derive the obligatory ends from the Formula of Universal Law, but he does it by a curiously roundabout procedure in which someone is imagined formulating a maxim of rejecting them and then finding it to be impermissible. This argument does not show that there would be a moral failing if the agent merely unthinkingly neglected rather than rejected these ends. The point about the pervasiveness of these ends in the moral life is a more complicated one, one that follows from their adoption by this route: among the obligatory ends is our own moral perfection. Pursuing ends that are determined by reason, rather than merely acceptable to it, cultivates one's moral perfection in the required way (*MMV*, 380–81/37–8; 444–7/108–11).

It is important to point out that even if this is the correct way to understand Kant's ideal theory, it does not imply that Kantian ethics commands a life of conventional moral "good deeds." The obligatory ends are one's own perfection and the happiness of others; to be governed by them is to choose instantiations of these larger categories as the aim of your vocation and other everyday activities. It is worth keeping in mind that natural perfection is a large category, including all the activities that cultivate body and mind. Kant's point is not to introduce a strenuous moralism but to find a place for the values of perfectionism in his theory. But this perfectionism will be a part of ideal theory if the argument for it is based on the Formula of Humanity and cannot be derived from that of Universal Law. This seems to me a desirable outcome. People in stultifying economic or educational conditions cannot really be expected to devote all their spare time to the cultivation of perfectionist values. But they can be expected not to do what is impermissible, not to violate the Formula of Universal Law. Here again, the Formula of Humanity sheds light on the situation even if it is not directly applied: it tells us why it is morally as well as in other ways regrettable that people should be in such conditions.

Conclusion

If the account I have given is correct, the resources of a double-level theory may be available to the Kantian. The Formula of Humanity and its corollary, the vision of a Kingdom of Ends, provide an ideal to live up to in daily life as well as a long-term political and moral goal for humanity. But it is not feasible always to live up to this ideal, and where the attempt to live up to it would make you a tool of evil, you should not do so. In evil circumstances, but only then, the Kingdom of Ends can become a goal to seek rather than an ideal to live up to, and this will provide us with some guidance. The Kantian priorities – of justice over the pursuit of obligatory ends, and of respect over benevolence – still help us to see what matters most. And even in the worst circumstances, there is always the Formula of Universal Law, telling us what we must not in any case do. For whatever bad circumstances may drive us to do, we cannot possibly be justified in doing something which others in those same circumstances could not also do. The Formula of Universal Law provides the point at which morality becomes uncompromising.

Let me close with some reflections about the extent to which Kant himself might have agreed with this modification of his views. Throughout this essay, I have portrayed Kant as an uncompromising idealist, and there is much to support this view. But in the historical and political writings, as well as in the *Lectures on Ethics*, we find a somewhat different attitude. This seems to me to be especially important: Kant believes that the Kingdom of Ends on earth, the highest political good, can only be realized in a condition of peace (*MMJ*, 354–5/127–9). But he does not think that this commits a nation to a simple pacifism that would make it the easy victim of its enemies. Instead, he draws up laws of war in which peace functions not as an uncompromising ideal to be lived up to in the present, but as a long-range goal which guides our conduct even when war is necessary (*PP*, 343–8/85–91); *MMJ*, 343–51/114–25). If a Kantian can hold such a view for the conduct of nations, why not for that of individuals? If this is right, the task of Kantian moral philosophy is to draw up for individuals something analogous to Kant's laws of war: special principles to use when dealing with evil.

Notes

1   Where I cite or refer to any of Kant's works more than once, I have inserted the reference into the text. The following abbreviations are used:
    G: Foundations of the Metaphysics of Morals (1785). The first page number is that of the Prussian Academy Edition Volume IV; the second is that of the translation by Lewis White Beck (Indianapolis: Bobbs-Merrill Library of Liberal Arts, 1959).
    C2: Critique of Practical Reason (1788). Prussian Academy Volume V; Lewis White Beck's translation (Indianapolis: Bobbs-Merrill Library of Liberal Arts, 1956).
    MMV: The Metaphysical Principles of Virtue (1797). Prussian Academy Volume VI; James Ellington's translation in *Immanuel Kant: Ethical Philosophy* (Indianapolis: Hackett, 1983).

MMJ: The Metaphysical Elements of Justice (1797). Prussian Academy Volume VI; John Ladd's translation (Indianapolis: Bobbs-Merrill Library of Liberal Arts, 1965).

PP: Perpetual Peace (1795). Prussian Academy Volume VIII, translation by Lewis White Beck in *On History*, edited by Lewis White Beck (Indianapolis: Bobbs-Merrill Library of Liberal Arts, 1963).

SRL: "On a Supposed Right to Lie from Altruistic Motives" (1797). Prussian Academy Volume VIII; translation by Lewis White Beck in *Immanuel Kant: Critique of Practical Reason and Other Writings in Moral Philosophy* (Chicago: University of Chicago Press, 1949; reprint, New York: Garland Publishing Company, 1976).

LE: Lectures on Ethics (1775–80). Edited by Paul Menzer from the notes of Theodor Friedrich Brauer, using the notes of Gottlieb Kutzner and Christian Mrongovius; translated by Louis Infield (London: Methuen & Co., Ltd., 1930; reprint, New York: Harper Torchbooks, 1963; current reprint, Indianapolis: Hackett Publishing Co., 1980).

2   I defend it in "Kant's Formula of Universal Law," *Pacific Philosophical Quarterly* 66, nos. 1 & 2 (January/April 1986): 24–47.

3   I am relying here on the assumption that when people ask us questions, they give us some account of themselves and of the context in which the questions are asked. Or, if they don't, it is because they are relying on a context that is assumed. If someone comes to your door looking for someone, you assume that there is a family emergency or some such thing. I am prepared to count such reliance as deception if the questioner knows about it and uses it, thinking that we would refuse to answer his questions if we knew the real context to be otherwise. Sometimes people ask me, "Suppose the murderer just asks whether his friend is in your house, without saying anything about why he wants to know?" I think that, in our culture anyway, people do not *just ask* questions of each other about anything except the time of day and directions for getting places. After all, the reason why refusal to answer is an unsatisfactory way of dealing with this case is that it will almost inevitably give rise to suspicion of the truth, and this is because people normally answer such questions. Perhaps if we did live in a culture in which people regularly *just asked* questions in the way suggested, refusal to answer would be commonplace and would not give rise to suspicion; it would not even be considered odd or rude. Otherwise there would be no way to maintain privacy.

4   In fact, it will now be the case that if the murderer supposes that you suspect him, he is not going to ask you, knowing that you will answer so as to deceive him. Since we must avoid the silly problem about the murderer being able to deduce the truth from his knowledge that you will speak falsely, what you announce is that you will say whatever is necessary in order to conceal the truth. There is no reason to suppose that you will be mechanical about this. You are not going to be a reliable source of information. The murderer will therefore seek some other way to locate his victim.

On the other hand, suppose that the murderer does, contrary to my supposition, announce his real intentions. Then the arguments that I have given do not apply. In this case, I believe your only recourse is refusal to answer (whether or not the victim is in your house, or you know his whereabouts). If an answer is extorted from you by force you may lie, according to the argument I will give later in this article.

5 Kant himself takes notice of this sort of problem in a footnote to this passage in which he criticizes Golden-Rule type principles for, among other things, the sort of subjectivity in question: such principles cannot establish the duty of beneficence, for instance, because "many a man would gladly consent that others should not benefit him, provided only that he might be excused from showing benevolence to them" (G, 430n./48n.).

6 Sometimes it is objected that someone could assent to being lied to in advance of the actual occasion of the lie, and that in such a case the deception might still succeed. One can therefore agree to be deceived. I think it depends what circumstances are envisioned. I can certainly agree to remain uninformed about something, but this is not the same as agreeing to be deceived. For example, I could say to my doctor: "Don't tell me if I am fatally ill, even if I ask." But if I then do ask the doctor whether I am fatally ill, I cannot be certain whether she will answer me truthfully. Perhaps what's being envisioned is that I simply agree to be lied to, but not about anything in particular. Will I then trust the person with whom I have made this odd agreement?

7 A similar conclusion about the way in which the Formula of Humanity makes coercion and deception wrong is reached by Onora O'Neill in "Between Consenting Adults," *Philosophy & Public Affairs* 14, no. 3 (Summer 1985): 252–77.

8 *Immanuel Kant's "Critique of Pure Reason,"* translated by Norman Kemp Smith (New York: St. Martin's Press, 1965) A738–9/B766–7, p. 593.

9 It is perhaps also relevant that in Kant's discussion of perfect moral friendship the emphasis is not on good will toward one another, but on complete confidence and openness. See *MMV,* 471–2/138–9.

10 Some evidence that Kant is concerned with this sort of thing may be found in the fact that he identifies two meanings of the word "prudence" (*Klugheit*); "The former sense means the skill of a man in having an influence on others so as to use them for his own purposes. The latter is the ability to unite all these purposes to his own lasting advantage" (G, 416n./33n.). A similar remark is found in *Anthropology from a Pragmatic Point of View* (1798). See the translation by Mary J. Gregor (The Hague: Martinus Nijhoff, 1974), p. 183; Prussian Academy Edition Volume VII, p. 322.

11 I call this view Socratic because of Socrates' concern with the differences between reason and persuasion and, in particular, because in the *Apology*, he makes a case for the categorical duty of straightforwardness. Socrates and Plato are also concerned with a troublesome feature of this moral view that Kant neglects. An argument must come packaged in some sort of presentation, and one may well object that it is impossible to make a straightforward

presentation of a case to someone who is close to or admires you, without emphasis, without style, without taking some sort of advantage of whatever it is about you that has your listener's attention in the first place. So how can we avoid the nonrational influence of others? I take it that most obviously in the *Symposium*, but also in other dialogues concerned with the relation of love and teaching such as the *Phaedrus*, Plato is at work on the question whether you can use your sex appeal to draw another's attention to the reasons he has for believing or doing things, rather than as a distraction that aids your case illicitly.

12   Of course you may also resist force with lies, if resisting it with force is not an option for you. This gives rise to a question about whether these options are on a footing with each other. In many cases, lying will be the better option. This is because when you use coercion you risk doing injury to the person you coerce. Injuring people unnecessarily is wrong, a wrong that should be distinguished from the use of coercion. When you lie you do not risk doing this extra wrong. But Kant thinks that lying is in itself worse than coercion, because of the peculiarly direct way in which it violates autonomy. So it should follow that if you can deal with the murderer by coercion, this is a *better* option than lying. Others seem to share this intuition. Cardinal John Henry Newman, responding to Samuel Johnson's claim that he would lie to a murderer who asked which way his victim had gone, suggests that the appropriate thing to do is "to knock the man down, and to call out for the police" (*Apologia Pro Vita Sua: Being a History of His Religious Opinions* [London: Longmans, Green & Co., 1880], p. 361. I am quoting from Sissela Bok, *Lying* [New York: Vintage Books, 1979], p. 42). If you can do it without seriously hurting the murderer, it is, so to speak, cleaner just to kick him off the front porch than to lie. This treats the *murderer himself* more like a human being than lying to him does.

13   I owe this example to John Koethe.

14   For a discussion of this question see Barbara Herman, "Mutual Aid and Respect for Persons," *Ethics* 94 (July 1984): 577–602.

15   In the *Lectures on Ethics*, Kant takes the position that you may lie to someone who lies to or bullies you as long as you don't say specifically that your words will be true. He claims this is not lying, because such a person should not expect you to tell the truth (*LE*, 227, 229).

16   John Rawls, *A Theory of Justice* (Cambridge, MA: Harvard University Press, 1971). Section and page numbers referring to this work will appear in the text.

17   In a nonideal case, one's actions may be guided by a more instrumental style of reasoning than in ideal theory. But nonideal theory is not a form of consequentialism. There are two reasons for this. One is that the goal set by the ideal is not just one of good consequences, but of a just state of affairs. If a consequentialist view is one that defines right action entirely in terms of good consequences (which are not themselves defined in terms of considerations of rightness or justice), then nonideal theory is not consequentialist. The

second reason is that the ideal will also guide our choice among nonideal alternatives, importing criteria for this choice other than effectiveness. I would like to thank Alan Gewirth for prompting me to clarify my thoughts on this matter, and David Greenstone for helping me to do so.

18   See the "Dialectic of Pure Practical Reason" of the *Critique of Practical Reason*, and the *Critique of Teleological Judgment*, sec. 87.

19   Bernard Williams, in *Utilitarianism For and Against*, by J. J. C. Smart and Bernard Williams (Cambridge: Cambridge University Press, 1973), pp. 75–150.

20   Williams also takes this issue up in "Ethical Consistency," originally published in the Supplementary Volumes to the *Proceedings of the Aristotelian Society* XXXIX, 1965, and reprinted in his collection, *Problems of the Self* (Cambridge: Cambridge University Press, 1973), pp. 166–86.

21   It is important here to distinguish two kinds of exceptions. As Rawls points out in "Two Conceptions of Rules" (*The Philosophical Review* 64 [January 1965]), a practice such as promising may have certain exceptions built into it. Everyone who has learned the practice understands that the obligation to keep the promise is cancelled if one of these obtains. When one breaks a promise because this sort of exception obtains, regret would be inappropriate and obsessive. And these sorts of exceptions may occur even in "ideal" circumstances. The kind of exception one makes when dealing with evil should be distinguished from exceptions built into practices.

22   Kant's argument depends on a teleological claim: that the instinct whose office is to impel the improvement of life cannot universally be used to destroy life without contradiction (*G*, 422/40). But as I understand the contradiction in conception test, teleological claims have no real place in it. What matters is not whether nature assigns a certain purpose to a certain motive or instinct, but whether everyone with the same motive or instinct could act in the way proposed and still achieve their purpose. There is simply no argument to show that everyone suffering from acute misery could not commit suicide and still achieve their purpose: ending that misery.

Index